Language Testing and Assessment

ALSO AVAILABLE FROM BLOOMSBURY

Developing Materials for Language Teaching, edited by Brian Tomlinson
Teaching and Learning the English Language, Richard Badger
Teaching English to Young Learners, edited by Janice Bland

Language Testing and Assessment

From Theory to Practice

AEK PHAKITI

BLOOMSBURY ACADEMIC
LONDON • NEW YORK • OXFORD • NEW DELHI • SYDNEY

BLOOMSBURY ACADEMIC
Bloomsbury Publishing Plc, 50 Bedford Square, London, WC1B 3DP, UK
Bloomsbury Publishing Inc, 1385 Broadway, New York, NY 10018, USA
Bloomsbury Publishing Ireland, 29 Earlsfort Terrace, Dublin 2, D02 AY28, Ireland

BLOOMSBURY, BLOOMSBURY ACADEMIC and the Diana logo are trademarks of Bloomsbury Publishing Plc

First published in Great Britain 2025

Cover design and illustration by Olivia D'Cruz

A catalogue record for this book is available from the British Library.

A catalog record for this book is available from the Library of Congress.

ISBN: HB: 978-1-4742-9011-1
PB: 978-1-4742-9012-8
ePDF: 978-1-4742-9009-8
eBook: 978-1-4742-9010-4

Typeset by Integra Software Services Pvt. Ltd.
Printed and bound in Great Britain

Contents

Figures

Tables

Acknowledgements

First and foremost, I would like to express my appreciation and gratitude to many notable scholars who have led and significantly advanced various philosophical stances, innovations, conceptions, principles and methodologies in language testing and assessment (e.g. Charles Alderson, Lyle Bachman, Micheline Chalhoub-Deville, Carol Chappelle, Alan Davies, Cathie Elder, Liz Hamp-Lyons, Antony Kunnan, Constant Leung, Jim Purpura, Elana Shohamy, Bernard Spolsky, Merrill Swain, Cyril Weir and Paula Winke, to name just a few). Their significant contributions to the field have influenced my understanding of language testing and assessment. Special thanks to the anonymous reviewers for their constructive feedback, which greatly improved this book.

Secondly, since my formal study of language testing and assessment started at the University of Melbourne, Australia, I thank my academic supervisors and teachers, Brian Lynch, Tim McNamara and Paul Gruba, whose insights and knowledge in language testing and assessment were profound. This book is dedicated to Tim McNamara, who inspired me to pursue this field of research. I would like to thank my dear colleagues and friends Carsten Roever and Talia Isaacs for their academic and emotional support.

I would like to thank my editorial colleagues in *Language Assessment Quarterly*, for which I served as Associate Editor for several years. My heartfelt thanks go to Jim Purpura, who kindly mentored me in managing manuscript reviews and teaching me how to communicate with reviewers and authors. I have also learnt a lot about academic writing from Jim as well as Antony Kunnan. I would also like to thank Constant Leung, whom I have been working with very closely in the past few years. Thanks also to past and present Associate Editors of *Language Assessment Quarterly* (Claudia Harsh, Gary Ockey, Lia Plakans, Yasuyo Sawaki, Elvis Wagner and Sara Weigle) who I used to work with very closely. My experiences as Associate Editor have expanded my horizons on issues and knowledge in language testing and assessment beyond my research interests.

It would not have been possible for me to complete this book without support from the Sydney School of Education and Social Work at the University of Sydney, where I work. I would like to express my gratitude to my mentors (Brian Paltridge, Janette Bobis and Jackie Manuel) and my TESOL colleagues (Marie Stevenson, Jack C. Richards and Ken Cruickshank) for their continuous friendship and support. I am also indebted to students who took the language testing and assessment unit for nearly two decades. It was them that inspired me to write this book. They read many chapter drafts of this book and provided constructive feedback.

Next, I thank Guy Middleton, who helped read through and edit earlier chapter drafts. I would also like to thank Bloomsbury's current and past team, including Gurdeep Mattu, Andrew Wardell, Morwenna Scott, Helen Sanders, Becky Holland, Laura Gallon, Maria Brauzzi and many more. They have been very supportive during this book-writing period.

I thank my mum, sisters, niece and nephew for their support and love. My special thanks go to Damir Jambrek, who has provided emotional support and my dearest dog – Nero – and now my new cat – Leilah – who have been with me day and night while writing this book. Last but not least, I would like to thank the readers of this book. Without you, this book would not have been written, and without you we cannot improve language testing and assessment practices worldwide.

1

Language Testing and Assessment

Overview

This chapter introduces the fundamental concepts and practices of language testing and assessment (e.g. language assessment literacy, types of language testing and assessment). It aims to establish a foundational framework for the subsequent chapters of this book.

Guided questions

1. What is language testing and assessment?
2. Why are language tests and assessments used in education or society?

Introduction

There are two possible ways to examine the notion of 'language testing and assessment'. On the one hand, it can be understood as an academic discipline in applied linguistics, which focuses on a theoretical and methodological understanding and practice of testing and assessing language use and learning in educational and social contexts. On the other hand, it can be understood as the practice of using language tests and assessments for various purposes by test and assessment developers, language practitioners and policymakers, for example, to make informed, evidence-based decisions such as teaching and learning purposes, selection, certification and improvement. Language tests and assessments, accordingly, are techniques, methods and tools to collect information in language testing and assessment. In this book, 'language testing and assessment' is seen as a singular term (i.e. the practice).

Several national and international language assessment associations worldwide have been established to promote high-quality language testing and assessment practices (e.g. the International Language Testing Association (ILTA), the European Association for Language Testing and Assessment (EALTA), the Asian Association for Language Assessment (AALA) and the Association for Language Testing and Assessment of Australia and New Zealand (ALTAANZ). Academic journals such as *Language Testing* and *Language Assessment Quarterly* have long been devoted to advancing research and practice in language testing and assessment.

The current book synergizes the author's knowledge of language testing and assessment in the applied linguistics field, experiences of English language teaching, and training language teachers to use language tests and assessments, to help readers interested in language testing and assessment explore its applications, potentials and limitations. This chapter provides some basic information about language testing and assessment as a field of study and educational and social practices for decision-making. For example, it aims to clarify the definition of testing and assessment, some insights from the language testing and assessment field of study, reasons for using tests and assessments and an overview of the remaining chapters.

Aims of the book

This book promotes 'language assessment literacy' (LAL) by providing a practical, theoretical guide to developing and using language tests and assessments in language teaching and educational contexts. Essential frameworks and principles in language testing and assessment are discussed and articulated (e.g. types of assessment, assessment qualities and techniques for assessing language skills). The topics covered in this book have been given prominence in language assessment (e.g. assessing language proficiency and skills and technology-enhanced language assessment).

Language assessment literacy

LAL commonly describes the knowledge about language testing and assessment in terms of how to design or use test and assessment tasks suitable for an intended purpose or use and what quality standards to consider before, during and after an assessment activity (Harding & Kremmel 2017; Inbar-Lourie 2017; Taylor 2009). Fulcher's (2012a, p. 125) definition of LAL is adopted in this book:

> The knowledge, skills and abilities required to design, develop, maintain, or evaluate large-scale standardised and/or classroom-based tests, familiarity with test processes, and awareness of principles and concepts that guide and underpin practice, including ethics and codes of practice. The ability to place knowledge, skills, processes, principles, and concepts within wider historical, social, political, and philosophical frameworks in order to understand why practices have arisen as they have, and to evaluate the role and impact of testing on society, institutions, and individuals.

Based on Fulcher's (2012a) definition, teachers with LAL should be able to apply the processes and principles for appropriate and practical designs and classroom practices. LAL is critical for teachers and assessment users due to the ever-changing needs and demands of assessing the twenty-first-century classroom and society.

Use of 'additional language' in this book

In this book, the term 'additional language' (AL) is preferred for describing learning and using another language. The traditional way to describe language learning and using another language is to differentiate the first language (L1) from the second language (L2). L1–L2 terms describe the different nature and characteristics of language development and language processing (e.g. differences in acquiring native and non-native languages; see Ellis 2015). In the twenty-first century, such distinction can be limited or blurry because people may acquire two or more languages simultaneously or sequentially from birth. However, they may not be equally good at these languages. Hence, using a second language (L2) can be limited or misleading in understanding the nature of the target language of interest.

The language teaching and learning literature also often differentiates foreign language (FL) from second language (SL) contexts by identifying whether a language is used officially in every communication. For example,

English as a foreign language (EFL) refers to how people learn or use it in a country where English is not an official language or people's native language (e.g. China, Thailand, Japan). In contrast, English as a second language (ESL) refers to the context in which English is an official or common language for communication for all people (e.g. the UK, USA, Canada, Australia and New Zealand). English as an additional language (EAL) is arguably more *neutral* than ESL or EFL. AL is context-neutral and can describe learning and using a language of interest. Therefore, in this book, the use of 'L2', 'ESL' and 'EFL' appearing in the literature will be replaced with AL when the meaning is clear.

Language testing versus language assessment

In its early conception, language testing was related to designing, developing and using a language test to collect individuals' language ability, knowledge or skills, for example to inform a decision-making process (e.g. selecting applications for admission and employment). The origin of language testing is associated with the structuralist view – each individual differs in the quality and quantity of what they can do when using a given language. The key interest in language testing and tests is objectively collecting evidence of language ability. The terms 'language testing' and 'language tests' are typically used as standardized tools or instruments for assessing and evaluating abstract abilities such as language proficiency, language skills and language learning achievement.

Language testing follows prescribed standardized procedures for collecting, scoring and interpreting scores. For instance, except for particular groups of students or test takers (e.g. those with disabilities), all students or test takers usually complete the same test (or parallel forms of the same test) within the same time limitation and their responses or performances are evaluated and interpreted in the same manner. Commonly known English language tests include commercialized standardized English proficiency tests (e.g. the International English Language Testing System (IELTS), Test of English as a Foreign Language (TOEFL) and Pearson English Test (PTE).

The term 'language assessment' is broader than 'language testing' because assessment does not rely on tests alone. It can range from a more formal, standardized collection of language use or learning performance (e.g. through examinations and official submission of work) to a less informal, non-standardized manner (e.g. informal inquiry such as teachers' use of questions in the classroom and students' self-assessment). Often, informal assessment is used for formative purposes, such as when teachers check whether student learning is formed and take subsequent actions by providing feedback for teaching and learning. Classroom language assessment can have a sociocultural origin, arguing that the development of humans, particularly of their higher mental functions, is fundamentally shaped by their cultural, institutional and historical contexts. Classroom contexts, therefore, provide tools of intellectual adaptation that shape how students think and communicate.

In summary, in the current book, language assessment is a broad term that includes language testing – a specific procedure for collecting information in a standardized manner (e.g. Bachman & Damböck 2017; Bachman & Palmer 2010; Brown & Abeywickrama 2019). While 'language testing' and 'language assessment' overlap, it remains true that people do not necessarily conceive tests in the same way as assessment and vice versa. Although some language testing and assessment scholars may not want to use 'language testing' (given that assessment already includes testing and tests), this book explicitly uses both terms. It aims to help readers recognize the similarities and differences between language testing and language assessment from an education-oriented standpoint.

From theory to practice

Readers new to language testing and assessment should know some background of language testing and assessment, which informs how it has been theorized and practised in educational and social situations. Testing and assessment has existed in educational and social contexts for centuries (Kunnan 2018; O'Sullivan 2012a; Phakiti & Leung 2024; Spolsky 1995, 2017). The following are significant themes of language testing and assessment research and development that have influenced the content of the current book.

Development of language proficiency and its testing and assessment

In Anglophone applied linguistics, language testing was formally established around 1961 with the publication of a book on language testing by Lado (1961). Lado's book, however, took a primarily structural view of language, such as testing lexico-grammatical knowledge, which is now considered to be narrow for testing and assessing language proficiency by the modern language testing and assessment approach (Davies 2014).

Since Lado's (1961) publication, the language testing and assessment field has advanced both theoretically and methodologically (e.g. Fulcher & Harding 2022; Read 2015). Between the 1960s and 1980s, the field moved from being structural (e.g. testing grammatical and vocabulary knowledge) and psychometric (e.g. focusing on objectively assessing individuals' underlying traits or predispositions free from context) toward being more psycholinguistic (psychological aspects of language use and learning) and sociolinguistic (social aspects of language learning and use; see Spolsky 1977).

In the 1970s, unitary L2 proficiency traits (one underlying L2 proficiency trait residing in the human brain) influenced many testing methods. For example, discrete-point and objective-scoring techniques (e.g. multiple-choice questions) were commonly used in language tests. Bachman (2000) pointed out that in the 1980s language testers started to critique the problems of adopting the unitary trait hypothesis of L2 proficiency to inform what to assess and how to interpret test scores. This led to what is known today as multi-componential *communicative competence*. For example, Canale and Swain (1980) and Canale (1983) proposed that communicative competence consisted of grammatical, sociolinguistic, strategic and discourse competence:

- *Grammatical competence* is the ability to use target language knowledge to form correct utterances or sentences.
- *Sociolinguistic competence* is the ability to use socially appropriate language in a given situation.
- *Strategic competence* is the ability to use communication strategies to compensate for the lack of necessary language knowledge and to overcome communication difficulties or barriers.
- *Discourse competence* is the ability to use language or express meaning cohesively and coherently in a specific context or situation.

In the 1980s, language testing and assessment researchers focused on identifying a general factor model of L2 proficiency and gathering empirical evidence to verify competence-based language models (Skehan 1988, 1989). Davies (1982) pointed out that in the 1980s, language tests were developed to measure communicative competence (also known as L2 proficiency), which was theorized to go beyond simply understanding the grammar and vocabulary of a given language.

Test and assessment standards

Testing and assessment qualities have been pinnacles in a language test and assessment use. Since the 1990s, there have been several significant developments and movements in establishing essential standards and qualities for language testing and assessment (see Alderson & Banerjee 2001, 2002; Bachman 2000; Kunnan 1999; Leung 2022). According to Green (2014, 2020), *standards*, on the one hand, are the criteria for achieving an acceptable quality level (e.g. relevance and adequacy of language tasks or activities that measure the target language constructs). Conversely, qualities, on the other hand, are whether and to what extent the target standards are surpassed (Green 2014, 2020). In other words, standards represent desired quality levels, whereas qualities represent the levels themselves (e.g. poor to excellent). Therefore, understanding common standards for evaluating language testing and assessment is critical for effective testing and assessment. Standards and qualities are discussed in more detail in Chapter 4.

- *Reliability* refers to how a given test and assessment consistently elicits students' or test takers' performance. It is related to the precision of scoring methods.
- *Validity/trustworthiness* refers to meaningful inferences about students' or test takers' target ability, constructs of interest, or achievement levels based on test and assessment scores or performance. In classroom assessment, *trustworthiness* is often used instead of validity because it concerns the relevance of the evaluation to localized teaching, learning and assessment.
- *Authenticity* refers to the extent to which test and assessment tasks are similar to real-world language tasks and processes. Authenticity in classroom assessment can be defined as the resemblance of test and assessment tasks to classroom teaching and learning activities.
- *Practicality* refers to whether tests and assessments are *cost-* and *time-efficient* (e.g. easy to develop, administer and score). It is also related to the feasibility and timeliness of developing, administering, scoring and using a given test and assessment.
- *Fairness* refers to equality of treatment to all students or test takers (e.g. before, during and after the test and assessment). It includes avoiding bias against a specific student group and considering accommodations for students with disabilities or special needs.
- *Impact* refers to the influence of testing and assessment practice (i.e. consequences) on stakeholders (e.g. students, teachers, parents and the general public). Impact includes considering the stakes of decisions and washback effects (e.g. teaching or learning to succeed in the test or assessment).

- *Ethics* concerns the broad social responsibilities when using language tests and assessments for decision-making, including whether tests and assessments are abused by those responsible or the authorities.

Factors affecting language performance

Since the 1990s, researchers have aimed to explain the reasons for variations in language performance by investigating factors affecting language test performance (e.g. test methods facets such as choices of test and assessment techniques and scoring methods) and test-taker characteristics such as personal attributes). There has been emerging innovation in using computer technology in large-scale standardized test development, delivery, administration and scoring. Some assessment areas have been developed (e.g. cross-cultural pragmatics and language for specific purposes). In standardized AL proficiency tests, authentic language-use tasks have been recognized for assessing writing and speaking skills. There has been an increased interest in using non-standardized assessment methods for classroom assessment (e.g. portfolio assessment). Researchers have begun investigating the impact of language testing and assessment on language teaching and learning.

Needs to understand and assess complex language constructs

Constructs refer to abstract abilities, skills or attributes that cannot be observed directly but inferred from responses to questions, tasks or situations (see Chapter 2). Since the 2000s, language constructs have expanded beyond language skills (Bachman 2010; Davies 2014; Douglas 2010). For example, the conceptualization of assessment constructs (e.g. the linguistic nature of language ability, and the social roles of interactional competence and content knowledge) are more critically evaluated. A socio-interactional approach (Kramsch 1986), which argued that interactional competence should be viewed as a joint co-construction of performance, has raised significant questions for testing and assessment practices, such as how to assess and interpret interactional competence.

Current and emerging practices

In recent years, several research issues and practices in language testing and assessment, discussed above, remain relevant to the present situations, which are constantly evolving (e.g. assessing pronunciation, pragmatics and integrated skills; assessment in global contexts; social consequences of assessment use; and technology in language testing and assessment; see Brown & Abeywickrama 2019; Fulcher & Harding 2022; Purpura 2016, Green 2020). For example, assessment issues of the changing workforce and educational demands for high-level language skills continue to challenge language testing and assessment designs and practice (Purpura 2016). The current book explores these issues across various chapters (see also Chapter 10). This section introduces themes such as multilingual competence, the impacts of uncertain situations and the influences of computer technology in language testing and assessment practice.

Multilingual competence

Another interest in language testing and assessment relates to *multilingual competence*, which requires a new perspective on knowing multiple languages (Lopez, Turkan & Guzman-Orth 2017). Multilingualism denotes a person's use of various languages and skills for language communication. The Council of Europe (2020) proposes plurilingualism to represent a multilingual notion. Both terms describe a movement away from the ideal native-language proficiency model for assessing non-native speakers of that particular language (Leung 2022). Chalhoub-Deville (2019) argued that language testing and assessment approaches should uphold the presence of multilingualism. A pressing challenge for assessment developers and users is, for instance, how translanguaging (systematic and non-systematic switching of multiple languages used among multilinguals to communicate in a given task or situation) can be integrated into language testing and assessment (Chalhoub-Deville 2019).

Impacts of uncertain situations

It has become clear that we live in an uncertain and ever-changing world, so language testing and assessment practice needs to be flexible to adapt to changing situations. Consequently, teachers and educators need language testing and assessment skills to deal with uncertain situations. The Covid-19 pandemic, for instance, has significantly impacted language teaching and assessment practice. In a large-scale standardized test, issues of test deliveries and security have been investigated, and technology such as proctor software has been used. The quality of formative assessment (FA) during online teaching and learning was also challenging, given the social and physical distancing between teachers and students. How can teachers assess students' learning status and provide effective feedback when they cannot see their students (e.g. when students turn off their cameras)?

Roles of computer technology

Technological advancement has changed how students learn and process another language and how they are assessed or tested. In many language teaching or learning situations today, it is hard to imagine that teachers only use paper-based tests or assessments and students handwrite their answers or assignments. One of the most challenging issues in language testing and assessment today is the influence of generative artificial intelligence (AI). Because the internet, computers, tablets, smartphones and software, including Grammarly and ChatGPT, have become more affordable and accessible, traditional language testing and assessment practices that worked several decades ago may no longer work or remain as relevant to the current situation. For example, synchronous and asynchronous teaching and learning are now integrated through a learning management system (e.g. Blackboard, Canvas) and a cloud-based video conferencing platform such as Zoom and Microsoft Team. This changes the nature of traditional embedded classroom assessment.

Changes in technology to enhance language testing and assessment can be seen in large-scale standardized examinations that can be administered with more robust remote proctoring software (e.g. ProProctor and ProctorU) to monitor students taking remote online tests (without human proctors in an exam room). Furthermore, AI and corpus-based technology have allowed the possibility of developing automated scoring programs for assessing productive language skills, such as writing and speaking and providing automatic feedback, which students can receive more promptly. The ever-changing language teaching, learning and assessment situations are exciting yet concerning. It is exciting because of its convenience and flexibility. Yet, it is *concerning* because of the many unknown consequences and decision-making outcomes. For example, what credible mechanisms are there to ensure that test takers or students do not cheat using AI technology? Chapter 10 further discusses opportunities and challenges in adopting technology in language testing and assessment.

In summary, the past decades have seen ever-changing situations impacting language testing and assessment research and practice (e.g. multilingualism and technological advancement). These situations will continue challenging language testing and assessment research for several decades. This book aims to apply knowledge and insights from language testing and assessment theory, research and from professionals to help teachers inform their language testing and assessment practice.

Practices of testing and assessment in the language classroom

It is essential to understand the connection between teaching, testing and assessment practice in classroom contexts and to realize how testing and assessment principles presented in this book can be applied to enhance effective classroom teaching and learning. This section explores the relationship between language teaching and assessment.

Teachers' and students' perceptions about assessment

To explore language testing and assessment concepts, we examine how teachers and students explain testing and assessment.

Excerpt 1: Testing is about sitting in an exam room. We have a limited time to complete the test. We have to sit in a row, and we cannot ask our friends for answers to test questions. We cannot cheat on a test as it is a kind of dishonesty, and it does not show our actual ability. Testing is stressful for me because I have much pressure from my parents, and I often have to compete with my friends due to rankings of test scores. (Wei, high school student)

Excerpt 2: Testing is also about checking if I can remember what I have studied, explain something well, or use what I know to do something successfully. Self-testing needs to be realistic about what I can and cannot do. For example, I test myself by answering practice tests and checking if I answer them correctly using the provided answer keys. I then tried to figure out why I was wrong in some questions. (Rafael, university student)

Excerpt 3: Clearly, testing is different from assessment. We tell our doctor we want a 'blood test', not a blood assessment, right? In this case, testing seems related to something quite technical and standardized. A tool is needed to test something. However, the doctor needs to assess and evaluate the blood test results. So, in this case, the doctor needs to have some expert knowledge about what is in the analysis, for example. He is assessing and evaluating the blood test results. Similarly, when testing our students, we may use a test, but we need to know how to judge students' test responses. (Ann, a teacher)

Excerpt 4: Maybe assessment is broader than testing. We have to follow a procedure when we test something. Testing may be more concrete and specific than assessment because a test is a tool. Assessment can sometimes be less formal. For example, I often ask my students to recall the concepts I have just taught them, and I may correct them when they are wrong. In this case, I may assess if they have learnt something, but I won't fail them if they are wrong, as I would in a test. (Tyler, a teacher)

As can be seen from these excerpts, there are different situations in which language testing and assessment is employed. Excerpt 1 relates to educational testing or standardized examination that the student experiences. This type of assessment refers to summative assessment (or assessment of learning), which focuses on collecting evidence of performance resulting from learning. Excerpt 2 is a self-assessment for monitoring, evaluating and modifying learning or performance. Excerpt 2 also suggests that language testing and assessment is not necessarily restricted to a controlled testing condition (as in Excerpt 1). This type of assessment refers to formative assessment (or assessment for learning), which produces feedback for learning and teaching. Excerpts 3 and 4 suggest possible distinctions between testing and assessment from a teacher's perspective.

Formal and informal assessment

Several language testing and assessment practices are formally or officially required by an educational policy, curriculum or syllabus (e.g. to determine students' achievement level or attainment of the course learning outcomes or objectives). Formal assessment is also known as planned and mandatory assessment. Such language testing and assessments can be standardized examinations, coursework and performance-based tasks. In formal assessment, students usually know when assessments will occur in advance. However, in the language classroom, many assessment activities can be informal and are implicitly embedded in the language classroom. The following scenarios illustrate how assessment is an informally or embedded part of teaching and learning:

Scenario 1: Students are completing a classroom exercise that focuses on the use of 'didn't' in English.
Student: I didn't ated breakfast this morning.
Teacher: Didn't eat or ate?
Student: Oh, I didn't ate breakfast this morning.
Teacher: Should it be 'eat'?

In Scenario 1, the teacher reacts to the student's error by asking for clarification, prompting the student to notice a mistake. If the student still cannot recognize the error, the teacher may intervene by explicitly giving the correct form, explaining the grammar rules and providing several examples. In second language acquisition (SLA), teachers' explicit correction is considered negative evidence (signalling a problem or error) or implicit correction as *recast* (offering implicit corrective feedback), thereby encouraging students to notice their language output (Gass & Mackey 2006). Teacher assessment in Scenario 1 is embedded within teaching and learning activities and is also known as formative assessment.

Scenario 2: Students are taught to use comparative adjectives (e.g. better, happier, more beautiful and less accurate) and superlative adjectives (e.g. best, the biggest, the most expensive and the least influential) in English. They are next asked to complete a quiz at the end of the lesson. Examples of the quiz questions are:

Instruction: Complete each sentence using the comparative or superlative form of the adjective given in brackets.

1 John can swim ____________ than Jeff. (fast)

2 Jane is ___________________ student in the class because she is extremely quiet. (talkative)

3 I think swimming is ____________ than diving. (exciting)

4 Sydney is _______________ city to live in Australia because of high rental rates and food prices. (expensive)

Answers:

(1) faster; (2) the least talkative; (3) more/less exciting; (4) the most expensive

Suppose teachers discuss the quiz questions and answers with students and explain correct and incorrect answers so students can learn the concepts and improve their future learning and performance. In that case, this action is related to formative assessment.

Consider the following Scenario 3, which incorporates formative and summative assessments for evaluating students' learning and achievement.

Scenario 3: As part of the project-based assignment in an English for Ecotourism unit of study, students are asked to collect information about wildlife in their local context. This assessment task is considered formal. They are asked to write a 1,000-word report in English about the wildlife they have chosen by:

1 describing its physical characteristics, habits and habitats (400 words).

2 discussing whether it is endangered or threatened by the tourism industry (300 words).

3 suggesting how to help protect it from irresponsible or unregulated tourism business (300 words).

Criteria for assessing students' reports are provided and discussed with students from the beginning and periodically. Students are asked to submit a draft of each section over one month and the complete report for feedback or comments by a specified date. In the end, students are asked to submit a portfolio that includes the final piece incorporating previous feedback for grading, all their earlier drafts with teacher feedback, and sources they have used for their projects. This is an example of a portfolio assessment (discussed further below and in Chapter 2).

Based on these sample scenarios, the central purpose of language testing and assessment is to provide evidence on which decisions are based. Such decisions may improve learning and teaching or be made for accountability purposes.

Language testing and assessment as a bridge for effective language teaching and learning

Language testing and assessment mediate teaching, learning and use. The concepts of formative and summative assessments are introduced below. This section introduces language classroom assessment purposes (illustrated in Figure 1.1).

Formative assessment/assessment for learning

Formative assessment (FA) or assessment for learning (AFL) focuses on learning and development. FA, which subsumes AFL, will be used for ease of writing. For example, teachers use FA to inform how well students learn and devise feedback to help them improve their learning. Teachers may use display questions – pedagogical questions for checking student learning or

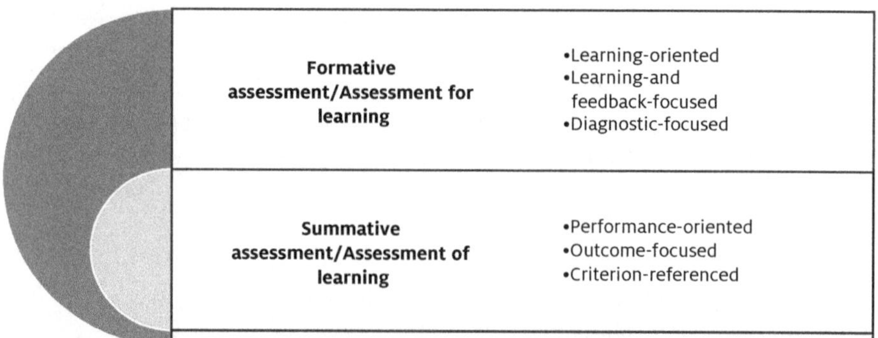

FIGURE 1.1 *Formative assessment/assessment for learning versus summative assessment/assessment of learning.*

understanding (e.g. do you know the meaning of this word?), quizzes and class exercises to provide feedback to their students. Teachers may observe that students make some common errors in the classroom, point these out to them and suggest ways for them to minimize such errors. FA also focuses on challenges students may face as they learn inside and outside the classroom. For this reason, FA can serve as a diagnostic strategy for understanding students' current learning and experience and for helping them overcome challenges or barriers affecting their learning. FA also assists teachers in modifying their future teaching directions, since teaching can be adaptive to students' current learning situations. This formative practice can result in increasing students' language accuracy, fluency and appropriacy.

Summative assessment/assessment of learning

Summative assessment (SA) or assessment of learning (AOL) focuses on a sum of learning outcomes or results of classroom instruction and learning. SA, which subsumes AOL, will be used for ease of writing. SA is explicitly related to the learning objectives or outcomes that inform assessment criteria. That is, teachers make a decision about students' attainment levels by checking whether students have met the required achievement criteria. SA is another common type of classroom assessment that bridges teaching and learning. SA aims to evaluate students' knowledge or performance at the end of a lesson, unit of study and term or semester. Teachers are often required to make decisions about their students at the end of their study programme. Therefore, SA, such as mid-term and final examinations and assigned tasks, is used to officially evaluate student learning attainment or achievement at the midpoint and endpoint of their learning (Lewkowicz & Leung 2021).

It should be noted that some SA can be used for FA. For instance, students' performance on the mid-term test can also be used as feedback to students to help them understand their strengths and weaknesses during a pressured assessment situation. Data from the mid-term test can also help teachers adjust their teaching content and activities so that students can be better prepared to do well in the final test. Such examples help to bridge teaching and learning processes. Based on this discussion, it is not useful to polarize FA and SA.

In-between FA and SA

Some classroom assessment tasks can encompass both FA and SA. For example, portfolio assessment in Scenario 3 above illustrates the application of FA as instructional for checking learning progress and improving learning and SA as it serves an administrative purpose for decision-making on student achievement grades. In Scenario 3, FA is achieved when the teacher reads students' drafts, applies some criteria or standards as students' drafts are read, provides comments or feedback on the drafts, and suggests what students should do next. Students can also engage in their FA (see 'Student-led assessment as a form of FA' below) as they plan their essay projects and use the scoring criteria to evaluate their current work. SA is achieved in the final project evaluation by considering students' submitted portfolios using the scoring criteria (Curtis 2018).

Student-led assessment as a form of FA

Much of the information discussed above has been largely *teacher-led*, but not all assessments in the language classroom are teacher-led. Students can lead their own assessment practices. For example, they can independently engage in assessment activities on their own, both inside and outside the classroom. Some scholars have used terms such as self-assessment, self-test, self-monitoring, self-evaluation, peer assessment and peer feedback to describe student-led assessment (also known as assessment as learning (AAL). In this book, FA encompasses AAL as formative in nature. For example, students may independently complete a mock test and check their performance at home. They can pay attention to areas or questions in which they did not perform well and try to improve. Another example is when students evaluate one another's essays and give feedback to one another regarding the level of task fulfilment, grammatical accuracy and input for further revisions. Student-led assessment, therefore, serves as a bridge between language learning and teaching.

Purposes of language testing and assessment practices

This section presents two broad purposes of language testing and assessment that will be expanded throughout this book:

1 *Accountability*: Accountability is related to ensuring that individuals (e.g. teachers and students) or institutions (e.g. departments and schools) that provide educational services are responsible for their roles and actions relevant to teaching and learning. This is also seen as *internal accountability* as it takes place in a local context. For example, teachers are responsible for providing high-quality teaching, learning and assessment activities in their teaching (e.g. teaching accurate content knowledge, monitoring students' progress and using

fair assessment). In language teaching, achievement tests and other forms of classroom assessment (as illustrated above) are used for accountability. Students are also responsible for their commitment to studying the learning content, participating in classroom activities, attending classes regularly and completing assessment tasks honestly. An educational institute is also responsible for checking students' academic progress, providing appropriate infrastructure that supports teaching and learning, and ensuring high-quality assessment and grading processes. Official acknowledgement of study completion, such as official certificates, course grades and academic transcripts, are commonly provided as accountability evidence.

External accountability can be related to mandatory examinations (e.g. literacy and numeracy tests) that governments, for example, ask students to take to measure their knowledge and progress. For governments, standards-based assessments are often served to account for education reform, which is usually one of the national strategic priorities. Governments argue that countries need to have knowledgeable and skilful citizens to compete economically with other countries. In Australia, for example, NAPLAN (National Assessment Program – Literacy and Numeracy) is an example of an annual standards-based assessment for Years 3, 5, 7 and 9; see https://www.nap.edu.au/naplan). When governments mandate standards-based assessments for schools, we need to ask critical questions about equality issues among schools or educational institutes.

Professional accreditation and licensing are other examples of external accountability. Accreditation or licensing purposes outside classroom contexts are associated with specific-purpose L2 proficiency tests (Douglas 2000). In Australia, for example, non-English-speaking healthcare professionals must take and pass the Occupational English Test (OET) criteria to register and practise their professions (i.e. licensing). Other examples of commercial specific-purpose tests are the Test of English for Aviation and the Michigan English Test (MET) for Healthcare.

2 *Selection*: In educational contexts, the notion of selection first relates to ensuring that students or applicants are suitable for a given language programme, position or job. It may also have a gatekeeping function in that only some may be selected. In education, it is often the case, for example, that only a certain number of students, candidates or applicants will be chosen or accepted due to limited classroom spaces and funding. Familiar to teachers are admission tests and university entrance examinations. These tests provide accountability for collecting evidence to determine whether students or applicants

have the necessary knowledge or skills and for deciding which students or applicants will be selected. International English language proficiency tests such as the Test of English as a Foreign Language (TOEFL) and International English Language Testing System (IELTS) are used to select applicants for university admission. Language aptitude tests (discussed below) are used to select military personnel with language talents to learn new languages before placement.

Placement has an element of selection. A placement test is particularly relevant to a situation where students or applicants who have already been selected or admitted into a programme must be placed in a suitable class or workplace. Tests used for this purpose are known as placement or screening tests. For example, it will be challenging for students with a low language level to be placed in an advanced language class because they will need help understanding the content and participating in classroom activities. Therefore, knowing whether a student's current knowledge and skills are suitable for a given study programme is crucial. Tailored placement tests may be developed locally based on the syllabus of a given course. Commercial placement tests are, for instance, the Oxford Placement Test (OEPT) and the Michigan English Placement Test (Michigan-EPT).

Tests and assessments can be used to diagnose students' or individuals' strengths and weaknesses of knowledge or skills. A diagnostic test or assessment has a selection purpose in that some students or test takers may be identified as being at risk of failing or being unsuccessful. Unlike a placement test, a diagnostic purpose does not have the primary aim of placing students into a specific programme. Instead, it is used to identify whether further academic support is probably needed. The Diagnostic English Language Needs Assessment (DELNA) is an example of language testing and assessment for this purpose. Students are first screened (Part 1) whether they should be further diagnosed (Part 2). Part 2 of the test can identify what students or candidates can and cannot do in a given language area (e.g. strengths and weaknesses). This information then provides a decision on further language support to areas needing improvement. In some classroom situations, self-assessment is a simple method for a diagnostic purpose (e.g. a self-assessment questionnaire that asks students to complete can-do statements). Dialang is an online diagnostic self-assessment on L2 proficiency levels based on the Common European Framework of Reference (CEFR) (https://dialangweb.lancaster.ac.uk/), which includes a self-assessment of eighteen European languages.

It should be noted that the term 'diagnostic' can have a negative connotation to some stakeholders, including students and parents, since it implies a deficit model (a lack of something). This term is often associated with medical assessment and evaluation of a symptom. Given this, it may be more strategic not to include the word in the test or assessment name.

Overview of this book

This book is a comprehensive yet introductory guide to language testing and assessment, with ten chapters that explore the interconnectedness between theory and practice for testing and assessing language proficiency and skills. Each chapter highlights important considerations, practices and the essential features of language tests and assessments. At the end of each chapter, discussion questions and resources for further reading are provided. The book also includes a glossary of language testing and assessment at the end and an appendix.

Chapter 1 (Language Testing and Assessment) has discussed various language testing and assessment purposes, ranging from accountability to selection. It has introduced the concept of language assessment literacy, emphasizing its significance for people involved in language testing and assessment.

Chapter 2 (Theoretical and Methodical Considerations) further discusses essential considerations in language testing and assessment, such as constructs to be tested or assessed, types of language tests and assessments, methods and techniques for eliciting language information or ability, and perspectives for interpreting language performance.

Chapter 3 (Test and Assessment Design) explores practical developmental and design stages in language testing and assessment (e.g. strategic planning, test design, test standards and qualities, test construction, test validation and revision, test administration, scoring and analysis, decision-making, report, feedback and test use). It introduces test and assessment specifications and quality criteria such as reliability, validity, practicality, fairness, impact and ethics.

Chapter 4 (Standards and Qualities) explores in further detail the seven aspects of language testing and assessment standards introduced in Chapter 3: reliability, validity and trustworthiness, practicality, ethics, fairness and impact. It aims to demystify these concepts with several examples and guidelines for applying them in language testing and assessment practices.

Chapter 5 (Testing and Assessing Reading) presents key considerations in testing and assessing AL reading. It explains the theoretical nature of reading and reading comprehension and reading purposes and discusses techniques for testing and assessing reading.

Chapter 6 (Testing and Assessing Writing) considers how to develop writing tests and assessments. It discusses the nature of writing, including views of writing assessment (e.g. product or process approach), and techniques to elicit and evaluate writing performance.

Chapter 7 (Testing and Assessing Listening) explores test and assessment methods for collecting and evaluating listening abilities. It discusses types of listening, listening test and assessment techniques, test administration and scoring methods.

Chapter 8 (Testing and Assessing Speaking) focuses on methods for testing and assessing speaking. It discusses the nature of speaking, its purposes and critical considerations in testing, assessing and evaluating speaking performance.

Chapter 9 (Test and Assessment Analysis) suggests ways to enhance and improve language testing and assessment practices by discussing quantitative and qualitative analysis of test and assessment data.

Chapter 10 (Challenges and Opportunities) concludes the book by discussing challenges in language testing and assessment and showcasing how the testing and assessment standards discussed in this book can be used to evaluate computer-assisted language testing and assessment (CALTA). This chapter also discusses further opportunities for language testing and assessment.

YouTube and Facebook

YouTube Channel: https://www.youtube.com/@LanguageTestingandAssessment

Facebook: https://www.facebook.com/Languagetestingandassessment/

Discussion

1 What have you learnt about the history of language testing and assessment as a field of study?

2 Give and discuss examples of classroom language testing and assessment activities in your classroom contexts.

3 What are language testing and assessment purposes?

4 Explain the following tests and assessments in your own words:

   a Achievement tests

   b Diagnostic assessment

   c Formative assessment

   d L2 proficiency test

   e Summative assessment.

5 What are some advantages and disadvantages of computer technology for language testing and assessment designs? Would you consider computer technology in your future test/assessment? If so, in what way?

Further reading

Bachman, L. & Damböck, B., 2017, *Language assessment for classroom teachers*, Oxford University Press, Oxford.

Chapter 2 (Using classroom-based language assessments) of this book discusses some basic concepts and issues in classroom-based assessments, such as the relationship between teaching and assessment and the relative importance of decisions based on assessment (e.g. formative and summative assessment).

Khan, R., 2018, 'What is assessment? Purposes of assessment and evaluation' in *The TESOL encyclopedia of English language teaching*, eds J.I. Liontas and C. Coombe, Wiley, Oxford, pp. 1–7.

This chapter complements the current chapter, providing an accessible introduction to language testing and assessment in an educational setting. It defines testing, assessment, and evaluation, and discusses their roles in teaching pedagogy.

McNamara, T., 2000, *Language testing*, Oxford University Press, Oxford.

This book is a seminal work that provides an accessible introduction to language testing. It addresses the critical role of language testing in educational and social contexts.

Phakiti, A. & Leung, C., 2024, *Assessment for language teaching*, Cambridge University Press, Cambridge.

This book explores the key concepts of assessment approaches for language teaching practice (e.g. theory of language proficiency, roles and methods of assessment in language teaching).

Phakiti, A., Fernandez, C. & Steinhoff, A., 2021, *Language assessment: A practical approach* (RELC New Portfolio Series 10), SEAMEO Regional Language Centre, Singapore.

This book is an accessible introduction to language testing and assessment. It emphasizes translating language testing and assessment theory and methods into a real educational assessment practice.

Comments/suggestions

The author highly values your feedback and suggestions regarding this book. Your insights are crucial in improving the content and ensuring its relevance to your learning needs and interests. If you have any questions or inquiries, please do not hesitate to contact Aek Phakiti at aek.phakiti@sydney.edu.au. Your input is greatly appreciated.

2

Theoretical and Methodical Considerations

Overview

This chapter discusses pivotal considerations in using language testing and assessment to make decisions about students or test takers. Key considerations include delineating the constructs or content to be tested or assessed, understanding appropriate testing and assessment tools and methods, effectively interpreting scores or performance and recognizing the social dimensions of language testing and assessment practices.

Guided questions

1 What does 'construct' refer to in language testing and assessment?

2 What is your understanding of test and assessment techniques?

3 What do 'high-stakes' and 'low-stakes' tests mean?

Introduction

As discussed in Chapter 1, language testing and assessment is crucial in various decision-making contexts, such as certification, evaluation, admission and employment. These processes can significantly impact students or test takers, even in the case of formative assessment (FA; Phakiti & Leung 2024). This chapter explores essential theoretical and methodical considerations in language testing and assessment. It begins by discussing the nature of constructs in language testing and assessment (what to test and assess). It then explores test and assessment techniques for evaluating different language skills. The norm- and criterion-referenced approaches to assessment purposes and use are considered in detail, as they are closely associated with score or performance interpretation and decision-making processes. Finally, the social dimensions of language testing and assessment are articulated.

Constructs of language testing and assessment

Knowing what to test and assess in language testing and assessment practice can lead to effective and practical assessment. A construct is an abstract concept that cannot be directly observed but inferred from systematic or accurate observation of language behaviours. For example, teachers may want to check whether students can accurately use subject–verb agreements in English (e.g. he/she/it is/does, they are/do), which is part of the learning outcomes of the course. The construct in this situation is grammatical knowledge in subject–verb agreements. Students may be asked to write an essay about their hobbies or to talk about their last holiday. Teachers can evaluate the correctness or appropriateness of subject–verb agreements in their writing or speaking. Accordingly, students' judged performance may imply the current level of this grammatical knowledge.

The following section explores three areas explaining three language constructs often tested and assessed: AL proficiency, standards-based frameworks and Bloom's taxonomy used to inform learning outcomes.

AL proficiency

As introduced in Chapter 1, AL proficiency represents language knowledge and communication skills (e.g. speaking, listening, reading and writing). It is an accumulative outcome of various language learning and use experiences. Understanding AL proficiency is crucial, as it is a complex construct involving linguistic, cognitive, affective and social dimensions (discussed further below and in subsequent chapters). Several terms have been used to denote AL proficiency, such as *communicative competence* (e.g. Canale & Swain 1980; Hymes 1972), *communicative language ability* (e.g. Bachman 1990; Bachman & Palmer 1996, 2010) and *plurilingual competence* (e.g. Council of Europe 2020). For simplicity, this book uses AL proficiency to encompass these notions collectively. AL proficiency can be used for general communicative (e.g. everyday language skills) and specific-purpose situations (e.g. academic and professional). This section aims to help readers familiarize themselves with some academic terms associated with AL proficiency in the language testing and assessment literature.

General and specific-purpose AL proficiency

General AL proficiency, on the one hand, is the ability to use a given language (e.g. English), for example, to obtain, understand, process information and interact with others. General AL proficiency allows us to communicate effectively. On the other hand, specific-purpose AL proficiency is domain-specific AL proficiency for a given profession or context (e.g. English for business, tourism or medical professionals; see Douglas 2000). People in a specific profession tend to understand certain expressions or vocabulary, but an outsider may not make much sense when they hear them. Understanding these different types of AL proficiency can help us appreciate the diversity and complexity of language use in other contexts.

Sub-constructs of AL proficiency

Both general and specific-purpose AL proficiency are multi-componential as various competence components are required at any time in language use (e.g. Bachman 1990; Bachman & Palmer 1996, 2010; Purpura 2008, 2016). They can be specific for different language skills (e.g. reading versus speaking). For readers new to theory in language proficiency, it is useful to know the following competence components:

1. *Organizational competence* refers to the ability to control the formal structure of language based on its rules. This competence is required to produce or recognize grammatically correct utterances or sentences and comprehend their propositional content to form texts (Bachman 1990). This competence has two subcomponents:
   a. *Grammatical competence* refers to linguistic competence involved in language usage. It includes knowledge of (1) vocabulary, (2) morphology, (3) syntax and (4) phonology (for speaking and listening) and graphology (for reading and writing). These linguistic competencies allow people to control their language choices to express or understand language forms, utterances or sentences. Examples are: 'That girl is taller than this boy' (grammatically accurate), compared to 'That girl *more taller* than this boy' (grammatically inaccurate, but understandable).
   b. *Textual competence* refers to the knowledge of the conventions or rules of cohesion and rhetorical organization for combining

utterances or sentences to form or create a unified text or unit of language. Cohesion includes using reference, conjunction and lexical cohesion, whereas rhetorical organization includes narrations, descriptions and explanations. In a conversation, such textual competence includes attention-getting, topic nomination, conversation maintenance and turn-taking.

2 *Pragmatic competence* refers to the ability to use and understand language in context. Pragmatics denotes the relationships between (1) utterances or sentences and (2) the act or function a speaker or writer intends to perform/achieve. Pragmatic competence, therefore, requires people to understand a pragmatic condition in which an utterance(s) or a sentence(s) with an intended function is acceptable to, as well as realized by others (e.g. listeners or readers). It includes two subcomponents:

a *Illocutionary competence* refers to producing and understanding speech acts in a given situation. It requires knowing the relationship between two or more speakers in a conversation or shared background or experience.

b *Sociolinguistic competence* is the ability to appropriately use, express and understand the language in various language functions in a given convention or situation. This ability requires appropriately formulating an utterance or a sentence for a given context or audience (e.g. listeners, interlocutors or readers). It may concern knowledge of how to behave socially and appropriately use language in a given situation (e.g. at a funeral or wedding ceremony).

3 *Strategic competence* refers to metacognitive strategies for managing language use and cognitive processes. According to Bachman and Palmer (1996, 2010), metacognitive strategies comprise goal setting, planning, assessment and appraisal (or evaluation). These strategies help people regulate their processing and use of required or available resources to accomplish a communicative goal.

4 *Interactional competence* refers to the ability to interact with other interlocutors or audiences, usually in face-to-face or technology-mediated communication (see also Salaberry & Kunitz 2019). Celce-Murcia (2007) presented two subcomponents of interactional competence:

a *Actional competence* refers to the knowledge of performing various speech acts.

b *Conversational competence* refers to the knowledge of the conventional turn-taking system.

5 *Intercultural competence* refers to recognizing, respecting and understanding that other people have different cultures, values, beliefs and cultural identities (Fantini 2009). Therefore, people should be able to use appropriate and sensitive language to a given audience.

AL proficiency tests

Most AL tests and assessments are standardized and used to serve purposes of accountability. There are situations in which it is useful to know people's AL proficiency to make decisions about them (e.g. education, employment and migration). Test and assessment developers use theories of AL proficiency as discussed above, and target language-use situations to inform their test design and administration. AL proficiency tests assess people's proficiency independent of a specific language syllabus or curriculum. They focus on people's accumulative language knowledge and skills that may result from formal and informal learning of a given language. Their performance represents their current AL proficiency (e.g. beginner, intermediate or advanced). AL proficiency tests and assessments separately measure receptive and productive language skills (e.g. listening, reading, writing and speaking). Still, there is a recent trend to assess integrated language skills, which combines receptive and productive skills. The Test of English for International Communication (TOEIC) is an example of a general English proficiency test. Specific-purpose AL proficiency tests include the TOEFL and IELTS tests (academic purpose), the Occupational English Test (OET; for medical professionals), and the Aviation English Proficiency Test (e.g. for pilots, air traffic controllers and flight engineers).

It should be noted that the theory of AL English proficiency (e.g. Hyme 1972) was initially rooted in a monolingual or monoglossic view of language proficiency (see also Leung 2022; Shohamy 2013). Multilinguals – individuals who can communicate in more than two languages with varying degrees of proficiency (see Chapters 1 and 10) – differ significantly from monolinguals who speak only one language, typically their mother tongue. Multilinguals have differential access to multiple language systems, both internally (cognitively) and externally (socially and culturally), which enhances their ability to navigate diverse communicative contexts (Leung 2022; Grosjean 1989). Unlike monolinguals, multilinguals constantly negotiate their identities and strategically use various languages during interactions, adapting to different audiences and environments (Lopez, Turkan & Guzman-Orth 2017). This dynamic and flexible approach to communication sets multilinguals apart, providing them with unique cognitive and social advantages. The complex nature of AL proficiency among multilinguals affects the validity or trustworthiness of language testing and assessment (see Chapter 10).

Standards-based frameworks

Standards are prescriptions of learning outcomes, objectives, competencies, skills or abilities that students or individuals should possess. Standards are used as benchmarks for teaching and designing assessments in educational contexts. They can be categorized into progressive levels of competencies (Levels 1, 2, 3 and 4; Years 1, 2, 3 and 4, etc.) and may have some content level overlaps (e.g. some similar competencies between Levels 1 and 2). Based on Popham (2017), it is useful to be able to distinguish two types of standards.

1. *Content standards* specify a set of competencies, skills or abilities that educators, teachers or governments want students to learn or possess. They can be part of the learning outcomes or objectives.
2. *Performance standards* focus on the desired competencies, skills or abilities described in the content standards.

The following are examples of standards-based frameworks for teaching and assessing English language:

- The American Council on the Teaching of Foreign Languages (ACTFL) Proficiency Guidelines (https://www.actfl.org/resources/actfl-proficiency-guidelines-2012) describes a continuum of proficiency levels in four language skills (speaking, writing, listening and reading) from advanced to intermediate to novice, with sublevels of high, mid and low.
- Australia's *ESL Scales* (https://education.nsw.gov.au/teaching-and-learning/curriculum/multicultural-education/english-as-an-additional-language-or-dialect/resources) describe nine levels of English language development of English as an additional language or dialect (EAL/D), in speaking, listening, reading and writing, ranging from the beginning level to Level 8. The scales serve as a benchmark for programme and curriculum development and assessment.
- The *Canadian Language Benchmarks* (CLB) for English as a second language for adults (https://www.canada.ca/content/dam/ircc/migration/ircc/english/pdf/pub/language-benchmarks.pdf) describe three stages (basic, intermediate and advanced) and sublevels (initial, developing, adequate and fluent) across the four language skills.

- The *Common European Framework of Reference for Languages* (CEFR; https://www.coe.int/en/web/common-european-framework-reference-languages) includes fourteen languages. The CEFR divides AL proficiency into six levels: A1 and A2 (Basic), B1 and B2 (Independent) and C1 and C2 (Proficient), with three additional 'plus' levels (A2+, B1+, B2+) related to language reception, production and interaction.
- The UK's *EAL Assessment Framework for Schools* by the Bell Foundation (https://www.bell-foundation.org.uk/eal-programme/eal-assessment-framework/) provides standards for teaching and assessing EAL students. See also EAL Proficiency Assessment Tool.

Across the globe, a government-prescribed standards-based framework often plays a significant role in how schools, universities or educational institutions use various forms of language testing and assessment for their students. Standards-based frameworks can also be connected to Bloom's taxonomy, which will be discussed next.

Bloom's taxonomy for teaching, learning and assessment

While Bloom's taxonomy has influenced the formulation of learning objectives in general education, it has not been commonly applied in many language teaching, testing and assessment practices. However, it can potentially inform standards for language classroom contexts, particularly when setting up learning outcomes or objectives that give what to assess. Therefore, this chapter introduces Bloom's taxonomy as it can determine higher-order thinking (Phakiti 2018). Familiarity with Bloom's taxonomy gives language teachers several advantages, especially for classroom assessment.

Bloom et al. (1956) produced a taxonomy or framework for educational objectives, which focused on six accumulative hierarchical levels of thinking and learning from the most basic and concrete to the most complex and abstract (i.e. from knowledge, comprehension, application, analysis and synthesis to evaluation). These objectives are also abstract. Bloom's taxonomy gained popularity among educators as it helps define learning objectives or outcomes across disciplines. Bloom's taxonomy was revised and updated by Anderson et al. (2001). In the revised taxonomy, the original levels are expressed in verb forms to represent active processes. Figure 2.1 illustrates the six levels in a pyramid. The taxonomy is accumulative in that lower-order levels are prerequisites to mastery of higher-order thinking and learning. In this revised version, comprehension concepts form part of 'understanding' and synthesis forms part of 'creating'.

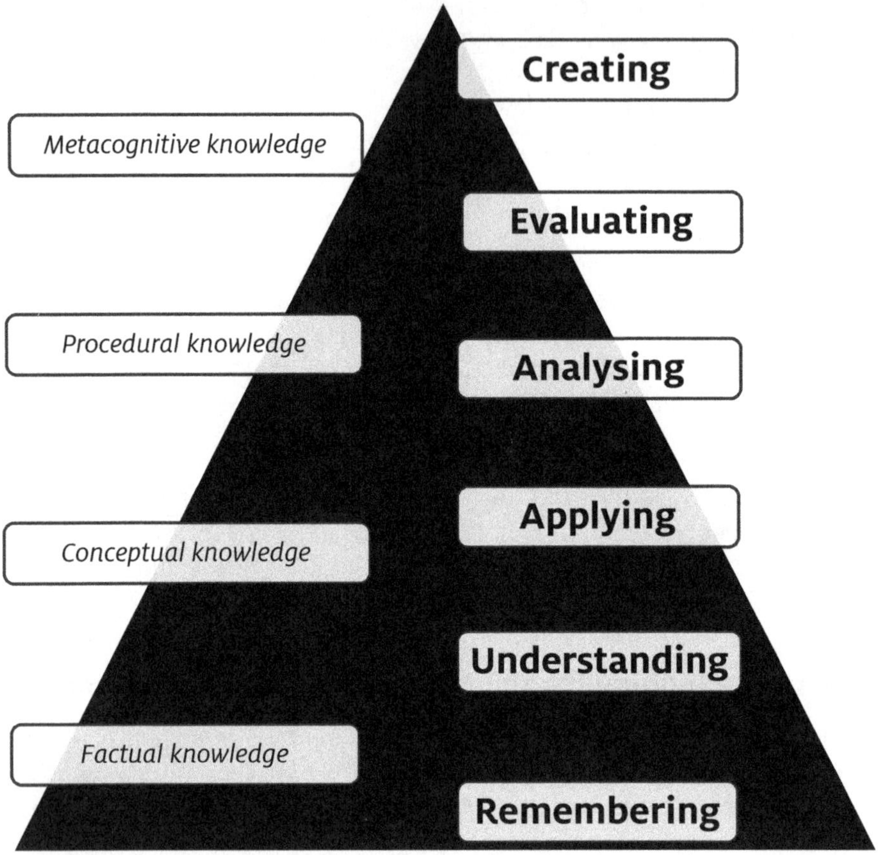

FIGURE 2.1 *Mapping of Bloom's (2001) taxonomy.*

The revised taxonomy is two-dimensional. The first dimension is the six levels of thinking and learning, and the second is the four knowledge dimensions (i.e. factual, conceptual, procedural and metacognitive).

Six levels of thinking and learning

The six levels of Bloom's revised taxonomy are as follows:

1. *Remembering* is related to memorizing new information and recalling information (e.g. factual and conceptual knowledge) from long-term memory.
2. *Understanding* relates to perceiving the intended meaning from oral, written or graphical texts. Understanding requires basic rhetorical skills such as interpreting, exemplifying, classifying, summarizing, inferring, comparing and explaining.

3. *Applying* is related to the act on an assigned or assessment task. Students use relevant knowledge and appropriate procedures from levels 1 and 2. They should be able to apply their knowledge to a new but similar problem structure or task.
4. *Analysing* involves breaking down materials and tasks into smaller units. Students should be able to see how different parts relate to one another and the overall picture. Analysing also includes differentiating facts from opinions and bias, organizing task completion and structures, and attributing, prioritizing or assigning values or importance to information and tasks.
5. *Evaluating* is related to monitoring, checking, judging and critiquing one's or others' performance using criteria such as quality, quantity, time and cost, and effectiveness and success levels.
6. *Creating* involves producing a new outcome, product or creative work using the above levels. Creating is the highest order of thinking and ability, requiring goal setting, planning, designing and producing an outcome.

Four levels of knowledge

The four levels of knowledge intersect with each of the six thinking levels:

1. *Factual knowledge* is students' basic knowledge to understand a task or solve a problem. It includes knowledge of the world.
2. *Conceptual knowledge* is related to understanding the interconnectedness among various factual knowledge. This knowledge requires students to know about principles that describe and explain knowledge, behaviours or expectations.
3. *Procedural knowledge* is related to the how-to knowledge. It requires knowledge about key and essential steps to accomplish a task. Students need to acquire domain-general and -specific knowledge to utilize it.
4. *Metacognitive knowledge* is the knowledge of one's knowledge (e.g. knowing what one knows and does not know). This knowledge requires students to apply appropriate strategies to enhance their task completion and decision-making.

Translating Bloom's taxonomy into learning outcomes

Learning outcomes are a set of statements of what students are expected to learn, understand or be able to do to complete a subject within a defined period of learning (e.g. term or semester). They are related to the aims of the subject syllabus and cover the range of abilities essential to pass the course. They must be feasible for students to meet and measurable by test or assessment tasks or activities. The following example shows three interrelated learning outcomes in EAL reading using Bloom's taxonomy that can be useful for formative and summative assessment practices. Table 2.1 illustrates how the three learning outcomes can be aligned with Bloom's taxonomy dimensions, and a higher outcome level requires a lower cognitive and knowledge level:

1 *Outcome 1*: Students can remember a topic and some factual information from the text they read.
2 *Outcome 2*: Students can summarize the general idea about the text they read.
3 *Outcome 3*: Students can write a summary of the text with some factual information and examples from the text.

Bloom's revised taxonomy helps formulate learning or outcomes for various levels or grades of students. Since it emphasizes the need for students to acquire some basic levels before a higher level, assessment can be tailored to match students' levels and readiness. It allows teachers to assess the right level of students' expected performance as they progress through learning objectives and classroom activities. Another benefit of the revised taxonomy is that each level can overlap, so students do not need to acquire one level before engaging in a more complex process. It is worth noting that Bloom's taxonomy was not designed to provide feedback for learning, making it difficult for teachers or practitioners to know when and what kind of feedback should be provided to students at different cognitive levels (Duckor & Holmberg 2023).

In summary, the first step in language testing and assessment is to clarify what to test and assess. However, successful language testing and assessment considers the alignment between the language constructs of interest, real-life language situations and assessment tasks. In classroom contexts, the learning outcomes, teaching and learning activities, and testing and assessment tasks must be aligned (Biggs & Tang 2011; Fulcher 2010). Figure 2. 2 further demonstrates such an interrelationship.

Teachers and assessors should consider (1) the intended learning outcomes, (2) teaching and learning activities that enable students to accomplish the learning outcomes, and (3) assessment tasks that match and facilitate both the learning outcomes and the teaching and learning activities (Biggs & Tang 2011; Fulcher 2010; Green 2020). For example, when a learning outcome aims to help students develop a skill to write a reflective essay about language learning, teaching and learning activities should help students compose a

TABLE 2.1 Aligned Applications of Bloom's (2001) Taxonomy Knowledge Dimensions

Knowledge	Remembering	Understanding	Applying	Analysing	Evaluating	Creating
Factual	Outcome 1	Outcomes 1 & 2	Outcomes 1, 2 & 3	Outcomes 1, 2 & 3	Outcomes 1, 2 & 3	Outcomes 1, 2 & 3
Conceptual	Outcome 1	Outcomes 1 & 2	Outcomes 1, 2 & 3	Outcomes 1, 2 & 3	Outcomes 1, 2 & 3	Outcomes 1, 2 & 3
Procedural	Outcome 1 (reading skills, how to extract information)	Outcomes 1 & 2 (concept maps, how to summarize)	Outcomes 1, 2 & 3 (summary outline)	Outcomes 1, 2 & 3 (how to group factual information)	Outcomes 1, 2 & 3 (what makes some information questionable)	Outcomes 1, 2 & 3 (how to write a summary, criteria for judging a good summary)
Metacognitive	Outcome 1 (reading strategies)	Outcomes 1 & 2 (self-monitoring, self-evaluation)	Outcomes 1, 2 & 3 (planning/ outlining, evaluating the outline)	Outcomes 1, 2 & 3 (self-monitoring)	Outcomes 1, 2 & 3 (self-evaluating)	Outcomes 1, 2 & 3 (self-evaluating)

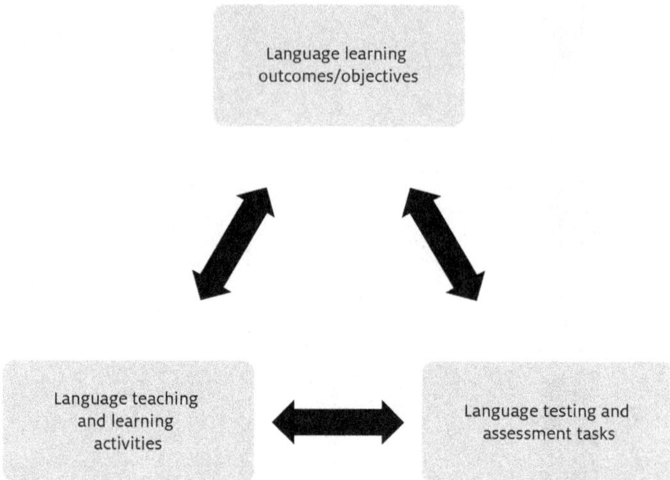

FIGURE 2.2 *Alignments between learning outcomes, teaching and learning experiences, and assessment tasks.*

reflective essay (e.g. what it should look like, such as common structures (introduction, body and conclusion), the content of their reflection and assessment criteria). Students should receive sufficient formative feedback on their learning and performance. The final evaluation of their reflective essays should be based on the criteria used during classroom activities.

Tools and methods for testing and assessment purposes

Tests and assessments are tools or elicitation methods to gather information from students or test takers. Tests are often administered in a standardized and planned condition using predetermined time for completion and scoring processes. They can be contrasted with non-test methods such as portfolios, assigned coursework and self- and peer assessments, which can be flexible to complete (Brown 2005; Douglas 2010; Green 2020). The following provide examples of language tests and assessments that are used in language education.

Language tests

This section presents achievement and language aptitude tests. AL proficiency tests have already been presented above.

Achievement tests

Achievement tests are used to serve an accountability purpose and are connected to the learning outcomes of a course. In many educational settings, an official policy requires teachers to report students' learning achievement or attainment in a given subject or unit of study. This means that information about students' learning performance needs to be collected based on the course learning outcomes. In many English as an additional language (EAL) contexts, students are, for instance, required to take the mid-term and final examinations to fulfil this requirement. Typically, achievement tests are summative (the sum of what students have learnt). For instance, students' achievement scores are mapped with the grading system (e.g. fail, poor, average, good and very good). It should be noted that teachers and academic institutes do not necessarily rely solely on achievement tests to judge students' achievement or attainment. They may also use other assessment tasks to collect students' learning performance (e.g. assigned course work, portfolio assessment; further discussed below).

Language aptitude tests

Language aptitude tests do not measure the achievement of prior language learning but predict the likelihood of future language learning success. Language aptitude is a special trait, an innate or raw talent people possess in learning a second or foreign language, such as linguistic decoding ability (see Doughty 2018; Smith & Stanfield 2017; Winke 2018, who discuss language aptitude tests and issues related to language aptitude tests at greater length). Winke (2018) points out that language aptitude is particularly relevant in language instructional contexts.

Several language aptitude tests are largely psycholinguistic-oriented since they focus on individuals' cognitive and linguistic traits rather than on the role of social environments. Examples of language aptitude tests include the Modern Language Aptitude Test (MLAT), the Pimsleur Language Aptitude Battery (PLAB) and the Defense Language Aptitude Battery (DLAB). The High-Level Language Aptitude Battery (Hi-LAB) is also cognitive-oriented, as it measures an individual's cognitive and perceptual language aptitude (e.g. memory, speed, acuity, induction and fluency; see Doughty 2018).

The use of language aptitude tests in educational contexts is not widespread due to questions about their immediate usefulness for language teaching and learning, the technical nature of test administration and interpretation, affordability and availability. An unintended impact on students identified to have low language aptitude is demotivation to learn languages (see Winke 2018).

Teacher-led language assessments

Teacher-led language assessments such as FA and SA, as introduced in Chapter 1, can be described as assessments teachers use to collect student information. In the language testing and assessment literature, the term 'alternative' or 'non-traditional assessment' is often used to describe assessments that do not use test procedures and conditions (see Al-Mahrooqi & Denman 2018; Ariza & Morehouse 2018; Brown & Abeywickrama 2019; Curtis 2018; Fox 2017). The term 'alternative', however, can be misunderstood by some in that it suggests that it is the other option that can replace traditional language tests. The term alternative assessment is not used in this book to avoid misconceptions.

In addition to FA and SA, there are other assessment approaches related to teacher-led language assessments that are worth noting. For example, learning-oriented assessment (LOA; Chong & Reinders 2023; Turner & Purpura 2017) considers that all language testing and assessments (formative and summative) provide rich information that can facilitate students' linguistic, cognitive and social processes and development. With these broad approaches in mind, the following presents some teacher-led assessments often used in classroom assessments.

Assigned course tasks

Assigned course tasks require students to fulfil specific requirements (e.g. a review of a topic, an article or a library project). It can be achieved through task- or content-based assessment (e.g. Ellis & Shintani 2014). It may be in written, spoken or digital format. For example, in a written assigned task, students learn to analyse the task requirements, plan their task structure, gather information (library research, observation) for use, and draft and edit their work using assessment criteria. Assigned course tasks can be individual, pair or group work.

Portfolio assessment

As discussed earlier in the chapter, portfolio assessment utilizes FA and SA. A portfolio assessment is a continuous assessment of students' work until the end of the course. It helps teachers and students understand the progress leading to the final desirable products or performance. For example, on their own, students may be asked to complete a project by producing a brochure, advertisement, catalogue, poster, news article or digital story. In group work, students learn to collaborate, share responsibilities, delegate tasks and improve their social and communication skills in a group project. Teachers can monitor and check students' progress at various points in producing their portfolios, and early feedback can be provided to them.

In recent years, ePortfolios (i.e. electronic/online portfolios kept or stored in an online or cloud platform, e.g. Google Docs, SharePoint and OneDrive) have been adopted in various educational settings (see Lam 2023). Through an internet connection, teachers can assess students' submitted work through technology applications such as Turnitin (for checking plagiarism), online assessment rubrics, text editors and comments. With internet access, students and teachers can access ePortfolios anywhere (schools or homes) and anytime, making learning and assessment flexible. This area is of interest to several educational and professional contexts.

Learner-led assessment

Learner-led assessment can be defined as assessment activities that learners or students actively engage despite the presence or absence of teachers' regulation. In addition to the teacher-led assessments above, two learner-led assessments (also known as assessment as learning, discussed in Chapter 1) are commonly found to be used in and outside the classroom: self-assessment and peer assessment.

Self-assessment

Self-assessment is a learner-centred approach to FA that promotes the development of self-monitoring, self-reflection, self-evaluation and learner autonomy (see Midraj 2018). Students can monitor their learning, reflecting on both the success and challenges obtained during their learning. To promote effective self-assessment, teachers should guide how and what to do when engaging in self-assessment activities (e.g. recommending some initial plans and explaining criteria with meaningful examples for judging performance). Self-assessment allows students to familiarize themselves with expectations and improve their language knowledge and ability. There are various forms of self-assessment with which students can engage. For ease of informal placement, students may be asked to estimate their proficiency level (e.g. are you beginner, pre-intermediate, intermediate, upper-intermediate or advanced learners?). They may be asked to complete a self-assessment questionnaire with a series of 'can-do' statements using rating scales (e.g. disagree, unsure, agree). As discussed earlier, another form of self-assessment includes language tests such as quizzes or practice tests. This is known as *self-testing*, as it allows students to observe the level of their success objectively. They can focus on areas of weaknesses or difficulty.

Peer assessment

Peer assessment takes a similar approach to self-assessment. It is a formative approach and promotes students' ability to observe and evaluate the quality of their peers' work or performance (see Sun & Doman 2018). Peer assessment includes peer evaluation, peer review and peer feedback. Peer assessment requires teachers' ongoing involvement, including monitoring and scaffolding. Peer assessment fosters collaboration and teamwork. It helps expand students' works' audience (i.e. teachers are no longer the only audience). Peer assessment can be extended in oral classroom presentations. For example, students can rate their peer performance based on given criteria (e.g. clarity of presentation, level of engagement, use of visual aids, non-verbal communication skills and overall performance). Another example of peer assessment is peer editing. Students may work on the same essay task and then exchange their essays for peer assessment. Teachers can provide a checklist or guide for them (e.g. whether there are problems with subject–verb agreement, incorrect verb forms, word order, incorrect prepositions, spelling mistakes and incomplete sentences).

Non-linguistic assessments

Assessment in the language classroom cannot only focus on students' learning outcomes or language achievement. Teaching and learning are socio-cultural by nature (e.g. teachers play a significant role in helping students reach the desired learning goals by connecting with their cognitive and psychological processes). This section considers some useful non-linguistic assessments, including questionnaires, qualitative observations and interviews. Cognitive engagement and psychological processes have been recognized in SLA and language teaching (Dörnyei & Ryan 2015; Mercer, Ryan & Williams 2012) and language testing and assessment research (Bachman & Palmer 2010; Winke & Brunfaut 2021). Understanding students' cognitive and psychological processes allows teachers and students to understand students' task engagement levels, challenges and emotional responses (e.g. feelings and attitudes). The following are essential constructs associated with mental and psychological aspects relevant to classroom assessment. Teachers may implicitly or explicitly assess these constructs to inform their teaching and assessment decisions.

Personal characteristics

Personal characteristics refer to students' variables (e.g. age, gender, first language, cultural and socio-economic backgrounds, target L2 proficiency level, number of languages spoken, and literacy and educational levels).

Teachers should consider students' characteristics before designing a test or assessment because some topics may give advantages to only some students due to differences in personal traits.

Cognitive or mental processes

Cognitive processes are related to students' linguistic and mental processes in human information processing. For example, they are related to using information in working and long-term memory (e.g. to recall or remember information, to activate grammar rules for applications, to monitor and evaluate the quality of language use or responses to tasks). Cognitive processes may be considered in terms of metacognitive or self-regulatory strategies (e.g. planning, monitoring and evaluating language use or responses). In an essay test, successful students tend to develop an outline of what to write, consider coherence and use cohesive devices, and check their spelling or grammar as they write and after they have finished writing, for example.

Psychological characteristics

Psychological characteristics refer to abstract mental and affective dimensions that explain individual differences. They can be understood through students' self-concepts. The following are psychological characteristics that can be considered in language testing and assessment.

Cognitive learning styles

Cognitive learning styles refers to students' preferred ways and modes to obtain, process and retain information for learning, problem-solving and use. For example, some students prefer to learn and use some rules or principles first before looking at language examples. In contrast, others prefer to look at examples before determining the grammar rules. Some students read and listen to gain information, whereas others prefer interacting with others to learn. Cognitive learning styles may impact language performance because specific test formats and tasks may not suit some students' cognitive learning styles.

Motivation

Motivation refers to students' affective disposition that governs their decisions to take action to learn or complete tasks. It determines how much they are willing to devote themselves and persist in completing tasks or achieving their goals. Without motivation, students will not engage in language tasks.

Effort

Effort refers to students' time use and devotion to complete a test or assessment task. It can be observed by counting the hours and cognitive attempts or engagement to complete the test or assessment tasks. Students should be encouraged to make an effort to complete test and assessment tasks by helping them understand the relevance of the tasks to their future capacity and opportunities.

Self-efficacy

Self-efficacy refers to students' evaluative beliefs and confidence about their capability to accomplish a future learning activity or test task. Self-efficacy is affected by the accumulative level of past success (e.g. previous learning or test-taking success) and current perception of ongoing support to help them succeed.

Language test and assessment anxiety

Language test and assessment anxiety refers to students' extreme distress, apprehension and worries. It can be triggered by fear of failure and a perceived lack of ability, adequacy or preparedness to complete assessment tasks. Anxiety can happen before and during test-taking or assessment processes. Students tend to be anxious in high-stakes tests. While moderate anxiety helps students push the effort to complete test or assessment tasks, extreme anxiety affects performance since it can affect concentration levels (e.g. students struggle to recall information or produce responses to tasks promptly). Teachers and assessors must attempt to minimize test or assessment anxiety and offer anxiety-coping strategies to prepare students and test takers to manage during test and assessment periods.

In summary, language testing and assessment require a complex set of tools and methods to collect and evaluate a wide range of language and non-language information from students or test takers.

Norm-referenced and criterion-referenced approaches

In FA, tests and assessments are geared toward improving and promoting successful teaching and learning. In SA and externally standardized language testing and assessment, tests and assessments serve outcome-oriented decision-making. This section focuses on how students' scores or performance decide their learning success, achievement and language proficiency levels. Generally speaking, interpretation requires inferences about language performance or ability based on observations and test scores. Two common interpretive approaches useful to know are the norm-referenced and criterion-referenced approaches (Burkett 2018; Sawaki 2017). The key difference between these approaches does not lie in what tests or assessments are used, but in score or performance interpretations (e.g. the same test can be used, but score or performance inferences can be different, leading to different kinds of decision-making).

Norm-referenced approach

The norm-referenced approach was part of the earlier language testing and assessment theory development in the 1980s. It ranks test takers' or students' scores with those of other test takers or students. The norm-referenced approach is related to the 'normal distribution' of score spread, in which students' scores or performance levels are ordered from the lowest to highest. A normal distribution has a bell-curve distribution in which a mean score represents an average ability (placed at the 50 per cent point or in the middle of the bell-shaped curve). On the left side of the mean score are students who are below average, whereas on the right side of the mean score are those above average. Based on this, students' scores are interpreted with other students' performances. In the norm-referenced approach, percentiles are used. For example, a 90th percentile means that 90 per cent of all students in the dataset are equal to or lower than that score.

The norm-referenced interpretation is often adopted in standardized tests and assessments, such as large-scale AL proficiency and standards-based tests used nationally or internationally as discussed earlier. However, a decision based on the norm-referenced approach can also be applied even when the sample size of students or test takers is small, for example when only one scholarship is available. Still, there are a number of applicants to be considered. The norm-referenced approach is often considered when there are limited spaces, resources or a quota for a given study programme, employment or immigration. It is important to note that while standards and criteria for evaluating students or test takers are used in large-scale standardized tests (similar to the criterion-referenced approach as discussed next), the focus on the norm-referenced approach is comparing and ranking scores or performance of all students or test takers.

Criterion-referenced approach

The criterion-referenced approach does not aim to interpret test scores or make a decision the way it is for the norm-referenced approach (i.e. by ranking and comparing students to make a decision). The term criterion refers to an expected ability, achievement or standard to judge students' performance. People may use the same test in which the norm-referenced test (percentile) is adopted. However, in the criterion-referenced approach, percentages are used (not percentiles). For example, while the IELTS or TOEFL can rank-order test takers according to their proficiency levels (e.g. from beginners to advanced), selecting applicants who use these tests to demonstrate their English proficiency levels can be based on the criterion-referenced approach. For example, a university in the UK may specify that international applicants must have the minimum overall and skill IELTS bands of 7 to be admitted to a degree programme. In this example, applicants are not compared with each other but with the specified English proficiency criterion.

A cut-off point for passing (e.g. at least 60 per cent) or achieving a particular grade (e.g. 85–90% = A, 91–100% = A+) can be a criterion for decision-making. In classroom assessment, teachers should focus on whether students have achieved the desirable learning outcomes or the expected task requirements. In the criterion-referenced approach, the decision required tends to be dichotomous or binary (e.g. pass/fail, can/cannot). Figure 2.3 summarizes the differences between the norm- and criterion-referenced approaches.

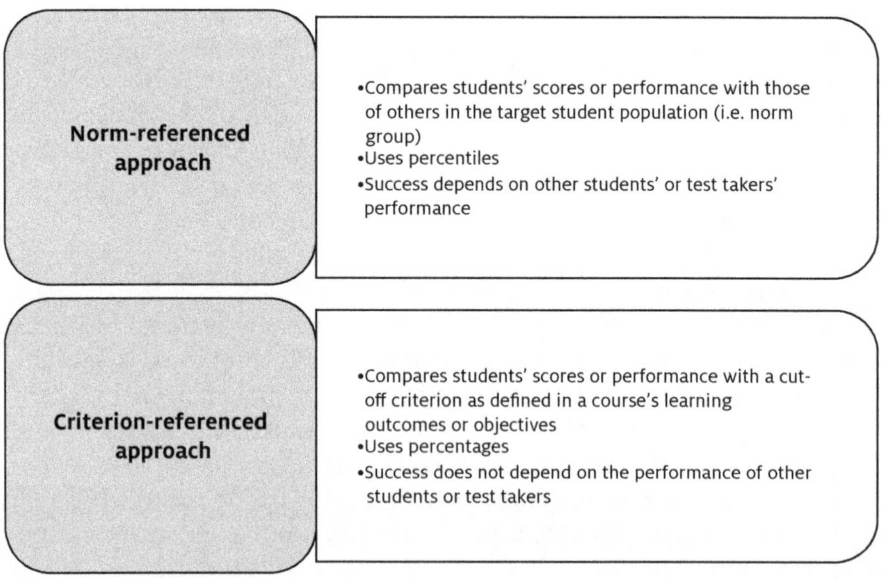

FIGURE 2.3 *Norm-referenced versus criterion-referenced approaches.*

In summary, the norm-referenced assessment approach compares students' scores or performance against one another. In contrast, the criterion-referenced approach compares students' scores against the criteria, learning outcomes or standards.

Social dimensions of language testing and assessment

The importance of social dimensions of language testing and assessment should be realized sooner rather than later (McNamara & Roever 2006; Young 2022). Language testing and assessment practice in any educational and social setting can also be highly political, as it is related to some form of power exercise (e.g. exhibiting authority). This section presents three social aspects of language testing and assessment: co-construction of language performance, stakes in language testing and assessment, and the socio-political nature of test and assessment use.

Co-construction of language performance

The social dimensions of language testing and assessment encompass a broad spectrum of considerations significantly influencing language test and assessment design, implementation and interpretation. These dimensions are integral to understanding the impacts of language assessments on individuals and societies. For example, the design of language tests and assessments often incorporates social and cultural contexts to ensure the assessments are equitable and relevant to students or test takers. The choice of questions, tasks and requirements imposing students or test takers to complete has a social origin. Language test and assessment performance depends on social aspects as well as students' or test takers' sole abilities.

In speaking tests and assessments, for example, the choice of interlocutors and raters can significantly affect performance outcomes. The interlocutor's behaviour, language proficiency and accent can influence students' or test takers' specific and overall performance. To illustrate, an interlocutor who uses complex vocabulary or speaks in a less familiar dialect may inadvertently disadvantage students or test takers. The social interaction between the interlocutor and the student or test takers needs to be recognized as a crucial element of language testing and assessment, potentially impacting test and assessment fairness and validity. Using human and computer raters also reflects the social dimensions of language testing and assessment. Human raters bring subjective interpretations, which can be influenced by their backgrounds, attitudes and experiences. They, therefore, potentially introduce bias into the scoring process (Phakiti & Leung 2024). On the other hand, computer raters, while offering consistency, may lack a nuanced understanding of authentic language use in social contexts, which can lead to the oversimplification of language proficiency assessments (Fulcher & Harding 2022).

High- and low-stakes controversies

The term 'stakes' has a social dimension in language testing and assessment. Stakes can be placed along a continuum of low and high degrees. Traditionally, language testing and assessment is considered high stakes if a decision can affect students (e.g. whether they will pass a given course, graduate, obtain a diploma or be admitted to an educational programme). Achievement tests and assessments tend to be considered high stakes for students and teachers. Issues in socio-political power can also be seen in classroom contexts. Teachers, for example, can decide whether students pass or fail a course. Given this, students may be unwilling to be critical of their teachers' perceived bias or unfair practice. Furthermore, assessments enforced by governments that hold a school, an educational institute, and teachers accountable for increasing students' academic achievement are considered high stakes because funding support decisions can be made on a given school depending on students' performance.

Low-stakes testing and assessments are often perceived not to have the same noticeable impact as high-stakes ones described above. They are often related to the discussion of FA, as introduced in Chapter 1. Teachers may, for example, ask their students questions about what they have been taught to know students' current learning. This form of assessment does not immediately radically impact students' lives.

It is important to stress that the distinction between high- and low-stakes assessment can be debatable, especially with the so-called low-stakes testing and assessment. For example, one may argue that FA should be considered low stakes (e.g. informal embedded assessment, such as teacher questioning and checking student learning). However, others may also argue that these types of FA can be high stakes because they are important for good learning and cognitive and emotional development, thereby impactful over time. They help students or individuals form and shape necessary knowledge or skills essential and critical for their future (see also Black & Wiliam 1998, 2009, 2018). Without FA, students can miss a critical opportunity to acquire and sustain accurate and valuable knowledge that helps shape their future lives and opportunities. In this sense, it is, therefore, high stakes. It can, therefore, be argued that all forms of testing and assessment are high stakes in that some can be immediately noticeable while others can be long term.

Socio-political power of language testing and assessment

Language tests and assessments have been used as 'a means of control' by authority, and their use has an attached socio-political power because test authorities (e.g. test developers, teachers, administrators, government officers and politicians) can decide the future of students or people who are required to take a test or assessment. Several policymakers (e.g. government ministers) can impose a compulsory assessment system for students or applicants. Such systems are, for example, standardized national tests or examinations, language tests for accreditation, visa, migration and citizenship applications (see Kunnan 2022).

To understand the socio-political impact of language testing and assessment, it is essential to consider and prevent unintended consequences. For example, language testing and assessment may unfairly and disproportionately disadvantage some minorities, specific races or students from a low socio-economic background. A particular language curriculum may be unintentionally narrowed down due to the assessment tasks and activities used for assessing students (e.g. compulsory tests by government agencies).

McNamara and Roever (2006) argue that, while necessary, traditional fairness in language tests is insufficient to address the broader social implications. They argue for a more comprehensive view that acknowledges the societal functions of tests, such as gatekeeping roles in immigration or employment (Fulcher & Harding 2022). Test designs must consider these roles to avoid disadvantaging any group. The social dimensions of language testing and assessment require careful consideration in the design and implementation of tests. By realizing the profound impact of social contexts on language testing and assessment, educators and policymakers can strive for tests and assessments that are fair, valid, socially responsive and inclusive.

In the light of the socio-political power of language testing and assessment, this book aims to raise awareness of language testing and assessment impacts, since a lack of this awareness can result in assessment misuse and unintended outcomes for students, stakeholders and society (see Fulcher 2010; Shohamy 1998, 2017, on critical language testing).

Summary

This chapter has extensively discussed essential considerations in language testing and assessment components. It has explained the concept of constructs in language testing and assessment, and the construct definition of AL proficiency. Other essential considerations include standards-based assessment, testing and assessment techniques, approaches to decision-making (norm- and criterion-referenced approach), and social dimensions of language testing and assessment. The next chapter considers stages in designing language testing and assessment.

Discussion

1. How has the discussion of AL proficiency and types of related competence influenced the way you understand the language performance of students or people?
2. Do you know any standards-based assessments in your home country? If so, what are the standards, what do they assess and what is their purpose?
3. Explore one of the standards-based frameworks by visiting the website(s) provided. Are there applications for teaching and assessment that you can utilize?
4. Can you think of a test or assessment task that may capture various levels of Bloom's taxonomy?
5. When do we use the norm-referenced and criterion-referenced approaches for decision-making on students or test takers?
6. Have you experienced or considered the socio-political roles of language testing and assessment? If so, in what way?

Further reading

Brown, H.D. & Abeywickrama, P., 2019, *Language assessment: Principles and classroom practices*, 2nd edn, Pearson Longman, White Plains.

Chapter 1 ('Assessment concepts and issues') provides an excellent overview of the types and purposes of language testing and assessment and considerations of some approaches to evaluation, such as integrative testing, performance-based assessment and computer-based testing. Chapter 4 ('Standards-based assessment') of this book discusses the nature of standards-based assessment, including its consequences and controversies.

Fulcher, G., 2010, *Practical language testing*, Hodder Education, London.

Chapter 1 ('Testing and assessment in context') introduces the roles and places of language tests and assessments, both in educational and social settings (e.g. test purposes and general testing activities). It also discusses the historical movements of language testing, including concerns about test consequences, politics of language testing, professionalism and validity of language testing.

Green, A., 2020, *Exploring language assessment and testing*, 2nd edn, Routledge, London and New York.

Chapter 2 ('Purposes for assessment') provides a rationale for the assessment needs and presents a useful discussion of assessment purposes and functions in an educational setting, including the relationships among assessment, teaching and learning.

Jeon, E.H. & In'nami, Y. (eds), 2022, *Understanding L2 proficiency: Theoretical and meta-analytic investigations*, John Benjamins, Amsterdam & Philadelphia.

This open-access, edited volume provides a theoretical, empirical, meta-analytic discussion of AL proficiency. The book explores various constructs of four language skills (reading, writing, listening and speaking).

Purpura, J.E., 2008, 'Assessing communicative language ability: Models and their components' in *Language testing and assessment*, 2nd edn, eds E. Shohamy & N.H. Hornberger, Springer Science + Business Media LLC, New York, pp. 53–68.

This chapter discusses models of communicative language ability and various approaches for assessing communicative language ability.

3

Test and Assessment Design

Overview

This chapter discusses essential design considerations in language testing and assessment. It presents major stages when creating a test or assessment for an intended use, test and assessment specifications, and the interior design concept for effective language test and assessment use.

Guided questions

1. What are essential stages in designing and developing a language test and assessment?
2. What does 'standardization' in language testing and assessment entail? What is 'non-standardized assessment' like?
3. What are 'test and assessment specifications' for?

Introduction

As seen in Chapter 2, language testing and assessment is multi-dimensional in that several considerations and practices shape a given test or assessment simultaneously. As discussed in Chapter 1, some assessment activities can be informally embedded in teaching and learning activities (e.g. through language tasks, exercises and informal questions). They are known as formative assessment and assessment for learning, highlighting the importance of being flexible, adaptive and dynamic in a teaching and learning situation.

However, there are situations in which formal language tests or assessments are needed to account for students' language proficiency, achievement or attainment levels. They have to be decided in advance (e.g. stated in the syllabus, mandated by a government policy). Knowledge of what is involved in formal language testing and assessment design is significant for effective assessment practice (Lanteigne 2018; O'Sullivan 2012b). Although language teachers are not always responsible for developing a test or assessment (e.g. formal tests or assessments may have been developed and prepared for them), it is helpful to have this knowledge because they may be asked to create one by their employers (e.g. admission or diagnostic tests) or they may be interested in creating their tests or assessments for their students.

This chapter provides an overview of the prescribed stages of language test and assessment design and development. It focuses largely on summative assessment (to formally evaluate students' learning achievements and language proficiency levels) and includes criteria for ensuring quality testing and assessment. It then presents the development of test and assessment specifications and interior design concepts.

Standardized versus non-standardized testing and assessment

Language testing and assessment can be placed along a standardized and non-standardized variation continuum. Standardized language tests or assessments are administered and scored based on pre-specified criteria. For example, all students respond to test questions or tasks in the same manner within the same time allowance. A common situation in which tests and assessments are standardized is when students need to complete them in an examination period in which various tests are scheduled to take place in the middle or at the end of the teaching period. In the so-called high-stakes situation (see Chapter 2), standardized testing and assessment is often considered objective and fair for all students as they receive the same test and assessment tasks to complete and are evaluated in the same way.

Non-standardized testing and assessment can be the opposite. Students, for example, can use as much time as they want to complete a test or repeat the same test until they have achieved the minimum expectation (e.g. at least 70 per cent correct). A non-standardized test can be designed or used by teachers and students to enhance or facilitate learning. It should be noted that a teacher may use a test designed to be standardized (e.g. IELTS) as a non-standardized practice test to help students learn or become familiar with the test tasks. Given this, standardization is not the test or assessment itself but how students or test takers are asked to complete it for a particular purpose.

Most language tests and assessments are neither standardized nor unstandardized. They can be placed along the standardized and non-standardized continuum. For example, in an assigned classroom task, students may be given a range of options on a topic of interest and opportunities to gather sources of information independently and outside a restricted time. This is an example of a non-standardized element. Still, some standardized procedures will be used to evaluate the quality of their work (e.g. using the assessment criteria and reporting the same grading system). Therefore, the extent to which a test or assessment is to be standardized will influence how it can be designed, developed and used.

Key design stages in language testing and assessment

Figure 3.1 presents an overview of the key stages in developing and implementing a language test or assessment for formal or summative assessment. Although Figure 3.1 suggests sequential stages (one leads to another), in practice they are *iterative* (going back and forth to what has been done in earlier or later stages) because a change or modification in one stage can require changing the previous work in other stages.

Planning

The first stage in language testing and assessment development is *planning*. Planning is a strategic process of brainstorming and considering the purposes of a given test and assessment relevant to, for instance, the curriculum, syllabus or policy. Planning also seeks to answer what and who will be involved in developing the test or assessment. The following are valuable questions that can guide the planning stage:

1. What is the intended purpose of the test and assessment (e.g. achievement, proficiency, diagnostic assessment; see Chapter 1)?
2. Who are the students or test takers?
3. What are the language constructs to be tested and assessed (see Chapter 2)?

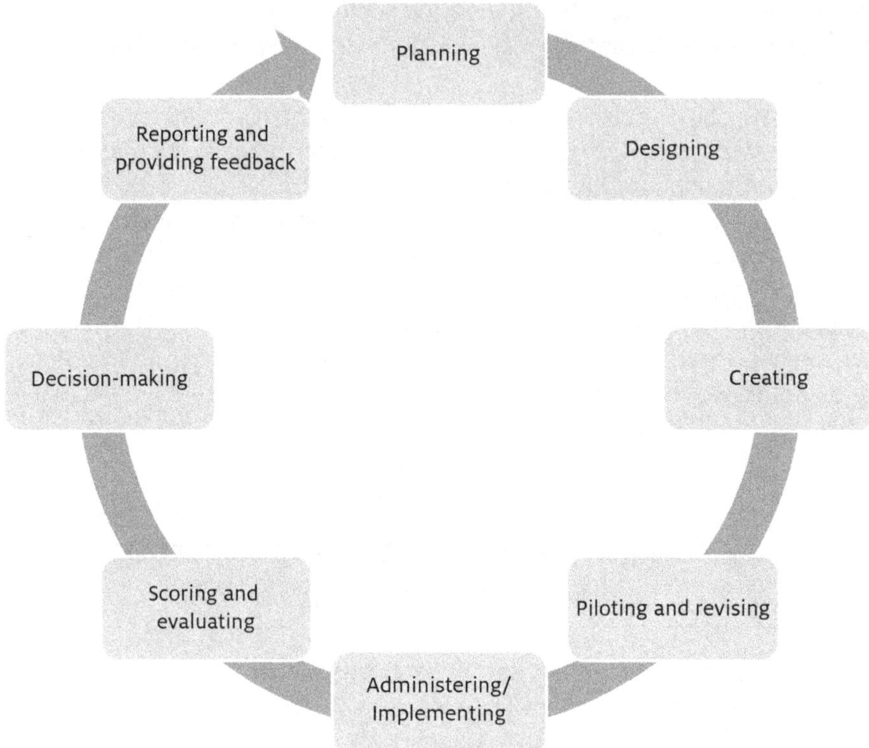

FIGURE 3.1 *An overview of the key stages in assessment development and implementation.*

4. Will the test and assessment be interpreted using the norm- or criterion-referenced approach (see Chapter 2)?
5. What resources are needed to complete the test and assessment (e.g. human resources, funding support, technology and educational resources)?
6. What are the significant timelines for completing the test and assessment design?

Designing

The designing stage includes developing explicit test and assessment specifications that outline the nature of test and assessment tasks. It also addresses what and how test and assessment quality criteria (e.g. reliability, validity and fairness) can be addressed (introduced in Chapter 1; to be discussed substantively in Chapter 4).

Test and assessment specifications

Typically, towards the end of the planning stage, a working document known as test and assessment specifications (or blueprints) will be created to guide how to produce test and assessment tasks and the overall structure of the test and assessment. Test and assessment specifications provide information such as the number of test tasks or significant sections, the sequences of test and assessment sections, the number of questions in each section, the types of test and assessment questions and tasks to be developed (e.g. restricted or constructed response; discussed further below) and the overall time allowed to complete the whole test and assessment. Test and assessment designers or developers may produce (1) an overall test and assessment specification that provides an overarching structure of the test, and (2) a set of test and assessment specifications for different sections (discussed in more detail later below).

Creating

After developing a test and assessment specification, the third stage is to write questions or tasks. For a language test, this involves item/task writing (see Shin 2012a). Test and assessment prompts include (1) an instruction that asks students to perform a task, (2) a written text about a topic, and (3) a set of questions or tasks that ask them to demonstrate their ability or knowledge. In performance assessments such as an essay or interview task, scoring rubrics that capture essential criteria (e.g. task fulfilment, content, cohesion, coherence and language use) should be developed for test and assessment task construction. We discuss scoring rubrics in Chapters 6 and 8.

Piloting and revising

The term piloting refers to a simulation of a test and assessment as if it were used. It aims to check and improve the quality of the test and assessment. Information from various sources, such as students, other teachers, administrators and assessment experts, can be collected in a pilot test. Preliminary analysis such as item difficulty (i.e. the ratio of correct responses among test takers, suggesting whether or not an item is easy or difficult) and reliability analysis (when sample size permits) can be calculated (further discussed in Chapter 9). This information improves test items, questions or tasks through revision processes.

Administering and implementing

Test and assessment administration refers to the actual use of the test and assessment in which students and test takers complete. O'Sullivan (2012b), for example, provides valuable practices for test and assessment administration:

1. *Check physical conditions that facilitate test and assessment performance* (e.g. the seating of students, lighting, noise control and room temperature).
2. *Ensure uniformity of administration* (e.g. monitoring test structures, proctoring, penalties for test cheating or dishonesty, physical conditions of a test room and timing).
3. *Warrant test and assessment security* (e.g. secure delivery methods and storage of test and assessment data).

According to O'Sullivan (2012b), administration must be uniform and strictly follow the specified procedure in standardized tests. Clear instructions for proctors or administrators are needed (e.g. check students' or test takers' identities and inform students at the beginning of the test about what will happen if they are dishonest). Dishonest behaviours include copying answers from other students, secretly copying prepared answers and taking the test materials without permission upon exiting the test room.

In classroom assessments, administration includes informing students how and when they need to submit their work for evaluation, explaining the policy on academic integrity (e.g. how dishonest behaviour is dealt with) and the penalty for late submission, and advising what they need to do if they experience a situation that affects their work completion (e.g. how to request an extension application).

Scoring and evaluating

Students' responses will be scored or evaluated once the test and assessment have been administered and submitted. Answer keys are typically used for scoring restricted-response tasks (e.g. true–false and multiple-choice questions). Scoring rubrics should be used in other open-ended or constructed-response assessment tasks involving productive skills such as speaking or writing. Scoring moderation can enhance the quality of subjective scoring processes as raters can compare their scores and discuss challenges or difficulties they face.

Next, raw scores or grades can be reported to students in achievement tests or non-standardized classroom assessments. In commercialized, standardized AL proficiency tests (e.g. IELTS and TOEFL), raw scores are typically converted into scales or bands with associate descriptors that explain the nature of performance. In a standardized test, score conversion is performed, for example, using an equating method.

Decision-making

The semi-final stage is related to decision-making, which is related to the intended purpose of a given assessment (see also Chapter 2 about the norm- and criterion-referenced approaches). Decisions can be associated with the certification of students' achievement or proficiency levels and with the selection and admission of applicants. Classroom assessment decisions are formative and summative (see Chapter 1). They are formative when teachers use test and assessment scores or observations to help students improve their learning (e.g. giving feedback and adjusting teaching content and activities). They are summative when teachers use test and assessment scores to form an overall achievement grade.

Reporting and providing feedback

This last stage includes how test and assessment results are communicated to stakeholders (e.g. students, teachers, administrators, parents, educational or government departments or officials, and future employers). In an educational context, results or grades are presented in an academic transcript. Test and assessment reports need to be accurate and credible. They should be formatted neatly because they provide the trustworthiness of the test and assessment. Another strategy to ensure stakeholders (e.g. students, test takers and selection committee) can use the assessment results meaningfully is to make an assessment manual or information available. In classroom assessment, feedback should focus on how to help students reflect on what they can do differently in further evaluations.

Test and assessment specifications in more detail

In the stages of test and assessment development, developing test and assessment specifications is critical for effective testing and assessment because they explain how a test and assessment should be constructed, administered, scored and used. Davidson (2012, p. 198) states that test and assessment specifications are 'a generative blueprint from which many equivalent test items or tasks can be produced'. They are working documents that can be adjusted or improved (Davidson 2012). They are 'the coding system [that] tells the item/tasks writer precisely what is and is not allowed' when creating test tasks (Fulcher 2010, p. 147). Owing to the space limitation for this chapter, the appendix presents examples of additional language (AL) tests and assessments by explaining the test and assessment purposes, what they test and assess, general test and assessment structures, the sequences of test and assessment sections, and administration and scoring. Readers are highly recommended to look at them before continuing the sections below because they will show concrete examples of test and assessment specifications.

Types of test and assessment specifications

This section explores six categories of test and assessment specifications (see Fulcher 2010) related to the complexity level of a given test and assessment.

General specifications

General specifications provide a holistic test and assessment framework. For example, the overall specification of the IELTS test includes information such as its intended purposes, what it measures generally and specifically in each test section, the number of test sections (e.g. Listening, Reading, Writing and Speaking), the overall test-taking time allowance, and how the test and assessment are administered and scored.

Section specifications

Section specifications provide specific, fine-grained designs for each section's components (e.g. test and assessment constructs and learning outcomes, number of questions, tasks or prompts, test and assessment techniques, and scoring methods; discussed further below).

Production specifications

Production specifications provide operational and technical instructions on how to put all test and assessment sections in order. For example, the production specifications of a computer-based reading test must indicate that students can scroll up and down to view or revisit the text as they complete the tasks. Production specifications also ensure a seamless transition from one section to another. Finally, they must provide a checklist for the overall appearance of the test and assessment.

Administration specifications

Administration specifications provide instructions for administering the test and assessment. Instructions should be unambiguous. For example:

1. How is the test and assessment delivered?
2. How can test and assessment security and fairness be ensured?
3. How should test desks and rooms be arranged?
4. How should equipment be tested and checked beforehand?
5. How should students' or test takers' identifications be verified?
6. How are students' or test takers' dishonest behaviours monitored?
7. How are cheating or dishonest behaviours dealt?
8. What must test administrators do after students or test takers have completed the test and assessment?

Scoring specifications

Scoring specifications can be a component of the overall specifications or section specifications. However, this type of specification may be necessary for a complex language test and assessment that includes many sections and test techniques and requires objective and subjective scoring methods. In performance assessment (e.g. speaking and writing), scoring rubrics must be specified and developed. Rater training and meetings should be considered and provided to ensure fairness and integrity.

Validation specifications

The term validation is associated with standardized or formal testing and assessment. Validation is a process which designers and developers use to ensure that their test or assessment can capture what they set out to measure, test or assess. For example, they are concerned with whether the test and assessment qualities have been met (e.g. reliability, fairness and impact). For example, test developers need to be able to show empirical evidence of test analysis or justify the use of the test and assessment (see Chapelle 2021; Chapelle & Lee 2022).

In summary, various test and assessment specifications are constructed to enhance the qualities of language testing and assessment. The following sections further explore components of general and specific section test and assessment specifications.

Components of general test and assessment specifications

Language testing and assessment experts such as Bachman and Damböck (2017), Bachman and Palmer (1996), Carr (2011), Davidson (2012), Davidson and Lynch (2002) and Fulcher (2010) provide various structures of assessment specifications and considerations in developing them. There is no one specific structure of a test and assessment specification to follow. Nonetheless, some standard components can be identified or considered when constructing them. They can be considered key ingredients for the readers to create their own test and assessment recipes.

Overall specifications

An overall assessment specification provides general details of an assessment (see Bachman & Palmer 1996; Brown & Abeywickrama 2010). The following are the essential components of an overall test and assessment specification:

1. *Title of the specifications*: Create a brief, meaningful title that captures the nature of the test and assessment. It is useful to include 'last update' information in a bracket.
2. *Purpose of the test and assessment*: Specify the purpose(s) in the evaluation (e.g. formative, summative, placement, diagnostic, selection). If the stake level of students or test takers is known, including it in this section is helpful.
3. *Students or test takers*: Describe the background characteristics of the students or test takers. If it is related to a given subject or unit of study, information about their language proficiency (e.g. beginner, intermediate, advanced) should be provided.
4. *Weight of the assessment*: Indicate the weight of the evaluation for decision-making (e.g. 10 per cent, 50 per cent, 100 per cent).
5. *Delivery mode*: Specify the test and assessment format (e.g. paper-based, computer-based, online assessment). Indicate how students or candidates can submit their work for non-test language assessments such as assignments, group projects and portfolios.

6 *Time allowed to complete*: Specify the time or period for completing the test and assessment. Students should be given a specified number of days and the due date for a non-test assessment.

7 *Test and assessment constructs*: Identify the constructs, abilities or skills tested and assessed (see Chapter 2). Learning outcomes can be used in classroom assessment. This section may include an overview of the criteria for judging responses or performance.

8 *Number of tasks or questions*: Specify the number of test questions or tasks that correspond to or are aligned with the test and assessment constructs.

9 *Assessment techniques*: Choose test and assessment techniques that best elicit performance or responses to the assessment task(s) (e.g. true–false, matching, multiple-choice, short-answers, interviews, pair-work, a written report or oral presentation; discussed further below).

10 *Scoring*: Indicate how students' or test takers' responses or performance are scored or evaluated (e.g. objective scoring, subjective scoring using rubrics or scales, automated scoring). In classroom assessment, specify the cut-off score for passing or meeting the requirement (e.g. 50 per cent, 70 per cent).

11 *Report*: Consider what will be reported to students (e.g. overall scores with an accompanied mean score and feedback on performance).

Table 3.1 is a simplified reading test specification that helps the reader visualize an overall test and assessment specification.

Section specifications

The structure of the overall test and assessment specifications can be adapted for section specifications. The main reason for constructing a section specification is that different sections in a given language test require descriptions of varying test and assessment constructs and techniques. It is simply too complicated to incorporate all in one specification. It is practical to have a section specification that describes what to test and assess specifically. In this section, Davidson and Lynch's (2002) specification approach is illustrated. Davidson and Lynch (2002) adopted Popham's (1978, 1981) test specification framework in their book *Testcraft*. The authors also considered the roles of context-specific mandates (e.g. policy on testing and assessment), the designer team and ownership in a given assessment

TABLE 3.1 An Example of an Overall Test Specification of a Reading Test

Overall specification Reading Comprehension Test	
Test purpose	To determine students' reading achievement levels in Basic Reading Skills (Eng101)
Test takers	Senior high-school students (Year 11) who are enrolled in Basic Reading Skills (Eng101)
Type of decision	Summative. If students fail the test, they must repeat the subject
Reading skills to be assessed	1 Scan and skim for information 2 Understand word meanings 3 Understand common abbreviations 4 Understand references 5 Identify topics 6 Identify main ideas or gist 7 Draw inferences from text 8 Extract specific information
Time allowance	1 hour
Topics	Family and friends, food and drink, travelling, culture, accommodation, party
Text types	Descriptive, narrative, explanatory
Number of test sections	4
Order of sections	Section 1: Family (10 questions) Section 2: Food and drink (10 questions) Section 3: Travel (10 questions) Section 4: Party (10 questions)
Number of questions	40
Source of texts	Newspapers, magazines, catalogues, advertisements
Text length and number	200 to 300 words × 4 passages
Text difficulty	Texts may be modified to suit students' level or similar to texts taught in the course
Test techniques	Multiple-choice, matching, gap-filling, information-transfer and short answers
Scoring procedure	Objective scoring with answer keys

specification (see also Phakiti & Leung 2024). There are five components to a section specification:

1. The *general description* (GD) includes information about the test's purpose and assessment and what language skills, knowledge or abilities will be collected and evaluated.
2. The *prompt attribute* (PA) provides information about assessment tasks students or test takers will respond to (e.g. questions or tasks, texts to be used and time allowance to respond).
3. The *response attribute* (RA) articulates what and how students or test takers will produce to illustrate their language skills, knowledge or abilities about the test questions or assessment tasks.
4. The *sample item* (SI) shows and describes examples of test questions or assessment tasks on which question or task writers can base when constructing test questions and tasks.
5. The *specification supplement* (SS) provides additional information to support successful item writing or task development. It can include more examples of test questions or tasks and scoring rubrics previously developed or used. In syllabus-based assessment, supplements may consist of lessons and activities, previously used tests and samples of students' responses.

Table 3.2 provides an example of these components.

TABLE 3.2 Illustrated Example of Specific Section Specifications

Components	Explanations and example
1. General description	A statement that describes target language skills, knowledge, abilities or behaviours to be tested. This may be related to the learning outcomes or objectives in classroom assessment. For example, 'This internet-based test measures test takers' ability to understand and extract key ideas from an audio text and a written text of the same or similar topic. Topics are general enough and should not be specific to a particular culture, religion or ethnic group. They should be neutral for all genders and not be highly provocative, sensitive or politically motivated. Through speaking, they are then to use their understanding and recall information to address their agreement or disagreement about the given issue.'

Components	Explanations and example
2. Prompt attributes	A complete description of test tasks, requirements or questions that test takers will do. For example, 'Test takers will be asked to listen to an audio recording (a talk) about a topic (approximately 2 minutes; once only). Then, they will read a 200-word non-specialized text on a related topic to the audio recording (recommended reading time = 5–7 minutes; the text is accessible at all times). They are allowed to take notes while both listening and reading. After that, they will be asked to read an opinion statement about the topic. They will be asked to state whether they agree or disagree with the statement using information from their listening and reading sources and their viewpoint (time allowance = 2 minutes for planning and 2 minutes to speak).'
3. Response attributes	A complete account of what test takers will do to address or answer test tasks, prompts or questions. Response attributes may be thought of as something along a continuum of 'completely selected or restricted response' format and 'completely constructed or productive response' format. It should be noted that information in the prompt and response attributes is often overlapped and inseparable. For example, 'Test takers will read the instructions of the test task. After test takers have finished listening and reading, they will read an opinion statement about the topic. They will decide whether they agree or disagree with the statement. They will use or extract information from their listening and reading in their speaking. They will plan their statement response within 2 minutes (a clock on the computer screen will be activated). The recording will start automatically after the 2-minute planning time has ended. They will talk within 2 minutes. Once the clock stops, their subsequent responses will not be recorded. They must click the "Next" button to move to the next test question or section.'
4. Sample items	An example of the test task that reflects this specification.
5. Specification supplement	Any additional information or resources to be useful for test constructions or item/task writing. The supplement may include lessons or classroom activities that resemble the test task, a guide of possible and avoidable topics, previous test samples or versions, resources for choosing audio and written texts and other similar test manuals.

Table of specifications

Although unnecessary, a specifications table is helpful as a quick reference for a given assessment (see Davidson 2012). It summarizes the assessment constructs, number of questions or tasks, test and assessment techniques (discussed further below), time allocation, sample questions or tasks, and percentage of relative contributions. Table 3.3 presents an example of the specifications for an EAL speaking test.

Common errors and mistakes in test and assessment specifications

It is helpful to recognize errors or mistakes in test and assessment specifications when planning and designing a new one. Common errors and mistakes by some language assessment students or teachers are as follows:

1 A new test and assessment specification is created by copying, imitating or mocking a well-established test (e.g. a TOEFL or IELTS-style test). This mistake can make the test and assessment unsuitable for the target language constructs and student or test-taker group. For classroom assessment, such test and assessment tasks may not match the learning outcomes and classroom activities with which students have engaged.

2 The assessment constructs are unaligned with assessment tasks or questions. For example, suppose the target reading construct is 'the ability to correctly identify the main idea of a given passage'. Yet, the selected test task is the 'cloze' technique (see Chapter 5) that asks students to complete a gap with one word only for every *nth* word (see Chapter 5). In that case, there may be an apparent unalignment between the target construct and the test task without further articulation or rationalization. Test tasks must be aligned with the target ability or skill of interest.

3 Test questions or tasks to assess the constructs of interest are not adequately included (e.g. very few questions or tasks). Insufficient questions or observations of language responses are related to the so-called construct-underrepresentation, discussed in Chapter 4. Students' ability or performance is not adequately collected, and their responses to assessment tasks can be random. In assessment, more questions lead to better performance observation. Having adequate questions is essential to avoid a decision error on students' achievement levels.

TABLE 3.3 Table of Specifications for an English as an Additional Language (EAL) Speaking Test

Test task	Construct	No. of questions or tasks	Test and assessment techniques	Time allocation	Examples	%
Task 1	Ability to appropriately engage in a general, everyday conversation	1 to 3 general questions	Interview-style	2 minutes	Tell me about yourself; what do you do in your free time? What is your favourite food?	10%
Task 2	Ability to produce intelligible pronunciation of individual words and sentences	2	Semi-constructed response	2 minutes (no preparation)	Read the following 10 non-specialized words aloud; read 10 sentences (including questions) aloud	15%
Task 3	Ability to describe and narrate a story	1	Descriptive, constructed response	3 minutes (including 1 minute preparation)	A series of four pictures about an event, process or person's activities will be provided	20%
Task 4	Ability to articulate and express viewpoints or opinions about a general social topic	1	Constructed-response	2 minutes	What are your opinions about the impacts of environments or surroundings on people's mental health or well-being?	25%
Task 5	Ability to extract critical information from a short, non-specialized written text (60–80 words) and articulate and express viewpoints	1	Constructed-response	6 minutes (2 minutes reading, 2 minutes preparation, 2 minutes speaking)	Read the following extract. Please tell me the main issues and your personal opinions about the issue. Do you agree or disagree with the author or people in the text?	30%
Total		8		Approximately 15 minutes		100%

4 Test and assessment specifications are written in essay form, including a lengthy paragraph without clear headings and subheadings. While there may be a place for theory, descriptions and explanations in assessment specifications, long essay-style paragraphs make it difficult for item/task writers, for example, to extract essential information about the characteristics of the assessment and questions/tasks. Therefore, the language used in assessment specifications must be precise and direct. Thus, headings, subheadings, numbers and bullet points can enhance communication. Headings and subheadings are essential for adequate assessment construction, use and operation.

5 Only restricted-response techniques are chosen (e.g. multiple-choice, true–false, matching; discussed further below) because they are commonly used in a particular educational setting or are easy to score. The main problem with narrowing test and assessment techniques to only restricted-response categories is that some essential skills cannot be captured appropriately (e.g. critical thinking and problem-solving skills, personal stance in a given issue). Assessment techniques should be chosen according to what they can best capture or elicit from students. Therefore, it is vital to have a balanced mixture of selective- and constructed-response tasks whenever possible because they complement each other's weaknesses and make testing activities more exciting and challenging for students.

6 Test and assessment instructions are not clearly and precisely explained, resulting in an incomplete understanding or expectation of the assessment. Assessment instructions should be explicit and clear to students. They need to be precise and direct to the point. Unclear instructions can result in undesirable responses or avoidable mistakes by students.

7 Insufficient time is given to students to complete the test and assessment tasks, making the assessment unneccessarily more difficult. For tests and assessments to be valid, sufficient time is needed for students to process assessment materials and respond to assessment tasks. Unrealistic time allowance results in speededness testing, which requires other irrelevant constructs, such as coping with pressure or anxiety and high-level attention. The difficulty of a test and assessment task can be increased by choosing more complex texts for students to read or listen to and incorporating more constructed-response tasks rather than restricting the time for completion.

Three principles for understanding testing and assessment techniques

This section now turns to how to assess. Techniques can be considered strategies that testers or assessors employ to stimulate language responses from students or test takers (see also Hughes & Hughes 2020; Weir 1990, 2005). Examples of testing and assessment techniques include multiple-choice, true–false, short-answer, cloze, dictation, translation, item matching, oral interviews, essays and role-play (further explored in more detail from Chapters 5 to 8). There are no perfect assessment techniques. This section presents three applicable principles when designing and developing language tests or assessments.

Direct and indirect principles

When students complete a language task, they activate language knowledge or skills to produce an appropriate answer. The principles of direct and indirect assessment are related to the extent to which a language skill or ability of interest is involved in completing a test or assessment task.

Direct testing and assessment

On the one hand, a direct testing and assessment approach refers to a situation in which students are asked to engage in a language skill of interest (e.g. reading, listening, writing or speaking). For example, if writing is the target skill in the assessment, students should engage in writing in a communicative context (they are asked to write). Hence, 'direct' is used when students are asked to demonstrate their ability in the target skill.

Indirect testing and assessment

On the other hand, indirect language testing and assessment does not require students to engage in a skill of interest directly. Indirect assessment includes language components that are part of language skills, such as grammar, vocabulary, spelling and pronunciation. For example, students may be asked to identify and correct sentence errors (e.g. subject–verb agreements, spelling mistakes, appropriate word forms).

I <u>dislike</u> people <u>which</u> toss their <u>rubbish</u> in public <u>areas</u>.

A B C D

In the above example, students' scores based on various test items may be used to infer some aspects of their writing skills, which are not directly assessed. Indirect assessment is often limited to assessing productive language skills. It can assess receptive language knowledge or components of language skills (e.g. grammatical and phonological knowledge). While indirect assessment is more convenient for completing, administering and scoring than direct assessment, it does not give a complete picture of how well students can speak or write in communicative situations.

Which one to choose in test and assessment design

Whether to adopt a direct or indirect testing and assessment approach in language testing and assessment depends on the purpose of the test and assessment. For example, if a grammar test is used to identify whether students have grammatical difficulties at the sentence level, then the grammar test as an indirect test will be useful. Direct testing and assessment is useful for understanding and interpreting students' communicative language performance, especially when it can identify how well students can use the target language in an authentic language-use situation.

On a final note, it is important to stress that there is no such a thing as a real direct test or assessment in testing and assessment because language learning and ability are abstract constructs. We cannot directly access them via our tests or assessment tasks. Students' observed performance is not equivalent to their abstract abilities or skills, whether we use direct or indirect testing and assessment.

Restricted- and constructed-response testing and assessment principles

The word 'restricted' suggests that students are provided options for answering test questions or tasks. For example, a four-option, multiple-choice question asks students to choose only one option out of the four provided. A true or false statement asks students to select either true or false as their answer. These test techniques have the advantage that they can be marked objectively, as there is only one answer to each question, but they are prone to the guessing factor. In a listening test, a multiple-choice question can tap students' comprehension since they do not need to construct their responses. A restricted-response technique may lack features of authentic language use and is affected by a guessing factor that reduces the reliability and validity of scores (discussed in Chapter 4). As discussed above, restricted-response techniques are often used in indirect testing and assessment.

A 'constructed-response' technique is one in which students are asked to answer test questions or to complete tasks by creating their answers or responses. Constructed-response techniques can be grouped into (1) short-constructed responses and (2) extended-constructed responses (Purpura 2016). Examples of short constructed-response techniques are short-answer questions (e.g. the answer is one word only, or no more than three words), cloze tests (one word per one missing space in a text), diagram completion (e.g. of no more than three words), sentence completion (e.g. supplying missing information in a conversation) and the translation of a given sentence into another language. Students' responses remain somewhat restricted in short constructed-response techniques, and scoring is relatively straightforward.

Extended-constructed response techniques include writing an essay or a report on a given topic, giving a short talk or presentation, doing a role-play on a given topic and answering interview questions. A key benefit of extended-constructed-response techniques is that the activity can resemble authentic language use or classroom learning contexts. However, a significant limitation of this technique is related to practicality and feasibility, especially when there are many students to be assessed. It can be time-consuming and expensive to develop, administer and score. Scoring constructed-response tasks also requires good training and consistent monitoring to ensure scoring accuracy and consistency.

Objective and subjective scoring principles

Types of scoring and evaluation are related to assessment techniques and tasks, which can be placed along a continuum of objective and subjective scoring. In language testing and assessment, it is important to realize that objective and subjective scoring methods are neither good nor bad; they are just ways to score or judge students' or test takers' responses to questions or tasks. Understanding objective and subjective scoring highlights the importance of transparent, well-documented processes for developing and validating scoring systems to maintain the reliability, validity and fairness of language tests and assessments.

Objective scoring

Objective scoring indicates that scorers do not require personal judgement on students' responses, which can be subjective, biased and inconsistent. Restricted-response techniques, such as the true–false and multiple-choice techniques, are related to objective scoring because answers are fixed (either right or wrong without rater judgement). Results should be highly consistent if the scorer uses duplicate answer keys. Again, it is important to note that there is no such a thing as objective scoring because, for example, designers and item writers subjectively select texts to write questions or tasks in a certain way (e.g. how questions are phrased). This is the inherent subjectivity in what might traditionally be considered objective scoring methods. This realization is crucial for test and assessment design, from selecting texts to formulating questions and task conditions, which involves subjective decision-making.

Subjective scoring

Subjective scoring requires teachers or raters to judge the quality of responses based on an assigned scoring rubric and a personal evaluation. It can be difficult to avoid personal perceptions about the quality or relevance of students' or test takers' responses. Constructed-response techniques (e.g. interviews, paired speaking tasks, essays, assigned course tasks and portfolios) require subjective scoring because standardized answer keys cannot be produced for judging such responses. Another way to illustrate why this type of scoring is subjective is to ask two teachers to evaluate the same students' essays. It is most likely that the two teachers do not give identical scores for all students and, even if they do, they may have different reasons for assigning the exact scores.

In summary, in choosing test and assessment techniques during the designing stage, it is critical to know three different aspects: (1) closeness to language use or skills of interest (question of directness), (2) expected responses to test questions or assessment tasks, and (3) how performance or responses are scored.

Computer technology use in language testing and assessment

Designing and developing a test or assessment in the twenty-first century can be unsuccessful without a computer or digital technology. In many educational settings, computer technology in the form of learning management systems such as Blackboard and Canvas has become widespread. Such systems not only store educational materials but also provide tools for both formative and summative assessments. Plagiarism-checking software such as Turnitin can be integrated into the learning system. Computer technology has significantly influenced various aspects of language testing and assessment (e.g. Chapelle & Voss 2017; Yan, Rupp & Foltz 2020; Sawaki 2012; Stevenson & Phakiti 2019; Van Moere & Downey 2017; Winke & Isbell 2017).

Basic computer-enhanced assessment

Historically, according to Sawaki (2012), the use and application of computer technology in language testing and assessment began in the early 1980s when large-scale standardized computer-based testing was introduced. At an early stage, when testing techniques were predominantly selective-response (e.g. multiple-choice), computer-based tests were no more than a conversion of paper-based tests. The computer was a new delivery mode or format to present test tasks and record responses. Therefore, early validation research aimed to compare performance between traditional paper-based and computer-based tests (Sawaki 2012).

Computer-adaptive assessment

Computer-adaptive testing or assessment was developed based on advancements in statistical analysis in item response theory (IRT) which can provide a robust statistical estimate of test takers' ability levels and test item difficulty levels (see Chapter 9). IRT information is used to select test items based on ongoing performance. In computer-adaptive testing, after an initial assessment of performance at the beginning of the test, test takers are given test items or tasks that are likely to match their current ability profiles (those items or tasks are selected so that they are not too easy or too difficult). Test completion is shorter than that for an equivalent paper-based test, which has led to more cost-effective test administration (Moere & Downey 2017).

Internet-based tests and assessments

Internet-based testing has also become popular in high-stakes, large-scale tests and classroom assessments (see Shin 2012). Its popularity and feasibility are mainly due to the recent significant improvement in internet infrastructure and services (e.g. broadband, 5G) and people's increased information technology (IT) literacy. During the Covid-19 pandemic, for example, internet-based testing was invaluable as it helped reduce the spread of the virus, as test takers, interviewers and test administrators did not need to meet one another physically.

Since the 2000s, internet-based testing and assessment (e.g. TOEFL iBT (internet-based testing) has been popularized in testing and assessing EAL proficiency worldwide. The TOEFL iBT, for example, introduces online complex language-use tasks, such as an integrated reading, listening, reading and speaking tasks, allowing the assessment of test takers' ability to synthesize information from various language modes to demonstrate a much fuller range of language-use commands.

When internet-based assessment is used, students can receive immediate results and feedback soon after submitting their answers; this can be immediate in the case of objective-response testing (see Stevenson & Phakiti 2014, 2019). This enables students to focus on specific areas for improvement straight after the test. Feedback given soon after the work is completed can have more effect than feedback provided at a later date. Internet-based testing also allows test designers to use real-life materials, such as video clips of authentic language use, including news events, public speeches and documentaries. When authentic material is used, performance-based productive tasks, such as speaking and writing, can appear more accurate and relevant to the test constructs of interest.

Automated scoring technology

Assessing productive language skills, such as writing and speaking, requires excessive time to score. It is also challenging for raters to maintain scoring consistency and accuracy. To address these issues, automated scoring technology has been developed and used in recent decades to assess speaking and writing performance. An automated scoring system is software that integrates technologies such as AI and natural language processing (NLP), corpus linguistics, automated speech recognition (ASR) technology (for speaking), acoustic models (for speaking), and some statistical methods such as regression models and n-gram analyses (i.e. analyses of sequences of items such as unigrams (e.g. rainy), bigrams (e.g. rainy day) and trigrams (e.g. a rainy day), for scoring constructed-response writing or speaking tasks.

In writing tests, automated essay scoring software can assess linguistic features (e.g. essay length, word count, parts of speech, spelling) and semantic content (e.g. content, word choice, task completion, sentence fluency and coherence). Similarly, automated speech-scoring software can score linguistic features (e.g. grammatical accuracy, sentence mastery, pronunciation, intonation, prosody, pausing, fluency and pragmatics) in speaking tests.

The development of automated scoring technology is highly complex as it requires computer programmers, language testing and assessment specialists to work together to validate and improve a given scoring program. Shermis (2014) and Zechner and Evanini (2020) provide comprehensive coverage of automated writing and speaking scoring software, respectively. Commonly used automated scoring programs for writing assessment include Erater, IntelliMetric, and Intelligent Essay Assessor, and for speaking assessment, SpeechRater, EduSpeak, ELSA, Liulishuo, Duolingo, SpeakingPal, Carnegie

Speech and Rosetta Stone. Therefore, test and assessment designers may consider using existing software for their assessment use.

In summary, it is important to consider what technological avenues are available for use or enhancement in language testing and assessment design. Chapter 10 discusses challenging issues associated with computer technology.

Interior design of an assessment

The final consideration presented in this chapter is related to the appearance of a test or assessment and the logical relevance of the test and assessment to stakeholders. It concerns emotional reactions by stakeholders, especially students or test takers. Poorly presented tests or assessments (e.g. unprofessionally formatted, erroneous, low-quality images) not only reduce the public credibility of the test and assessment but also adversely affect students' performance due to errors and unclear structures. Therefore, this section stresses the importance of the aesthetic and appearance side of the assessment. We start with the concept of visual design.

Visual design

Visual design can be considered in terms of (1) visual and (2) functional components (see Norman 2004, who presents principles of the emotional system in product design that can be applied to language test development). Figure 3.2 conceptualizes Norman's (2004) three interconnected aspects of the human emotional system that can be applied in a language test and assessment design. The brackets in the figure provide examples of students' perceptions associated with a given aspect.

The first emotional aspect is *visceral design*, which is related to the emotional or affective reaction of the user. It is about the appearance of the test and assessment as a product and the experiences of students, test takers and test users. This emotional aspect relates to the perceived quality of the test by students and other stakeholders. Simply put, it is about the branding of the test or assessment. Visceral design enhances the designer's ability to persuade students to take the test or assessment (e.g. 'I prefer to take Test X to Test Y because Test X looks more attractive and trustworthy').

The second emotional aspect is *behavioural design*, which is related to the usability or utility of the product. Behavioural design is concerned with the practicality and functionality of the test and assessment. Suppose a language test is complex and demanding to administer. In that case, it loses usability

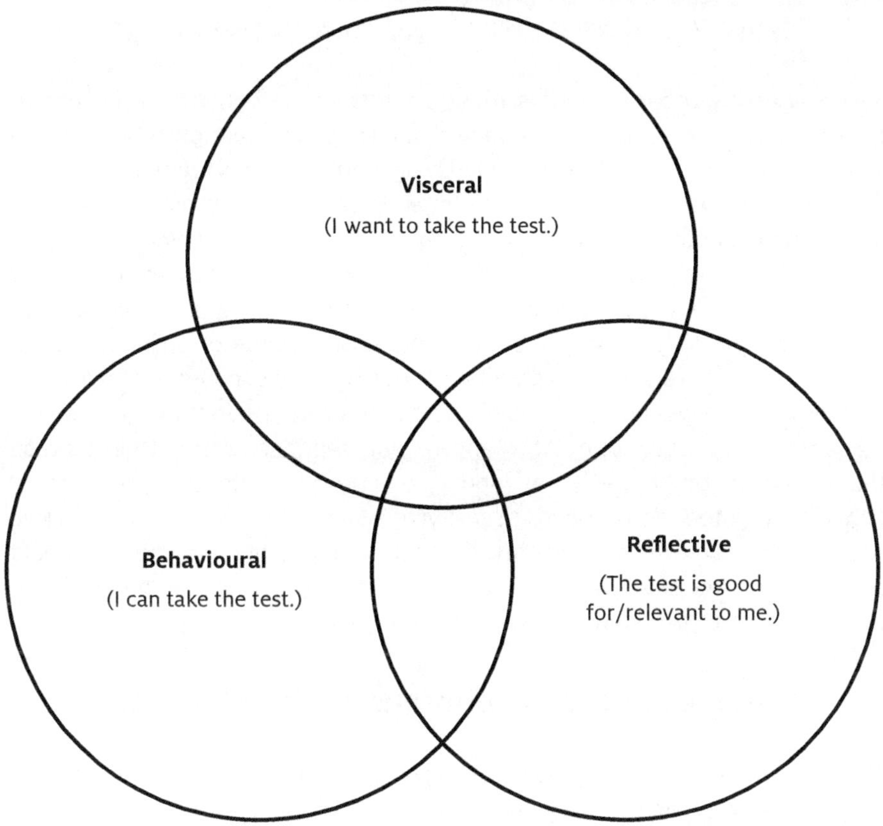

FIGURE 3.2 *Three interconnected levels of the human emotional system.*

because students may feel confused, stressed and underconfident about completing it before actually engaging in test tasks. Test and assessment administrators who are not involved in the assessment design may not be confident in explaining to students how to complete the test and assessment tasks. In other words, a test and assessment that is easy or less complex to administer and complete is more desirable than a highly technical and complex one.

Finally, the third emotional aspect is reflective design, which concerns students' and other stakeholders' rational and intellectual thinking about the product (i.e. the test and assessment). In everyday life, we ask what a product (e.g. a smartwatch or TV) is to us. Similarly, students, test takers or stakeholders ask what use the test and assessment they must complete or use is to them. This third level is the highest in assessment design because it is related to the relevance of the product to the target stakeholders.

How to balance visual and functional design

Test and assessment designers must be creative and artistic in presenting their tests or assessments. Language test and assessment designers should strive to balance not only the visual design but also the functional design. Regarding the visual component of test and assessment formats, a test and assessment should be visually pleasing to students (i.e. aesthetic). Titles, headings, test sections, appropriate line spacing, font sizes and margins or spacing should be visually attractive. In a computer-based test, the background should be plain (e.g. white). A background with patterns or dullness can be visually distracting and negatively affect performance (i.e. construct-irrelevant). Furthermore, a language test and assessment should be formatted to enable students to answer or submit their answers or responses correctly. To address the functional component of test and assessment formats, designers should consider its intended purpose, usability or utility. The test and assessment should communicate to students what it is about and how they should respond. For example, questions should be placed in a logical order where students or test takers would expect to see them.

Strategies to ensure high-quality interior design

The following are some valuable strategies when assembling and producing a test and assessment:

1. Order the test and assessment sections based on ease of test administration. Test sections that can be administered in a large group should be presented first, followed by sections to be administered individually. For example, listening, reading and writing test sections can be administered to a group of students, while a speaking test may be administered separately or in pairs afterwards. Therefore, for practical reasons, a speaking test (e.g. an interview and role-plays) is often the last section for students or test takers to complete. However, in a computer-based speaking test, the order of test sections may be more flexible, especially in integrated test tasks. In particular, a speaking test may be semi-direct (e.g. students respond to prompts by speaking to the computer via a microphone).
2. In each test and assessment section, easy questions/tasks should be presented before more complex questions/tasks. Placing less demanding or complex questions at the start of an assessment allows students to warm up to complete the test and assessment, giving them the confidence to complete the assessment (a psychological

principle to encourage students to engage in test and assessment tasks). Introducing the most complex task at the beginning can potentially demotivate students or test takers and demand cognitive and linguistic processing and resources, leaving students with little energy to complete less complicated questions/tasks later.

3 Use an appropriate font size and enhanced text (e.g. bold, italicized, underlined, coloured or capitalized) in test and assessment instructions to emphasize important information. This can help minimize students' incidental errors. Important information includes the number of words required in their responses (e.g. in writing), the time allowed and whether students can take notes or use external resources to complete the questions or tasks.

4 Use a clean and neutral background in language tests and assessments:

- Avoid bright colours such as yellow, orange, red, deep blue or bright green as the background, as they can strain students' or test takers' eyes over time.
- Use high-quality images/pictures. Poor-quality pictures (e.g. blurry and small) make it difficult for students to describe, explain or interpret them.
- Use colour pictures with a resolution of at least 300 dpi (dots per inch) whenever possible. Black-and-white pictures can influence students' understanding and interpretation.
- Use high-quality audio/video recording in a listening assessment. Poor recordings and graphics generate construct-irrelevant variance, interrupting comprehension and inhibiting memory processes.

5 Proofread the test and assessment carefully. As noted above, a language test and assessment that contains language errors will not be received well, and its results are unlikely to be trusted by students or other stakeholders. Do not rush to use a test if you have insufficient time to proofread it carefully.

Summary

This chapter has provided a comprehensive overview of the essential stages of designing and developing language tests and assessments. It has examined the characteristics of language testing and assessment specifications, principles that can inform decisions on adopting test and assessment techniques, the roles of technology in language testing and assessment design, and the importance of interior design. Since designers, teachers and assessors are responsible for interpreting test and assessment results and making decisions based on assessment scores, they must be able to articulate and defend the characteristics of their tests and assessments. The next chapter explores the standard and quality criteria for producing and evaluating the quality of language testing and assessment practices.

Discussion

1. Consider the cyclical stages presented in Figure 3.1. Which three stages are critical for successful design and development, and why?
2. Why are test and assessment specifications prerequisite to successful test and assessment design?
3. As discussed in this chapter, would you consider computer technology in your test and assessment design? If so, in what way?
4. What are the benefits of considering the interior design of a test and assessment? Why can't we focus only on testing or assessing the target language ability or construct of interest?

Further reading

Bachman, L.F. & Damböck, B., 2017, *Language assessment for classroom teachers*, Oxford University Press, Oxford.

This book provides an argumentative approach to classroom language assessment. In particular, it presents a template for creating a blueprint, successful strategies for making language testing and assessment tasks, and issues in test administration and scoring methods.

Brown, H.D. & Abeywickrama, P., 2019, *Language assessment: Principles and classroom practices*, 2nd edn, Pearson Longman, White Plains.

This book provides various test techniques and tasks for assessing language skills (chapters 6 to 10).

Carr, N., 2011, *Designing and analyzing language tests*, Oxford University Press, Oxford.

This book presents critical theoretical and practical issues in a language test design, including developing specifications for an overall test structure and individual tasks. The author offers examples of test techniques for use in item writing.

Dimova, S., Yan, X. & Ginther, A., 2020, *Local language testing: Design, implementation, and development*, Routledge, London and New York.

This book considers language testing and assessment designs in a local context. The authors present stages in test development, scaling, rater training, data management and score reports.

Lane, S., Raymond, M.A. & Haladyna, T.M. (eds), 2016, *Handbook of test development*, 2nd edn, Routledge, New York and London.

This book provides comprehensive coverage of test designs by focusing on essential fundamental considerations such as types of designs, content, item writing and scoring, and test production and administration.

4

Standards and Qualities

Overview

This chapter discusses seven standards and quality criteria of language testing and assessment: reliability, validity/trustworthiness, authenticity, practicality, fairness, ethics and impact. It argues that they help shape the usefulness and efficacy of language testing and assessment practices.

Guided questions

1. What makes a language test or assessment good or bad?
2. Why is it important to consider whether a test or assessment is reliable, valid, practical and fair?

Introduction

The previous chapter discussed the importance of carefully planning and designing a language test and assessment. As we plan and design a language test and assessment, we need to consider how to make it worthwhile for its intended purpose and fair for all students and test takers. When people question whether a given test or assessment practice is reliable, what does it mean? Is it valid? Is it fair? This chapter aims to articulate the answers to these questions further.

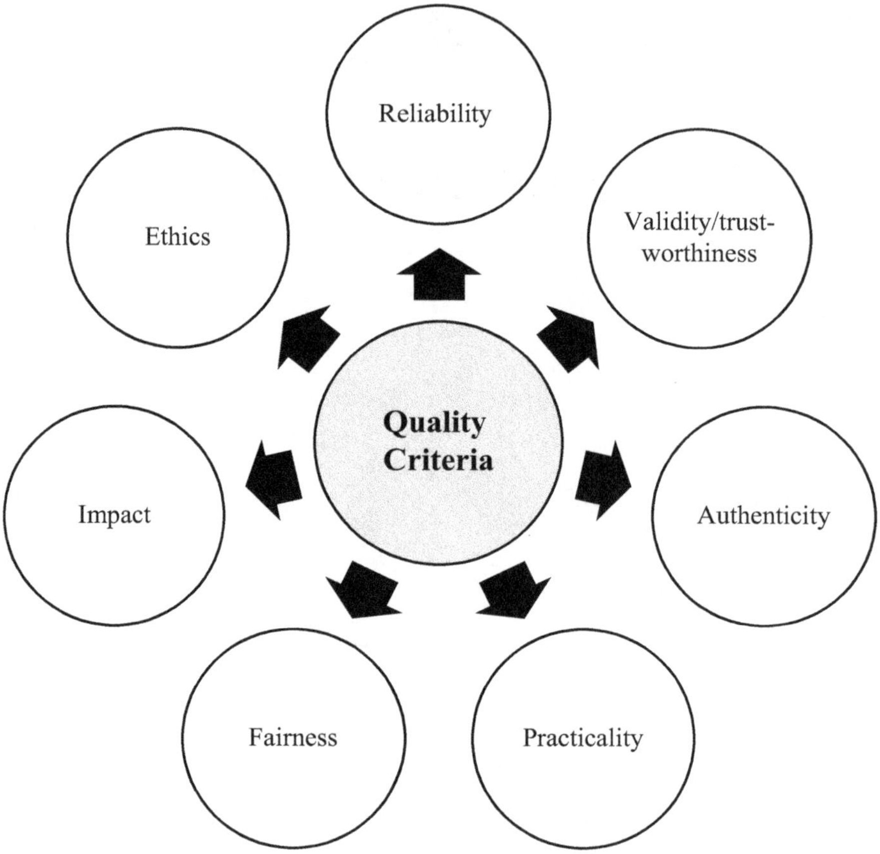

FIGURE 4.1 *Seven quality criteria for evaluating language tests or assessments.*

As part of language test and assessment design and use, establishing test and assessment qualities is arguably a critical foundation of good language testing and assessment practice. Figure 4.1 presents the seven quality criteria that are discussed in this chapter.

Reliability

Reliability is related to the consistency of a test or assessment in its capacity to collect or elicit relevant language data (e.g. skills or ability of interest) for use. Brown (2016, p. 149) pointed out that 'reliability is desirable because it helps ensure that all examinees will have the same treatment, opportunities and chances of success'. To be able to claim consistency, several questions, items or language behaviours, for example, need to be collected initially. If only one question or task, for instance, is given to students or test takers to collect their abilities or skills, it is unlikely to be reliable because there will not be enough information to ensure performance consistency. Also, errors made in observation will always interfere with information collection. Therefore, it is to be expected that many questions or tasks are included in language testing and assessment. In language testing and assessment practice, reliability is often discussed mainly in relation to marking procedures and marks (Bachman 1990; Brown 2005; Brown & Abeywickrama 2019; Roever & Phakiti 2018).

Nonetheless, reliability goes beyond giving many questions in a test or assessment instrument. Consistency of testing and assessment can be described in many holistic ways. Take an example of a classroom test. Teachers should consistently provide information about the test (e.g. what students need to do and what is in the test) because differences in the information produce a lack of consistency, which can influence students' performance.

Testing and assessment is not reliable without accuracy

When we define reliability in language testing and assessment, it is important to incorporate the notion of accuracy or 'correctness of information being gathered'. If a teacher always judges a student's response 'How is you?' as grammatically correct and awards one point to them, we can argue that the marking is consistent but inaccurate. In this example, we cannot say that marking is reliable. Another example of being consistent but inaccurate is when high-ability students consistently receive low marks, while low-ability students consistently receive high marks on the same test. Although the test marks are consistent for both groups of students, something is clearly wrong (error). We cannot say that the test marks are reliable, although they are consistent.

Therefore, when judging whether a language test and assessment is reliable, we should focus on both correctness and consistency. Reliability should be described as the *consistency of correctly or appropriately judging students' or test takers' performance*. While we can use 'correctly' for restricted-response techniques (discussed in Chapter 3), we may use 'appropriately' for constructed-response techniques, since scoring is subjective.

What are the true and error scores?

We have mentioned that when we collect information from students via tests and assessments, errors can affect the quality of information collected. We explain this by using classical test theory, which argues that a test and assessment score comprises (1) the true score and (2) the error score (see Brown 2005, 2022). The portion or part in the score highly relevant to the target ability or constructs of interest can be defined as the true score. In contrast, the score part contributed by measurement error (e.g. due to poorly constructed questions and test takers guessing the answers) can be described as the error score that can affect the reliability of a language test and assessment (Brown 2022). Errors can be explained as *uncertainty* in identifying and estimating students' learning achievement, abilities or skills of interest (Green 2020).

Figure 4.2 visualizes two measurement error types (see Brown 2005 for further explanations).

Systematic error occurs due to the characteristics of a specific assessment integrated into the test or assessment (e.g. clarity of instructions, administration procedures, choice of topics used, text lengths, assessment techniques and marking methods). This type of error is called systematic because it occurs across time, places and situations. For instance, we know that a multiple-choice question will produce some errors (e.g. chance error) as test takers can guess unthinkingly and will have a 25 per cent chance of being correct. This chance error is systematic.

On the contrary, random (or non-systematic) error results from specific situations and students or test takers. Situation-specific random errors include test room temperatures (e.g. scorching hot), lighting (e.g. too dark), noise (e.g. builders outside the test room), electricity blackout and slow internet speed on the test day. There are also personal-specific random errors, such as when a student is sick during test-taking or has an accident just before the test. While personal-specific random errors may impact only a specific student's scores or performance, situation-specific errors affect all students. In other words, random errors can be unpredictable and uncontrollable.

FIGURE 4.2 *Two types of error of measurement.*

What makes a test or an assessment reliable or unreliable?

Brown (2005) reiterates five potential sources of errors (illustrated in Figure 4.3). Understanding these sources explicitly helps the reader to improve the quality of test or assessment scores.

1 Test and assessment environment (e.g. test location, noise, space, ventilation, lighting and weather).

2 Test and assessment administration (e.g. unclear test instructions, faulty equipment and test proctors' attitudes toward the test or test takers).

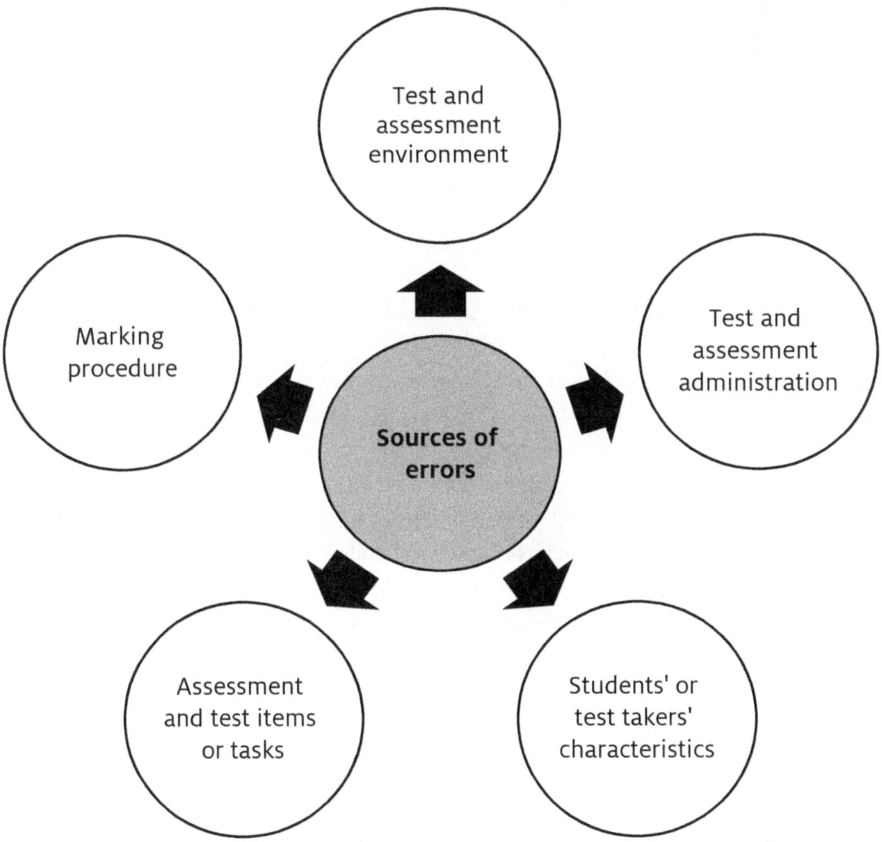

FIGURE 4.3 *Five potential sources of error variance (based on Brown 2005).*

3 Students' or test takers' characteristics (e.g. personal characteristics, test preparedness or motivation, fatigue, anxiety or health problems).
4 The assessment and test items or tasks (e.g. physical features of a given test and assessment, such as dull test papers, small font sizes or poor audio/video recording).
5 Marking procedure (e.g. incorrect answer keys, improper marking program and personal bias from teachers or raters).

It is important to note that this chapter does not comprehensively discuss the notion of dependability (see Brown 2005; Fulcher 2010), which is analogous to reliability but is used when talking about the criterion-referenced approach in classroom language assessment (see Chapter 2). Dependability is the consistency of decisions to classify students into, for example, passing or failing and mastery or non-mastery purposes. The primary focus is whether these decisions are dependable and trustworthy (further discussed below).

In summary, the reliability of a test or assessment refers to 'consistency in collecting, marking and evaluating language information of interest accurately or appropriately'. Chapter 9 revisits the concept of reliability by focusing on reliability analyses in language testing and assessment.

Validity and trustworthiness

This section presents two perspectives on test and assessment validity and trustworthiness. Validity is mainly related to standardized and summative language testing and assessment situations, while trustworthiness is associated with classroom and formative assessments. Both concepts are related to the purposes and use of tests and assessments for decision-making. They are also associated with reliability but are not the same as reliability. This section is an essential aspect of language assessment literacy (LAL) as it helps readers understand why it is problematic when validity and trustworthiness are ignored.

Validity of standardized and summative testing and assessment

The notion of validity is the most notorious and contentious concept in language testing history. It used to be defined as 'accuracy' (e.g. a test purports to test what it is set out to test), but it was soon realized that it was beyond that. Validity could not be a property of a test (see below). According to the Standards for Educational and Psychological Testing, published jointly by the American Educational Research Association (AERA), the American Psychological Association (APA) and the National Council on Measurements in Education (2014, p. 11), test validity is:

> the degree to which evidence and theory support the interpretations of test scores for proposed uses of tests. … It is the interpretations of test scores for proposed uses that are evaluated, not the test itself. When test scores are interpreted in more than one way (e.g., both to describe a test taker's current level of the attribute being measured and to make a prediction about a future outcome), each intended interpretation must be validated. Statements about validity should refer to particular interpretations for specified uses. It is incorrect to use the unqualified phrase 'the validity of the test.'

Stanley (2017) pointed out that the definition above remains relatively vague and is open to interpretation. The definition requires further unpacking for readers new to this concept. First, it suggests that what is being evaluated as validity is not the test or assessment itself but the interpretations of scores derived from the test or assessment. This statement indicates that test and assessment validity concerns the meaning and use of scores or assessment outcomes. Therefore, a language test and assessment is neither valid nor invalid, but interpretations and use of the test and assessment determine the extent of its validity. Second, validity is not an inherent property of a test and assessment (Newton 2012). Cronbach (1971, p. 447) also states, 'One validates, not a test, but an interpretation of data arising from a specified procedure.' (For extensive discussion, see Chapelle 2021; Chapelle & Lee 2022; Kane 2016, 2022; Lissitz 2009; Newton 2012; Stanley 2017.)

Types of validity in standardized testing and assessment

As the definition above shows, validity is a broad concept encompassing assessment use and interpretation. The testing and assessment literature has classified several associated types of tests and assessment validity useful for readers new to language testing and assessment (Bachman 2000; Brown 2005; Newton 2012):

1. *Construct validity* is the extent to which a construct of the test and assessment (see Chapter 2) can be elicited and captured correctly by testing and assessment. Test scores that accurately represent

the relevant linguistic, cognitive and social processes, behaviours or performances of students or test takers have strong construct validity (Cronbach & Meehl 1955). For example, students who have mastered the learning outcomes should have high scores or performance in the test and assessment, whereas those who have not mastered will not perform as well.

2 *Content validity* is related to whether test or assessment samples and tasks adequately represent the relevant language constructs or skills of interest. Content validity is significant for test and assessment quality because it is impossible or unrealistic to elicit all language behaviours in all language-use situations due to practical constraints (e.g. time, cost, location). To gather evidence of content validity, testers and assessment designers ask to what extent the sample content, tasks and situations used are appropriate and sufficient for eliciting or observing the target constructs that will be inferred and used for decision-making.

3 *Criterion-related validity* is the extent to which test scores or performance relate to other measures, tests or assessments. Two types of criterion-related validity are:

a *Concurrent validity*: the degree to which the test score of the same student correlates with their score from other tests or assessments that measure similar constructs or abilities. For example, as TOEFL and IELTS tests assess academic English proficiency, the same student should obtain a similar English proficiency level as identified by the two tests. A similar level based on both tests suggests a strong correlation. Another way concurrent validity can be examined is to correlate students' scores in two parallel forms of the same test (e.g. Forms A and B). As discussed in Chapter 3, test and assessment specifications can produce parallel test forms (e.g. there are many forms of IELTS tests worldwide). If students perform similarly in both forms, concurrent validity will be met.

b *Predictive validity*: a specific case of concurrent validity. It is the degree to which a score can predict future performance or success (e.g. performance in non-test situations, academic performance after programme admission). It aims to extend inferences of performance to other language use or language-related situations. In standardized language testing and assessment, predictive validity is related to generalizing students' performances in other non-assessment situations. For example, based on a given IELTS score, test users (e.g. admission officers) want to know whether a given applicant will probably succeed in their study in an English-medium university.

4 *Face validity* is related to the appearance of a test and assessment. See the interior design of tests and assessments discussed in Chapter 3. A language test and assessment should look credible to test and assess what it claims to be. For example, a speaking test should ask students to produce a speaking performance. A speaking test that asks students to answer written multiple-choice questions lacks face validity. It is important to note that face validity is not traditionally part of the broad concept of validity discussed above. It is, however, essential to consider. Face validity enables test and assessment validity because it promotes understanding the relevance of the test and assessment tasks. Face validity is also related to the concept of alignments between the constructs, real-world tasks and test and assessment tasks. When a test task does not seem relevant to the language situation of interest, it will not look right (i.e. lack of face validity).

5 *Consequential validity* is the extent to which a test and assessment impacts students, other stakeholders or society. The consequences of test and assessment use can be intended (see Chapter 1 about test and assessment purposes) or unintended (e.g. unrealized impact or side effects). Consequential validity is more observable when a decision is made based on the test and assessment. This type of validity will be discussed in 'Impact' below.

Threats to validity in standardized testing and assessment

Readers new to language testing and assessment may not be familiar with the term 'psychometrics', which is the field of study that focuses on the theory and methods for measuring constructs such as knowledge, abilities and psychological traits. Using mathematical and statistical models, psychometricians emphasize the importance of precise and standardized instruments such as tests that consistently measure and accurately reflect what they are designed to measure (see also 'Reliability' above). Based on the psychometric principles, two significant threats to validity are mainly considered: (1) construct-irrelevant variance and (2) construct-underrepresentation (Messick 1989, 1995). It is also helpful for teachers and readers new to language testing and assessment to realize the concepts related to these threats.

1 *Construct-irrelevant variance* results from test and assessment questions or tasks unrelated to the target constructs and language-use situations of interest. Suppose a language test measures students' listening comprehension skills but asks them to substantively write their answers as they listen and try to comprehend. In that case, test performance will also depend on the ability to write quickly and effectively. In this example, writing is not relevant to listening skills of interest. It should be considered construct-irrelevant variance or a threat to the test and assessment validity. In practice, several test and assessment characteristics can introduce construct-irrelevant variance. Earlier, we discuss them in terms of the inconsistency of test administration, the use of different test methods (e.g. paper versus computer), the impact of low or unstable internet speed during test-taking, and poor lighting in the test room.
2 *Construct-underrepresentation* occurs when little or insufficient information about the target constructs and language-use situations of interest is collected. It is related to content validity when language content, selected samples or tasks are insufficient for extracting students' or test takers' responses inferring what students can do. For example, a reading test with only one question asking students to answer the main idea question is deemed insufficient to decide whether they can identify the main ideas. This is because they may be able to answer it correctly by chance. The score does not give sufficiently sound information for use. Therefore, construct-underrepresentation is another threat to test and assessment validity.

Test and assessment validation framework

As discussed in Chapter 3, validation is the process that test or assessment designers use to ensure that the test or assessment can serve its intended purpose. Validation also minimizes the threats discussed above. Figure 4.4 presents a test and assessment validation framework for ensuring the validity of language testing and assessment. This framework is based on AERA, APA and NCME (1999, 2014):

1 *Evidence of test and assessment content* refers to the collection of information that evaluates the quality of test and assessment content (e.g. the target language ability, knowledge, skills of interest,

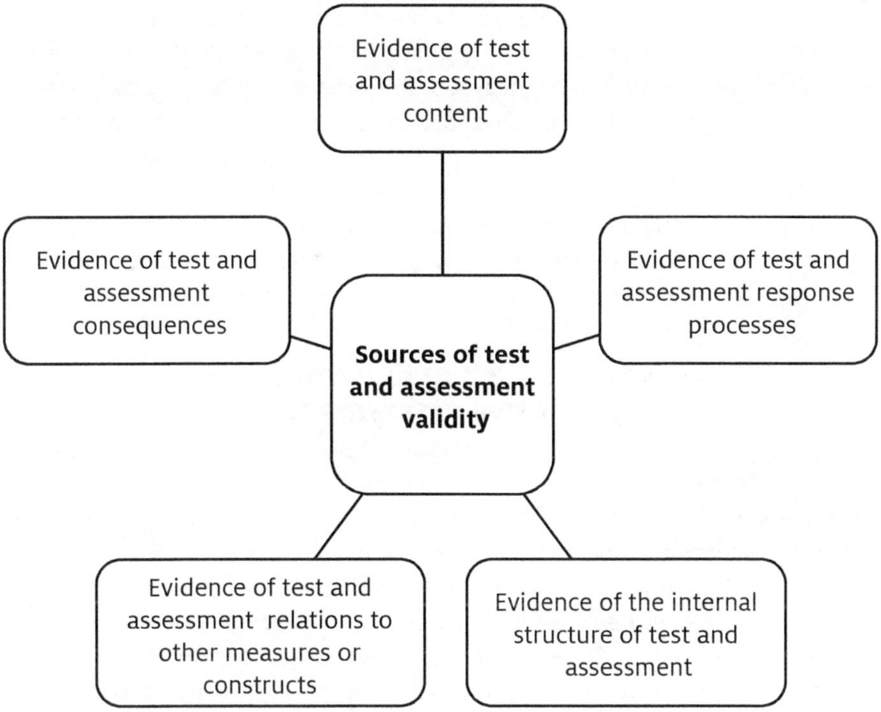

FIGURE 4.4 *Sources of language test and assessment validity.*

instructions, and questions and tasks that make up a given test and assessment). Test and assessment developers seek to ensure the extent to which the content of the test and assessment (e.g. language samples, behaviours, items, questions and tasks) is sufficient and appropriate in a given test and assessment context.

2. *Evidence of test and assessment response processes* is related to information about how students or test takers complete test and assessment tasks and whether they use the required knowledge or ability and processes necessary for demonstrating their performance.
3. *Evidence of the internal structure of the test and assessment* refers to the unity of the overall test and assessment, as well as the questions and tasks. This type of evidence can be addressed via complex statistical analysis (see Chapter 9).
4. *Evidence of test and assessment relations to other measures or constructs* concerns the criterion-related validity discussed above. Generally, this evidential source supports the generalizability and meaningfulness of the test and assessment results to the non-test and assessment situations (Bachman & Palmer 2010).

5 *Evidence of test and assessment consequences* is related to consequential validity and impact discussed below. Students' test and assessment data can be analysed over time to identify trends in their learning growth that are influenced by test or assessment use. They can be asked to provide their experiences, perceptions and opinions about the test and assessment (e.g. perceived fairness, relevance, usefulness and areas for improvement). Stakeholders (e.g. teachers, administrators and parents) can be interviewed to learn about their perceptions of the impact of the test and assessment.

Trustworthiness of classroom and formative assessments

As discussed in Chapters 1 and 2, classroom assessment is unique to a specific learning context (see Phakiti & Isaacs 2021; Phakiti & Leung 2024) as it focuses on formative and summative assessment. Bonner (2013) pointed out that teachers' testing and assessment practice is often judged as insufficient to meet the expected standards of validity by psychometricians who focus on standardized testing and assessment (as discussed above). However, it is important to note that not all language assessments are constructed according to strict psychometric principles (Green 2020). It is essential to recognize that classroom language testing and assessment does not function in the same way as large-scale, psychometric, standardized tests and assessments. Classroom testing and assessment is educational, as teachers and students focus on learning, improvement and development. For example, dynamic assessment (DA) can be adopted in formative assessment to assist students' unique learning processes. It devises instructional, mediating or interventive strategies to unlock students' potential for higher performance (e.g. Poehner & Infante 2017). A DA approach simultaneously promotes self-regulation through interaction with teachers and peers to transfer skills or knowledge to new contexts. The pure concept of validity discussed above cannot capture the usefulness of classroom testing and assessment.

The term trustworthiness, which was initially used to describe the validity of qualitative research (see Guba 1981; Guba & Lincoln 1989; Lincoln & Guba 1985), is a more appropriate and proposed term to describe the validity of classroom language testing and assessment (Phakiti & Leung 2024). Trustworthiness recognizes the socio-cultural nature of classroom teaching, learning and assessment. Five intertwined criteria can be used to describe the trustworthiness of classroom language testing and assessment. It should be noted that there is overlapping content between validity and trustworthiness since they are both concerned with the quality, relevance and usefulness of language testing and assessment.

1. *Credibility* refers to the fit between students' views of teachers' use of language testing and assessment to help them learn. The fit can be achieved through prolonged learning-testing-assessment engagement over time (e.g. throughout the semester or term). This process also requires member-checking of the usefulness of formative and summative assessments. Credibility is analogous to internal validity in standardized testing and assessment because it focuses on what happens during teaching and learning.
2. *Dependability* refers to the transparency of language testing and assessment in the classroom that stakeholders can trust. Students and teachers need to mutually understand why testing and assessment of various forms are used. Formative and formative assessments need to be logical, traceable and evidence-based. Occasionally, teaching colleagues may be invited to observe classroom testing and assessment practices. Since dependability focuses on consistent and appropriate practice, it is analogous to reliability in standardized testing and assessment.
3. *Confirmability* refers to the accurate, relevant and non-biased interpretation of students' performance based on observations (e.g. responses to questions in formative assessment, and mid-term and final test results). Conformability can be achieved when the credibility and dependability criteria have been produced. Since it is relevant to inferences and interpretation, confirmability is close to the definition of the broad validity discussed above. However, in the literature, confirmability is viewed to be similar to objectivity in standardized testing and assessment.
4. *Transferability* refers to how successful language testing and assessment can be useful in a new situation. It can be achieved by providing sufficient details of test and assessment use (e.g. quizzes used, nature of feedback for improving teaching and learning activities, and mid-term and final examinations, such as how they are administered and scored). Making test data and student records available helps other teachers decide the relevance of given classroom testing and assessment practices to be applied or considered in a new situation or context. Transferability is close to generalizability in criterion-related validity in standardized testing and assessment. However, unlike generalizability, which is an explicit and optimal aim of

standardized testing and assessment, trustworthiness does not aim to claim that testing and assessment is generalizable for students and contexts. Large amounts of descriptions and information are provided so that people can make their own decision whether a given testing or assessment practice can be used in their own situation.

5 *Authenticity* refers to the relevance or truthfulness of testing and assessment reflecting learning outcomes and classroom activities. It is, in fact, closely related to the concept of alignments discussed in Chapter 2. One strategy to ensure authenticity in testing and assessment practice is to ask students to write a diary or reflection about their engagement in classroom activities, including their participation in testing and assessment. Students' evaluations (e.g. end-of-semester surveys and emails to teachers) can be used to understand students' feelings or attitudes toward classroom testing and assessment practice, which can further improve teaching and learning. It should be noted that the authenticity discussed here is slightly different from how it is discussed below about test and assessment tasks (i.e. another dimension of authenticity is real-life language-use situations).

It is important to stress that using trustworthiness to discuss the qualities of classroom language testing and assessment does not mean that the test and assessment validity discussed above can be ignored entirely in classroom testing and assessment practice. This is because testing and assessment tools which disregard testing and assessment principles will affect the quality of classroom trustworthiness.

Guidelines to improve the trustworthiness of classroom language testing and assessment

Because there are guidelines to help enhance language test and assessment validity, some unique guidelines for trustworthiness can also be provided:

1 Focus on quality student learning rather than final test and assessment results (e.g. scores and grades). Quality learning includes students accessing the learning materials and resources required to successfully perform test and assessment tasks.

2 Use a criterion-referenced approach rather than a norm-referenced approach (see Chapter 2) because classroom assessment should not be used to compare students' relative performance and decide

on their achievement. The target language benchmark (e.g. learning outcomes or objectives) should be used to judge students' level of learning or mastery.

3 Align a specific learning outcome with teaching activities and assessment tasks. Teachers can use them to support their decisions on student learning or achievement levels and help students recognize the connections between test and assessment tasks and those in the language classroom.
4 Focus on the efficacy of teaching and assessment activities in improving the quality of student learning (e.g. how well students can become independent in learning and apply what they have learned in new situations).

In summary, this section has focused on ensuring the validity and trustworthiness of language assessments. This is crucial for assessment efficacy because it can warrant that testing and assessment can serve their intended purposes.

Authenticity

The authenticity discussed here is related to language-use situations and the nature of test and assessment tasks rather than the trustworthiness aspect discussed above. It is related to how meaningful language use is for communication. Bachman and Palmer (1996) argue that test and assessment tasks should be used to infer students' abilities outside the assessment tasks or situations. In communicative language testing, authenticity refers to the extent to which a test and assessment task is similar to a real-world language-use situation (see Bachman & Palmer 1996, 2010; Hasrol et al. 2022). Real-world tasks are needed because they can enhance the generalization or transfer of students' scores or performance for decision-making.

Using real-world source texts in test and assessment tasks is a common practice to enhance test and assessment authenticity. For example, authentic texts (written/spoken for native speakers and people in a given society) can increase the authenticity of language tests and assessment designs. McNamara (1996) stressed that testing and assessment can never be utterly authentic because they will always be simulations of language use under assessment conditions. For example, teachers and students know assessment tasks are for assessment purposes, not authentic communication.

Limits of being authentic in language testing and assessment

Although we can be excited about creating a test and assessment task to resemble a real-world situation, it is crucial to recognize that there are limits to authenticity in language testing and assessment. Language teaching and learning tasks that precisely resemble real-world tasks may not always be achievable simply because students (e.g. beginners) are not ready for authentic communication. Learning and assessment materials and tasks for some students may need to be tailored to suit their current learning level. Furthermore, in a context where the target language is not typical for everyday communication, test and assessment tasks cannot be the same as those faced by native speakers because students will not have a complete opportunity to use and practice them beyond their local contexts.

One may argue that some test and assessment tasks used in a classroom are far from being authentic. However, their use is justifiable and valuable for teaching and learning. For example, while true–false or multiple-choice questions are not authentic language tasks, they allow students to learn the target language appropriate for their current level (e.g. for beginners). In many countries, language teachers may not be proficient enough to use the target language authentically. Therefore, if such less authentic tasks help students understand the linguistic nature of the target language, they are useful. Authenticity of language test and assessment tasks is, at most, a simulation or imagination of communicative situations.

In summary, authenticity is vital in assessment qualities, especially in communicative assessment. However, not all assessment tasks can resemble real-life tasks or need to be authentic to be useful for teaching and learning. Some assessment tasks promote language learning and are tailored to suit students' specific needs.

Practicality

Two significant constraints or limitations that affect test and assessment validity and trustworthiness are cost and time in, for example, developing, administering and marking or evaluating a test. Therefore, in language testing and assessment, there is a need to consider practicality. Practicality relates to the feasibility and deliverability of an assessment in a given context (see Bachman & Palmer 2010; Brown & Abeywickrama 2019; Green 2020; Jin 2018). It can be understood as the ratio or proportion between available resources and resources necessary to develop, administer and score a test and assessment. For example, we need to consider how much it will cost to develop a test or assessment and how much time is required to create it. We also need to consider how it will be administered and scored. As discussed in Chapter 3, practicality should be considered during the planning and test development stages. A test and assessment that is expensive to develop and complex to administer and score can become impractical.

For a language test and assessment to be valid, students or test takers need to fully engage in answering test questions and tasks so that their performance can be collected. However, students can be exhausted from taking an extended test, and teachers need to spend a lot of time marking and evaluating students' responses. Practicality needs to be considered in this kind of situation. It is important to stress that if too much emphasis is placed on practicality (e.g. 'To save time and money, let's have a short test'), a given test and assessment may not serve its intended purpose but may have several serious unintended consequences (e.g. placing students in the wrong class or failing students who should not have failed).

Practicality in testing and assessment is related to Messick's (1989) proposition about avoiding construct-irrelevant variance (e.g. abilities or skills other than the constructs of interest) and construct-underrepresentation (e.g. too few items, questions or tasks for eliciting performance) discussed above. Therefore, test and assessment specifications should be carefully developed as it considers practicality, weighing cost and time as part of the whole test and assessment programme (see Chapter 3). Figure 4.5 summarizes some key questions relevant to test and assessment practicality.

The first question, 'How much will it cost to develop, administer and score the test and assessment?' is related to the affordability of a given test and assessment. It is crucial to have a budget that covers all costs involved in administration, marking and reports. To answer this question, one must check

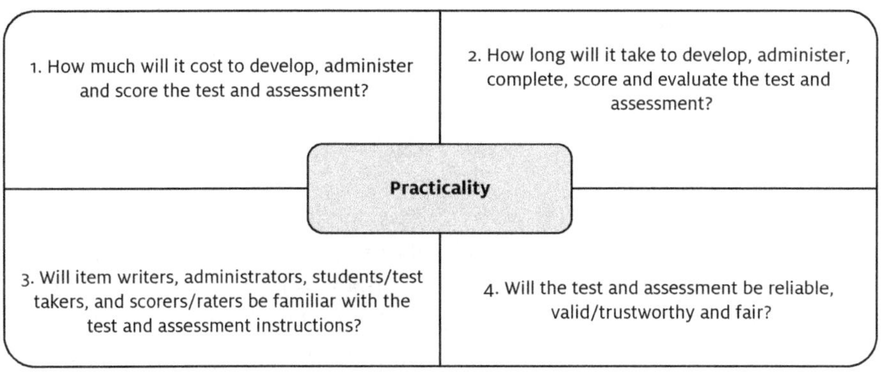

FIGURE 4.5 *Questions for evaluating practicality in language assessment.*

the available resources (e.g. materials, equipment and human resources) and the expenses to develop, administer and successfully score it. For example, suppose a computer-based test is to be used. A budget should cover all costs required for creating the test (e.g. programming, computer access for all students or test takers and reliable internet).

The second question, 'How long will it take to develop, administer, complete, score and evaluate the test and assessment?', can be asked in parallel with the first question. The purpose of a given assessment should determine this question (see Chapter 1). Additionally, it is related to whether the test and assessment can be reusable or adaptable in future assessment situations. If the assessment takes a lot of time to develop, administer and score, it cannot be easy to reuse or adapt it to a new or future situation.

The third question, 'Will item writers, administrators, students/test takers and scorers/raters be familiar with the test and assessment instructions?' is about the operationalization of a given assessment. For example, if there are no experienced item or task writers, it can be impractical to develop instructions effectively. If administrators are unsure how to deliver the assessment and cannot explain to students or test takers what to do in the assessment, the assessment becomes impractical. If students are unfamiliar with the test and assessment tasks, they will spend extra time understanding the task requirements. Still, they will not have enough time to engage in the actual functions (hence, underperform in the test and assessment). Finally, if raters evaluate students' responses for the first time but do not have adequate training to score them, it can take them a long time to navigate the evaluation process.

The last question, 'Will the test and assessment be reliable, valid/trustworthy and fair?' concerns the meaning and relevance of assessment scores. It considers, for example, whether the type of assessment tasks or questions matches the target constructs or learning outcomes and whether students are treated fairly when completing the assessment. The test and assessment can then be practical for use.

Fairness

According to Kunnan (2018), fairness is concerned with the concept of right (in parallel with the concepts of value and moral worth), which can be understood as the absence of bias (e.g. language bias, content bias, item/question bias and test format bias; see Hambleton & Rodgers 1995). For example, in an AL proficiency test, some topics may be more accessible for a particular group of test takers, but others find it more challenging to complete. Fairness can also be considered for accommodations for students with special needs or circumstances (e.g. physical or cognitive disability; Abedi et al. 2020). Test and assessment accommodations include providing hearing aids for students with hearing impairments and Braille question papers for test takers with visual impairments (see Abedi 2014; Taylor 2012). These students will not be treated fairly when accommodations are not provided.

Areas for examining fairness in language testing and assessment

Figure 4.6 presents significant areas in which test and assessment fairness can be considered (see AERA, APA & NCME 2014).

First, it can be examined in relation to the test and assessment process. Tests and assessments should maximize students' opportunities to exhibit their knowledge or target ability. In standardized language tests and assessments, transparent administration procedures and marking methods can enhance equal opportunities for students or test takers. Any variations, exceptions and accommodations should be specified and justified clearly and explicitly.

Second, fairness can be evaluated by investigating the level of measurement bias (e.g. reliability analysis to determine measurement error;

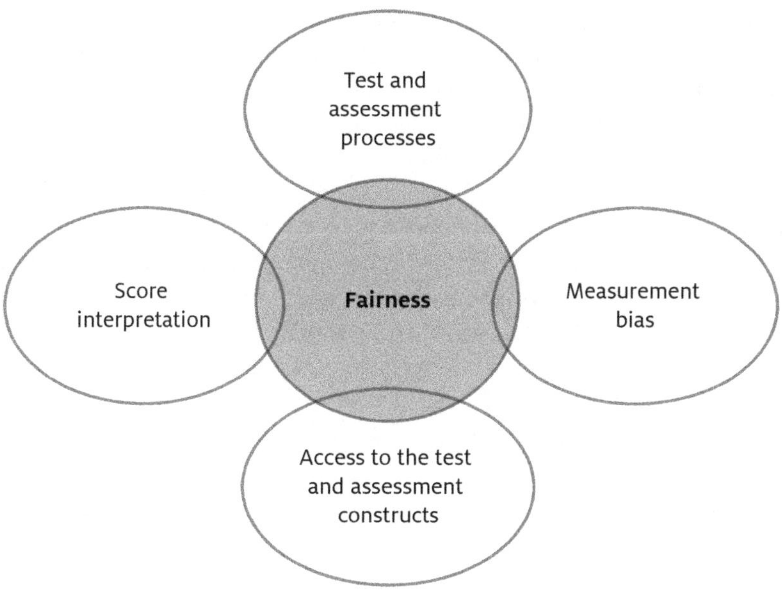

FIGURE 4.6 *Areas for examining fairness in language assessment.*

see 'Reliability' above). If assessment tasks are familiar to only some groups of students (e.g. test methods or techniques), there is an issue with measurement bias (see Kunnan 2018). Therefore, during language test and assessment development, it is essential to ask whether the given tasks and conditions are reasonable and fair for all students or test takers, regardless of their backgrounds (e.g. race, ethnic group, socio-economic status and disability). All students or test takers should be well-prepared to understand the test and assessment task conditions.

Third, the opportunity for students to access the target test and assessment constructs is critical to ensure fairness. The assessment is unfair if some students can access the material for test preparation while others cannot. Kunnan (2018) discusses this area in terms of opportunity-to-learn, which is underpinned by the principle stating that an assessment ought to be fair to all students and test takers.

Fourth, test and assessment results should be used meaningfully and fairly. Score or performance interpretations must be accurate, based on the assessment criteria and appropriate for a given purpose (see norm- and criterion-referenced approaches in Chapter 2). Without this consideration, a given test and assessment will face an issue of unfair treatment. In a standardized high-stakes language test, a typical test analysis often used to ensure fairness is called *differential item functioning* (DIF; discussed further in Chapter 9). Kunnan (2018) noted that DIF and differential test functioning (DTF) are post-hoc analyses, as they are performed after a given test has been administered and scored and after differences among groups have been detected. Therefore, performing these analyses in a pilot test and after the actual test is helpful. They should be performed in high-stakes test situations, as decisions can change individuals' lives significantly.

'The Code of Fair Testing Practices in Education' has been developed by the Joint Committee on Testing Practices, the American Psychological Association (APA; see https://www.apa.org/science/programs/testing/fair-testing.pdf). It provides a comprehensive set of guidelines regarding the critical considerations in educational assessment. The Code explicitly presents the expected responsibilities of test and assessment designers and users in four areas: (1) developing and selecting appropriate tests and assessments; (2) administering and marking tests and assessments; (3) reporting and interpreting test and assessment results; and (4) informing students or test takers about the results.

In summary, fairness is related to equal and equitable treatment and opportunity to perform at the highest level in a given test and assessment. All language testing and assessment practices (formative and summative) must be fair for all students or test takers.

Ethics

Ethical considerations are essential for good test and assessment practices. Such considerations are intertwined with fairness and impact. Ethics is related to moral practice. Ethical considerations should be part of every stage of assessment development discussed in Chapter 3 (see AERA, APA & NCME 2014; Davies 2012 2017; Kunnan 2018; Xi 2010). The International Language Testing Association (ILTA) 'Code of Ethics' presents nine principles to guide professional testing and assessment conduct (see https://www.iltaonline.com/page/CodeofEthics). The ILTA Code of Ethics allows test and assessment developers and users to realize the ethical dos and don'ts in language tests and assessments. The code expresses collective expectations of professional practice in language testing and assessment.

Principle 1: Respect the humanity and dignity of students or test takers. Developers should provide the best professional considerations and respect all persons' needs, values and cultures when providing their language assessment service.

Principle 2: Hold all information obtained about students or test takers confidentially and use professional judgement in sharing such information.

Principle 3: Adhere to all relevant ethical principles embodied in national and international guidelines when undertaking any trial, experiment, treatment or other research activity using language assessments.

Principle 4: Do not misuse professional knowledge or skills to cause harm or injustice to others.

Principle 5: Continue developing professional knowledge, sharing it with colleagues and other language professionals.

Principle 6: Share the responsibility of upholding the integrity of the language testing and assessment profession.

Principle 7: Strive to improve the quality of language testing and assessment and teaching services. Promote the just allocation of those services and contribute to the education of society regarding language learning and language proficiency.

Principle 8: Be mindful of their obligations to society while recognizing that they may occasionally conflict with their responsibilities to students, test takers and other stakeholders.

Principle 9: Regularly consider the short- and long-term potential effects on all stakeholders in their language tests and assessments.

As can be seen, ethical considerations in language assessment also overlap with assessment fairness because unethical use leads to unfair assessment. Ethical considerations are also related to testing and assessment impact, which will be discussed next.

Impact

The influences and impacts of language testing and assessment on students, individuals or society cannot be overlooked because there are consequences for students' or individuals' futures and society. Questioning language testing and assessment impacts is related to critical language testing. Based on Shohamy's (2017, p. 441) critical language testing

> emerged from realising that tests are powerful tools in education and society, which may lead to unintended consequences that must be examined and evaluated. It is the power of tests, especially those of high stakes, that causes test takers and educational systems to change their educational behaviors and strategies as they strive to succeed in tests given their detrimental impact.

As represented in Figure 4.7, intended and unintended consequences are discussed with impacts (see Saville & Khalifa 2017).

Intended consequences relate to the testing and assessment purposes – using assessment to inform decision-making (e.g. formative and summative assessment, achievement, admission and employment; refer to Chapter 1). Kunnan (2018) stresses that intended consequences should be based on moral grounds (see 'Ethics' above). For example, suppose a language test is

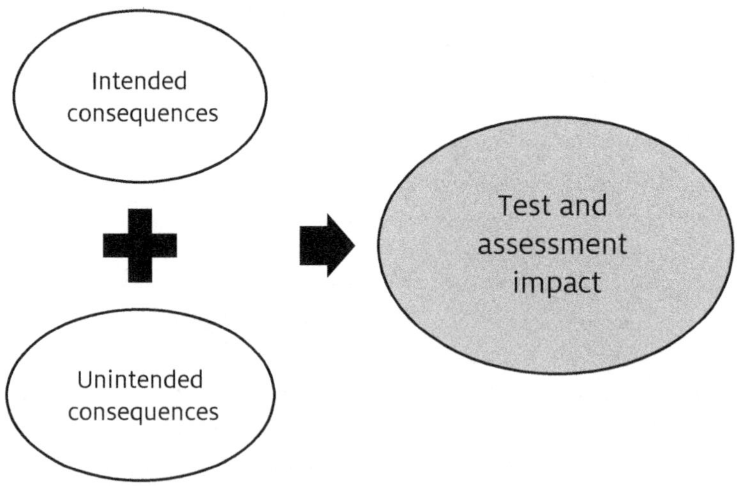

FIGURE 4.7 *Intended and unintended consequences of language test and assessment use.*

designed to exclude students with disabilities from the mainstream educational system to cut costs. In that case, the intended purpose is morally wrong because these students are being discriminated against and consequently will not have equal opportunities with others to be successful in their future lives. Kunnan (2012, 2018) pointed out that in many socio-political contexts, this type of immoral intended purpose is often hidden and denied when confronted with ethical scrutiny or public inquiry.

Unintended consequences arise when assessment results in other outcomes (similar to side effects in medicine). For example, students experience extreme test anxiety and worry that subsequently lead them to perform poorly. Another example of unintended consequences can be related to the result of an inaccurate test and assessment that produces significant errors in students' responses and marking. Owing to its use, some students fail the subject or course. In an admission test, they will be rejected from studying in a programme, thereby missing an opportunity to further their education.

Washback impact

In a language classroom context, the impact of tests and assessments is more felt regarding washback – the term used to describe how testing and assessment influences teaching and learning engagement and behaviours. Washback has been recognized in the field of language testing and assessment (see Cheng & Curtis 2012; Kunnan 2018; Rea-Dickins & Scott 2007; Saville & Khalifa 2017; Schissel 2018; Tsagari & Cheng 2017; Wall 2012). Washback can be considered as the extent to which testing and assessment influences:

1. what students invest in learning (e.g. only content covered in a given test).
2. what teachers decide to do to help their students pass the test (e.g. spending time with students on how to answer questions correctly and quickly).
3. how school administrators and parents behave to pressure teachers and students to do well on tests.

It is important to note that washback can be positive or negative (Bailey 1996; Wall 2012), depending on whether a given test and assessment promotes language learning beyond the test and assessment activities (i.e. positive washback) or impedes language learning or use as a result of the narrowly focused teaching and learning of material only applicable to the test and assessment (i.e. negative washback). If a test asks students to answer multiple-choice questions only, they will aim to learn how to answer them correctly. However, while they may pass the test, their knowledge of correctly answering multiple-choice questions may not be transferable to other real-life language-use situations.

Testing and assessment is not the only factor influencing teaching and learning behaviours. Social and educational conditions (e.g. how students are selected or rewarded) and teachers' beliefs and attitudes toward their professions (e.g. what helps them keep their current jobs and why they choose to become teachers), for instance, also significantly influence washback impacts. Test and assessment designers need to consider the potential impact of the assessment, especially on students, and ensure that positive washback is optimally promoted.

Practical tips for enhancing test and assessment qualities

We have discussed seven standards and quality criteria for language testing and assessment. It is now valuable to restate some practical tips that can enhance the quality of language testing and assessment using these standards. After language tests and assessments have been wholly created (see Chapter 3), they should be critically reviewed and evaluated before and after administration and evaluation (also known as validation in standardized tests discussed earlier). There are various types of reviews of language tests and assessment, including:

- *Assessment designer review*: Teachers and designers should critically review their test questions or assessment tasks to meet expected conventions and standards. They should also check language clarity and accuracy and instructions for item writers. Teachers or assessors may use a checklist to evaluate test items/tasks (e.g. item/task accuracy, clarity of questions/tasks, potential bias). They may initially complete the assessment, followed by an interview about the overall test and each question/task.
- *Language testing and assessment expert review*: Whenever possible, teachers and designers should ask language testing and assessment experts to review their tests and assessment tasks for appropriacy, adequacy and potential bias. Experts can comment on their understanding of the test instructions and questions/tasks and provide feedback on improving them.

- *Piloting the test or assessment*: Teachers or designers should pilot their tests or assessment tasks. In a standardized test, a relatively large sample size is desirable for statistical analysis (e.g. reliability and difficulty analysis; see Chapter 9). A reason for requiring a large sample size is the variations in observing various responses to the same question/task. Reliability or difficulty levels cannot be estimated accurately without score or performance variation. In performance assessment, a pilot study should be conducted on applying the marking rubrics and moderating raters' rating behaviours in performance assessments such as writing and speaking.
- *Continuously observe test and assessment use*: Since language tests or assessments can significantly impact students and test takers, monitoring their use and effectiveness is crucial. When situations and contexts change, the test or assessment may not function as it used to. Therefore, continuous observation and evaluation are needed.

Summary

This chapter has synthesized crucial considerations regarding the qualities of language testing and assessments that guide their design and implementation. It has underscored the interconnectedness among reliability, validity/trustworthiness, authenticity, practicality, fairness, ethics and impact, collectively forming the cornerstone of effective language testing and assessment practices. Each component represents a vital piece of the puzzle, and any omission or inadequacy can hinder a comprehensive understanding of the testing and assessment landscape. Thus, a holistic approach to addressing these qualities is essential for ensuring the integrity and effectiveness of language testing and assessment practices.

Discussion

1. What are the key themes and considerations in (a) reliability, (b) validity, (c) authenticity, (d) practicality, (e) fairness, (f) ethics, and (g) impact?
2. Can a language test be reliable but not valid? Why or why not?
3. Choose an example of a language test or assessment in your own context. What are its strengths and weaknesses regarding the quality criteria discussed in this chapter?

4 Name one important lesson you have learnt from this chapter and how you will apply it in your language testing and assessment practice.

Further reading

Bonner, S.M., 2013, 'Validity in classroom assessment: Purposes, properties, and principles' in *SAGE handbook of research in classroom assessment*, ed. J.H. Macmillan, SAGE, Los Angeles, pp. 87–106.

This chapter discusses critical issues in validity in classroom assessment. It stresses the importance of recognizing the nature of classroom assessment, which may not fulfil the validity criteria set in large-scale standardized tests. It proposes guidelines to evaluate validity in classroom assessment.

Green, A., 2020, *Exploring language assessment and testing: Language in action*, 2nd edn, Routledge, New York and London.

Chapter 4 ('The qualities of effective assessment systems') discusses four criteria for examining whether a test is adequate (practicality, reliability, validity and beneficial consequences, including washback).

Jones, N., 2012, 'Reliability and dependability' in *Routledge handbook of language testing*, eds G. Fulcher & F. Davidson, Routledge, London and New York, pp. 350–62.

This chapter provides a valuable discussion of test reliability and dependability. It connects test reliability with validity and offers future directions for test reliability applications and re-conceptualization.

Kane, M.T., 2013, 'Validating the interpretations and uses of test scores', *Journal of Educational Measurement*, vol. 50, no. 1, pp. 1–73.

This article comprehensively discusses test validity and an argument-based approach to test validation. Kane uses an interpretive/use argument to emphasize the equal importance of interpretation and use of test scores.

Kunnan, A.J., 2018, *Evaluating language assessment*, Routledge, New York.

This highly recommended book combines an integrative approach to test validity, impact, fairness and ethics. Kunnan provides a theoretical and practical discussion of these issues with concrete frameworks and examples.

Phakiti, A. & Isaacs, T., 2021, 'Classroom assessment and validity: Psychometric and edumetric approaches', *European Journal of Applied Linguistics*, vol. 10, no. 1, pp. 3–24.

This article discusses two approaches to assessment validity (psychometric and edumetric) for classroom assessment. It articulates debates, controversies and issues in assessment validity and discusses implications for classroom assessment.

5

Testing and Assessing Reading

Overview

This chapter discusses the nature of additional language (AL) reading, considering reading purposes and a sociocognitive model elucidating the bottom-up, top-down and interactive processes involved in reading within a social context. It also discusses reading skills and strategies, factors affecting reading, and testing and assessment techniques for evaluating reading comprehension with illustrative examples.

Guided questions

1. What is reading? What influences reading comprehension?
2. How are reading comprehension skills tested or assessed in your context?

Introduction

The previous chapters discussed general approaches, principles and considerations in language testing and assessment. The following four chapters focus on a specific language area that can be tested and assessed by applying those approaches, principles and considerations. This chapter discusses testing and assessing reading. The capacity to read in the first language (L1) is significant for people in the twenty-first century as it enables them to acquire new knowledge, develop critical thinking abilities and engage with diverse perspectives. Reading skills are commonly considered a fundamental literacy component across all education systems. The ability to read in an AL is equally significant as it enables people to develop a mutual understanding with other people using a lingual franca.

This chapter focuses on the essential considerations in testing and assessing AL reading. It first discusses the nature of AL reading because it is essential to know what to look for (i.e. constructs of reading) so that questions and tasks can be appropriate. Second, it considers the critical issues in designing reading tests and assessments. Finally, it presents some techniques for testing and assessing reading comprehension.

The nature of AL reading

Research into L1 and AL reading suggests that good readers extract information fluently and accurately and aim to interpret meaning from what they read (see, e.g. Alderson 2000; Alderson et al. 2015; Afflerbach 2016; Grabe 2009; Grabe & Stoller 2020; Hudson 2007; Koda 2005; MacMillan 2017). They also relate what they understand from the text to relevant knowledge, beliefs or experiences. Reading is, hence, a dynamic process that involves more than merely knowing or retelling what a text is about.

AL reading is multimodal, as reading can be nested with dynamic visual, audio or spoken texts. Urquhart and Weir (1998, p. 22) define reading as 'the process of receiving and interpreting information encoded in language form via the medium of print'. Grabe and Stoller (2020, p. 11) define reading for general comprehension as 'the ability to understand and interpret information from a text appropriately'. During reading comprehension, 'the reader extracts and integrates various information from the text and combines it with what is already known' (Koda 2005, p. 4). According to Alderson (2000), AL reading is a complex cognitive and social task, and it is not always easy to differentiate reading comprehension from retention (e.g. remembering and memorizing), understanding from inferencing, and inferencing from analysing and utilizing. For example, as AL students read multiple texts, they need to engage in more complex cognitive tasks such as remembering points of comparison or opposition, assessing the relative importance of the information, establishing the main concepts or themes, and addressing the real-work tasks (Grabe & Stoller 2020). To ease the complexity of testing and assessing reading comprehension, it is suggested that the purposes and types of reading be specified (Alderson 2000; Grabe 2009; Koda 2005).

Reading purposes

Reasons for reading or reading purposes can also explain the nature of reading. Figure 5.1 illustrates five essential purposes for people to read. Let's explore these purposes as they can shape what to test or assess:

1 *Reading to search for information* involves scanning (identifying specific or local information) and skimming (i.e. grasping general or global information; a microprocessor). This type of reading is considered expeditious reading (Urquhart & Weir 1998) because it is carried out at a high speed (e.g. 250 words per minute (wpm); Grabe 2009).

2 *Reading for general comprehension* is known as fluent or effortless reading comprehension. Advanced-level readers usually experience this kind of reading because they have a high level of automatic word recognition.

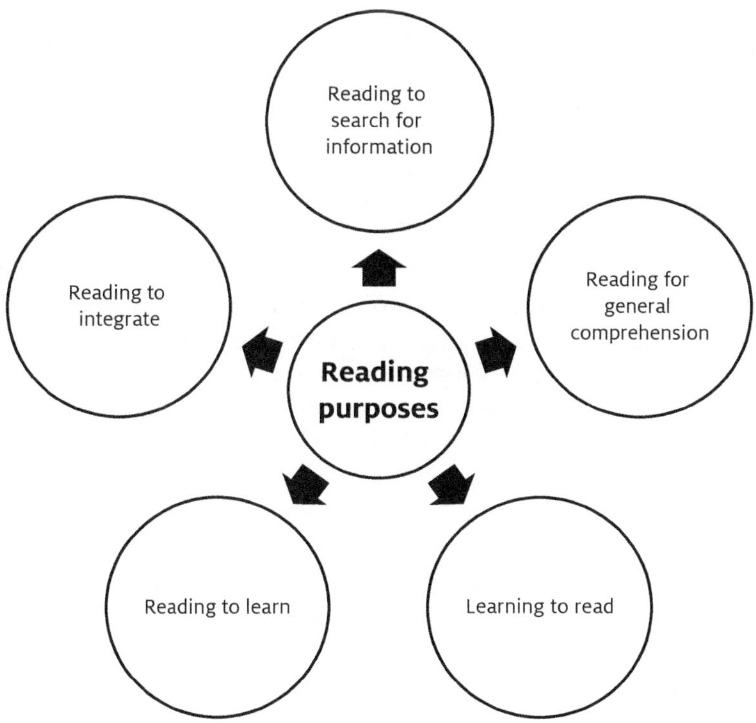

FIGURE 5.1 *Five key purposes for people to read.*

3. *Learning to read* requires readers to understand and acquire linguistics features of a text (e.g. lower-level, bottom-up processing) and the social use of language through mentoring, scaffolding or assistance from parents, peers and teachers. This reading purpose occurs in classroom and language learning contexts.
4. *Reading to learn* usually takes place in academic and professional contexts. It is generally much slower than the first two types of reading. It demands an effective use of memory for storing and retrieving information and invokes critical thinking for evaluating the validity of information. It also requires readers to be able to relate new information to existing knowledge or relevant background information. This reading purpose occurs in content and language-integrated learning (CLIL) situations.
5. *Reading to integrate information* has the same characteristics as reading to learn. However, the focus is on an output or product of language use (e.g. writing an academic assignment, thesis or dissertation, or presenting products or services to clients). This purpose can take place in educational, professional and personal contexts.

Reading purposes can, therefore, affect how people process and use information as and after they read. The following section discusses models of AL reading.

Models of reading

Several models of L1 reading have been used to explain AL reading (see Grabe 2009; Grabe & Stoller 2020 for comprehensive reviews). According to Koda (2005) and Grabe (2009), the critical differences between L1 and AL reading include the range and size of vocabulary knowledge, the types of responses AL readers need to provide, the levels of awareness of the AL, and the cultural knowledge relevant to a given AL. During an early development, AL reading tends to be less fluent and requires more attention and deliberation than L1 reading.

It is useful to know what may be involved in reading for effective testing and assessment. Figure 5.2 conceptualizes a sociocognitive model of AL reading that recognizes a social and cognitive dimension to reading. This model may be applicable for explaining aspects of other language skills, such as writing, which requires reading, and speaking, which requires listening. This model emphasizes reading as participation and interactions with a specific social context (i.e. a social dimension). Three sub-models of AL reading are further articulated as follows.

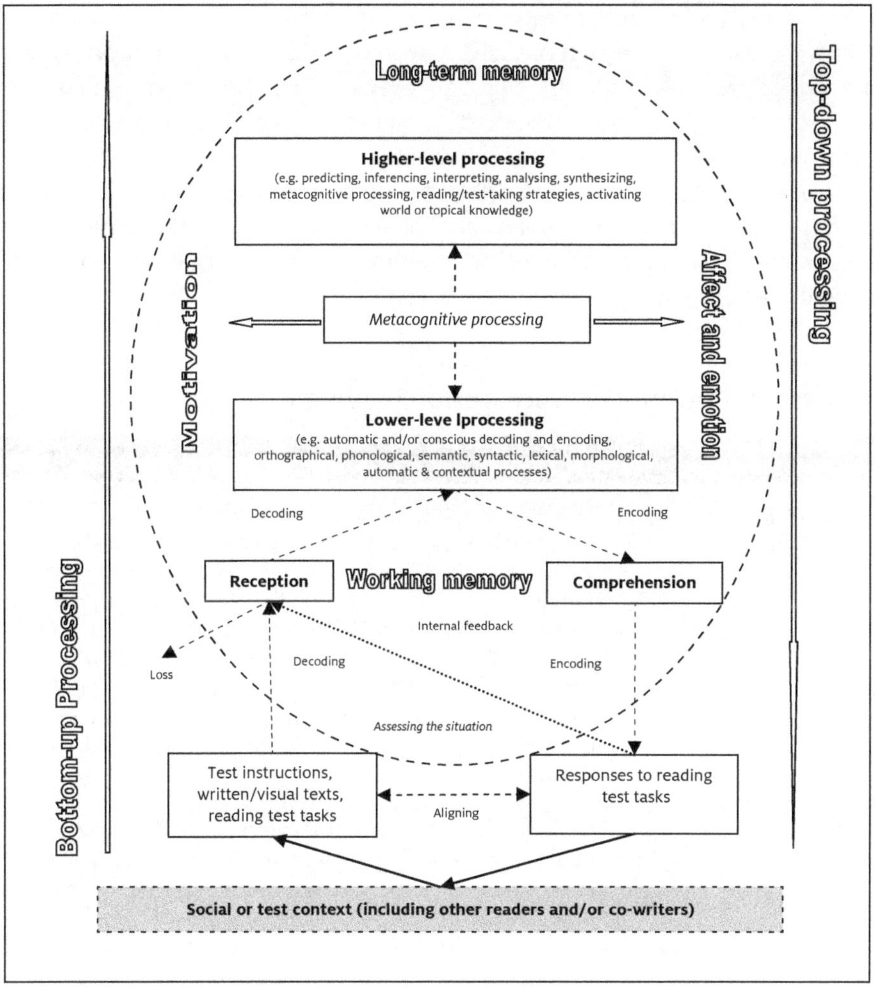

FIGURE 5.2 *A sociocognitive model of AL reading.*

The bottom-up model

Neurologically, AL reading starts from seeing (or touching for the blind), the primary physiological system that recognizes language symbols, orthography or semiotic signs containing meanings or messages. Information is passed through the visual cortex of the brain. Bottom-up processing takes place when AL readers receive and perceive text, progressing from the lower-level processes, such as automatic recognition and interpretation of words or language symbols, to the higher-level processes, such as assigning meanings to words, phrases and sentences, and the highest-level processes such as making inferences and interpreting. The role of executive control which regulates these processes, together with motivation and affect, are acknowledged in this model (see also Grabe 2009). Bottom-up processing suggests that AL readers must decode from graphic and phonemic to syntactic and semantic sequences (Alderson 2000).

Grabe (2009) presents the vital linguistic processes during bottom-up processing in reading comprehension. For skilful AL readers, these processes may operate without much directed attention or with minimal expenditure of cognitive effort (summarized in Table 5.1).

TABLE 5.1 Bottom-Up Processes of Reading

Processing	Explanation
Orthographic	The visual recognition and processing of words, their interconnections, orders and sequences in the text. Different languages have different characters and styles of their writing (e.g. reading comprehension (English), อ่านวิเคราะห์ (Thai), 阅读理解 (simplified Chinese Mandarin), ຄວາມເຂົ້າໃຈໃນການອ່ານ (Laotian) and စာဖတ်ခြင်းကိုနားလည်သဘောပေါက်ခြင်း (Burmese). Without orthographical knowledge of a given language, sight reading/reading aloud is impossible and information processing cannot proceed further.
Phonological	Recognition of a speech sound that creates a distinctive meaning in a word and between different words. It links a visual word or language input to the associated sound representation or pronunciation, which is then connected to meaning. This linguistic processing is key to word recognition.
Semantic and syntactic	The processing of a word that can be variable in (1) its semantic (i.e. some words may be concrete; others abstract), and (2) its syntactic (e.g. content words (e.g. nouns and verbs) versus function words (e.g. articles and prepositions). This type of processing allows readers to access and retrieve meaning and words (i.e. lexical access, presented below).
Lexical access	The process of matching a word with the reader's mental lexicon or cognitive representation of the word. It refers to the connection between the eyes (what word one sees) and the brain (what word one knows).

Processing	Explanation
Morphological	Processing morphemes, which are the smallest units of meaning. Some morphemes can stand alone (free morphemes, e.g. base words such as love and like), while others cannot (bound morphemes, e.g. prefixes such as re- and dis-; and affixes such as -ly and -ness). Early language learning helps readers realize that when two morphemes are combined, a new word can be created (e.g. news + paper). This processing also allows readers to make inferences about the meaning of unknown or unfamiliar words using available morphological knowledge.
Automatic	High-speed, effortless processing. This allows the reader to engage in multiple processes during reading (i.e. parallel, distributed processing) and does not take up working memory.
Contextual	The process occurs when the reader experiences word recognition difficulty; the context in which the word is located is considered to help support meaning-making. Contextual processing is also relevant to implicit or explicit awareness of a context, which gives meaning to a word beyond its literal meaning. Explicit contextual processing, therefore, slows down reading.
Syntactic	Parsing is the process that connects words (e.g. phrases, clauses and sentences), allowing meaningful meaning-making in a text. For example, 'I am taking a reading test' is more meaningful than 'reading is I a test-taking am'. Parsing allows readers to expect what can or cannot follow a word.

The top-down model

Figure 5.2 also depicts a top-down processing model in which the reader contributes to meaning construction and interpretation. This view is known as reading schemata – a network of knowledge (e.g. topical or world knowledge, experiences, knowledge of text types and writing styles; Alderson 2000). As AL readers read, they generate plausible hypotheses or predictions and use relevant and available knowledge to form inferences from the text. The top-down approach suggests that AL readers use what they think is related to their schemata and align information from the text with this network.

It is important to note that the extent to which the concept of reading schemata alone helps explain AL reading remains questionable (Alderson

2000) because it does not explain how different kinds of knowledge are called on for use. Grabe (2009) further points out that empirical evidence does not support the predictions of the Psychological Guessing Game Model (e.g. see Goodman 1967) in which higher-level processing is emphasized, whereby the reader first predicts upcoming texts, then samples from the text as needed, confirms his or her predictions, and then moves on to make new predictions. Grabe (2009) also argues that while this may be true for explaining AL reading of beginner-level readers, good readers do not typically engage in reading this way.

The interactive model

Figure 5.2 postulates that reading involves highly complex, dynamic and interactive bottom-up and top-down processes, which in one moment can be seen as serial or sequential and in the next moment as parallel or orchestrated (Alderson 2000; Clapham 1996; Phakiti 2007). The term interaction can be described in two related dimensions. The initial type of interaction is internal, involving various linguistic, cognitive, psycholinguistic and affective elements, depicted within the oval in Figure 5.2. Conversely, the second type of interaction is characterized as external and social, occurring within socially or educationally situated reading contexts. In this framework, the reader endeavours to unravel the text's intended meaning by deciphering both the explicit and implicit intentions of the authors. Subsequently, the reader leverages his or her comprehension abilities to craft responses to the reading purpose or provided task, such as answering questions or completing assigned tasks. This intricate cognitive endeavour is encapsulated within the delineated box in Figure 5.2.

In a reading assessment scenario, interactions may occur between the test takers and their perception of what the teacher or test designers expect them to exhibit. Such interactions, encompassing intrinsic and extrinsic factors, wield considerable influence over constructing meaning, interpreting a provided text, grasping encoded comprehension, and ultimately augmenting task proficiency (cf. Alderson 2000; Grabe 2009). In addition, interactions between top-down and bottom-up processes require (1) a cognitive mediator, which can be seen through the concept of executive control, and (2) an affective mediator, which can be seen through the roles of motivation, that energizes one's reading behaviours, and affect, which includes feelings. Grabe (2009) and Grabe and Stoller (2020) have advocated the roles of these mediators in AL reading.

Furthermore, a dynamic shift between conscious and automatic reading processes within a given individual, context and time must be recognized when explaining the nature of AL reading. When readers are aware of a difficulty affecting their reading processes and comprehension, their central executive takes over their reading processes, making their reading more and more strategic (e.g. by adjusting reading rates, previewing or planning to read, and monitoring comprehension), until the reading difficulty has been resolved. Reading strategies are likely to be activated despite no difficulty, especially in testing. This is simply because readers need to exhibit their ability to read and, to ensure this, they identify what they need to accomplish much sooner.

A significant limitation of reading models, including the current one, is that they describe skilful reading processes. However, such models do not suggest that unskilful readers do the opposite of skilful readers or do not possess the skills or engage in activities described in the model. Viewing models of unskilful readers – many of whom are AL readers – in that way presumes a deficit model of AL reading ability.

Two pivotal points should be noted. First, the multimodal, bilingual and multilingual nature of language use in a real-life context can shape AL reading. For example, in terms of multimodality, a written text may be read to edit, revise or rehearse for an oral presentation. While watching the news on TV, people also read what is written on the TV screen to gather additional information while simultaneously accessing audio-visual input. Second, it has been well theorized and acknowledged in bilingual reading that a bilingual reader is not two monolingual readers within the same person (Ortiz & Cehelyk 2024). Similarly, multilingual readers bring their languages, identities, cultural backgrounds and unique characteristics to reading and how they make sense of a text they read (e.g. Chalhoub-Deville 2019). Therefore, no single model or framework will ever be complex and sensitive enough to describe AL reading.

Reading skills and strategies

Skilful reading and strategic reading processes can be similar in comprehension processing but differ at the level of automaticity and attention. Skilful reading involves high-speed processing, whereas strategic reading tends to be attentional and thus slower because it involves some level of cognitive deliberation and intention. All readers use reading skills and strategies in a given reading situation. However, readers differ in the effectiveness of reading skills and strategies. Many reading skills and strategies aid successful reading (also depicted in Figure 5.2). These skills are classified as cognitive strategies in language learning strategies as they are directly related to the language (Oxford 2017). These reading skills and strategies include:

- recognizing or recalling word meaning
- skimming (quickly gathering the main ideas or the gist of a text) and scanning (quickly looking for specific information within a text)
- recognizing the use of references in a text
- being aware of the purposes of reading

- recognizing types of text and genres
- identifying topics, authors' purposes and tones, and the main ideas in a text
- distinguishing main ideas from supporting information
- distinguishing facts from opinions
- making appropriate inferences from a text
- linking texts to relevant prior knowledge or experience
- predicting upcoming topics or aspects of passages as the reader reads
- identifying or recalling specific information (e.g. persons, places, events and time) in a text
- guessing the meanings of unknown words using context clues.

Table 5.2 provides reading test and assessment constructs that share the characteristics of the reading skills and strategies.

TABLE 5.2 Examples of Types of Questions for Testing and Assessing Reading Constructs

Reading construct	Questions asked
Identifying main topics, ideas and purpose	What is the main idea of this passage? What is the writer's primary purpose in this paper?
Extracting facts from the text	According to the passage, where is XXX located? According to the passage, how many people were affected by the current flood? What is true about climate change, according to the passage? What is not true about XXX according to the passage?
Making inferences from the text	What can be correctly implied from the passage about XXX? Which of the following can be inferred from the passage?
Vocabulary-in-context	The word 'XXX' (line X) can be best replaced by … What does the word 'XXX' (line XX) mean?
Recognizing references in the text	The word 'them' (line X) refers to …

Factors affecting reading and reading comprehension performance

Reading comprehension is influenced by various factors, including reader and external factors (Alderson 2000), as summarized in Table 5.3. Test designers must consider these factors, as they have implications for the reliability and validity of testing and assessment.

TABLE 5.3 Reader Factors versus Textual, Contextual and Task Factors

Reader factors	Textual/contextual/task factors
Affect: Readers' emotions, anxieties and attitudes toward a text can affect their reading. Some topics can trigger negative or strong emotional responses, affecting people's reading.	*Choice of language in a text or task*: Texts or test instructions using highly complex sentence structures and unfamiliar vocabulary are more challenging to comprehend as they influence word and phonological identification. Texts and instructions with lay language are more accessible for comprehension.
Investment and identity: Readers may be highly motivated to read (see below) but do not desire to read a given text simply because it does not increase their personal or cultural identity empowerment. Therefore, they are not willing to invest in learning to read in that particular language.	*Literary and non-literary texts*: Literary texts such as fairy/folk tales, novels, poetry, plays and parodies can be more complex to read than non-literary texts, typically because they may include multi-layered meanings and are culturally specific in content and writing style.
Language knowledge and proficiency: Readers differ in vocabulary, grammar, pragmatics, discourse and L1-AL closeness.	*Medium of text representation*: How texts are provided to readers (e.g. prints on A4 paper, computer screens, screen resolution, mobile/cell phones, text background (e.g. colour) influences reading.
Level of motivation and interest: Even skilful readers differ in their motivation to read a text; in real-world reading, readers choose to read texts they are interested in, but in a reading test they are forced to read the texts in the test.	*Text organization*: How authors, and the extent to which they relate their paragraphs to one another, can affect reading comprehension and recall (e.g. text cohesion and coherence).

Reader factors	Textual/contextual/task factors
Literacy level: Literacy is related to knowledge of how language can be used as a means of communication. First-language literacy can influence how well a person can read in another language.	*Text readability*: Texts with high syntactic complexity and lexical density, including lengthy words and paragraphs, are more complex to read or extract information from than simplified and short texts.
Metalinguistic knowledge and metacognition: Some readers recognize parts of speech or language functions in a text, know the types of writing genres/ text types, use reading strategies to aid understanding, control their comprehension monitoring and evaluation, and notice text inconsistencies.	*Text topic, content and task*: Readers can understand familiar topics and content better than unfamiliar ones. Simple tasks such as answering true/ false questions are more accessible than answering short-answer questions.
Readers' skills, strategies, and experiences: As discussed above, reading skills and strategies are critical for success in reading comprehension. Opportunities to read and reading experience across various situations and tasks also determine the level of reading success.	*Text type and genre*: Written structures of narrative texts differ from expository texts that allow visualization or imagination for readers.
Topical, background and cultural knowledge: Some people have better knowledge of the world, general and specific content knowledge, and cross-cultural knowledge than others.	*Typographical features of text*: Features of prints, quality of prints, colours, fonts, font sizes, spacing, and layout impact reading comprehension.
	Verbal and non-verbal information in text: Graphical information such as headings and subheadings, highlighted direct quotes, use of tables, coloured versus black-and-white figures, and illustrations impact reading and reading comprehension.

Techniques for testing and assessing reading

Teachers and test and assessment designers should employ various techniques for testing and assessing reading skills because a particular technique has weaknesses (e.g. Brown & Abeywickrama 2010; Hughes 2003; Hughes & Hughes 2020; Weir 2005). This section presents restricted-response techniques, followed by constructed-response techniques.

Matching technique

This technique involves asking students to match two sets of information. It is useful for testing and assessing students' ability to identify topics and main ideas. For instance, they may match headings or titles to their corresponding paragraphs, insert a paragraph from a given list between two paragraphs in a text, or match events with places. This approach aids in assessing the ability to identify the main topic and topic sentences in reading and listening and evaluating text cohesion in writing. Additionally, this technique can be implemented as a drag-and-drop task in computer-based testing.

Instructions: Read the following paragraphs (1, 2, 3, 4) and match each with the appropriate title (A, B, C, D).

A Common human diseases

B Importance of sleep for overall health

C Stress management techniques

D The benefits of regular exercise

E Tips for healthy eating

1 _____ Routinized physical activity has numerous benefits for physical and mental health. Exercise helps strengthen your muscles and bones, improves cardiovascular health, and boost immune function. Additionally, it can reduce the risk of chronic diseases, such as heart disease, diabetes and certain cancers. Engaging in regular exercise also releases endorphins, which can improve mood and reduce stress.

2 _____ Consuming various nutrient-rich foods, including fruits, vegetables, whole grains, lean proteins and healthy fats, is essential. You should limit your intake of processed foods, sugary snacks and high-fat foods. Finally, you should pay attention to portion sizes and eat regular, balanced meals throughout the day.

3 _____ Adequate sleep supports cognitive function, emotional regulation and physical recovery. Insufficient sleep can affect concentration, memory and decision-making abilities. Planning a sleep schedule and creating a comfortable environment can promote better sleep quality.

4 _____ Strategies such as deep breathing exercises, meditation, yoga and progressive muscle relaxation can help reduce your stress levels. Engaging in hobbies, spending time in nature, and connecting with supportive friends and family can relieve stress.

Answers:

1. D; 2. E; 3. B; 4. C

Source: Modified AI text from ChatGPT 3.5

This technique offers several strengths. First, scoring is objective and efficient due to the limited response variation. Second, constructing items can be relatively straightforward, as authentic reading texts often already contain headings. Third, students may find this technique familiar, as they frequently encounter headings in reading tests and various classroom activities may already use them.

However, there are notable weaknesses to consider. First, students' overall performance hinges on the accuracy of matching each heading. One incorrect match can lead to failure on multiple items (a domino effect). Second, reading tasks using this technique require experienced item writers who can select suitable topics, text types, lengths and complexities tailored to the target test-taker group.

When constructing a matching task, consider the following recommendations:

1. Assign a letter representing each heading or paragraph (e.g. A to F) instead of requiring students to write the entire title or paragraph. This not only streamlines the task but also makes scoring quicker.
2. Avoid including unnecessary extra headings as distractors. Several distractor options can divert students' attention from completing the task efficiently within the allotted time frame.

True, false or not given technique

Unlike the true–false technique, which offers a dichotomous option and thus gives a 50 per cent chance of success through guessing, including an additional option labelled 'not given' introduces a more nuanced approach to testing and assessment. This option requires students to draw inferences based on the factual information presented in the reading text. Test questions or tasks may present statements that, while logically plausible, lack direct evidence within the reading material for students to verify their accuracy. This technique tests comprehension and the ability to discern between true, false and not given statements based on the information provided in the passage. The following is an example of this technique.

Instructions: Do the following statements agree with the passage below:

1 *True* if the statement agrees with the passage.

2 *False* if the statement contradicts the passage.

3 *Not given* if there is no information on this.

Passage

Climate change is a pressing issue that affects various aspects of our planet. Rising global temperatures, primarily due to human activities such as burning fossil fuels and deforestation, have led to more frequent extreme weather events, including heatwaves, hurricanes and droughts. The consequences of climate change are far-reaching, impacting ecosystems, economies and human health worldwide. Addressing climate change requires urgent action on both individual and societal levels, including reducing carbon emissions, transitioning to renewable energy sources, and implementing sustainable practices in agriculture and industry.

1 _________ Climate change has no impact on human health.

2 _________ Climate change only affects the environment but does not have economic consequences.

3 _________ Rising global temperatures are caused by human activities such as burning fossil fuels and deforestation.

Answers:

1 *False* because the passage mentions that climate change impacts human health, contradicting the statement.

2 *Not given* because the passage discusses the economic consequences of climate change but does not explicitly state whether it does not affect the economy.

3 *True* because the passage explicitly states that human activities primarily cause the rising global temperatures.

Source: Modified AI text from ChatGPT 3.5

The advantages of this technique lie in its simplicity of scoring and its applicability to formative assessment practices, which are seamlessly integrated into reading activities. Incorporating the 'not given' option reduces the likelihood of correct responses due to random guessing. Moreover, it encourages deeper cognitive engagement by critically evaluating whether 'not given' constitutes a plausibly correct answer.

However, this approach is not without limitations. Despite the inclusion of the 'not given' option, guessing that leads to a correct answer is not removed, posing a persistent challenge to testing and assessment validity. Reading texts that balance presenting factual information and allowing for plausible inferences can be challenging, particularly in true–false statements. This highlights the delicate balance required to use this technique for effective testing and assessment.

Multiple-choice techniques

This technique typically involves presenting a question followed by several plausible answer options, with students tasked with selecting the single correct response from the multiple choices provided. While the number of options can vary, ranging from three to five, four are most commonly employed. The widespread adoption of this method stems from its practicality in administration and scoring, particularly in large-scale testing situations where expedient results and decision-making are pressing. An example of a multiple-choice technique can be illustrated as follows.

Instructions: Answer the following questions by choosing A, B, C or D.

Coffee consumption has been linked to various health benefits. Studies have shown that moderate coffee intake may reduce the risk of certain diseases, such as Parkinson's disease, type-2 diabetes and liver cirrhosis. Coffee contains antioxidants that can help protect cells from damage caused by free radicals. However, excessive coffee consumption can lead to adverse health effects, including increased heart rates and disrupted sleep patterns.

1 Which of the following diseases has a moderate coffee intake been shown to reduce its risk?

A Alzheimer's disease

B Parkinson's disease

C Lung cancer

D Osteoporosis

2 According to the passage, what adverse health effects can excessive coffee consumption lead to?

A Increased frequency of urination

B Reduced cognitive function

C Increased heart rate

D Increased more nightmares

Answers:

1. B; 2. C

Source: Modified AI text from ChatGPT 3.5

Crafting high-quality multiple-choice reading questions demands considerable time and effort. Thus, pre-testing, careful editing and rigorous validation procedures are essential to the item-construction process. Validation steps, such as discrimination analysis, distractor analysis and cognitive interviews, are critical for ensuring the reliability and validity of this technique (see Chapter 9). Furthermore, pre-testing serves as an initial evaluation phase, allowing the test developer to gauge the effectiveness of the questions before their implementation. Following this, careful editing is essential to refine the questions, addressing any ambiguities or inconsistencies that may detract from their clarity or effectiveness. Incorporating these validation measures into the question development process can improve the quality and reliability of the multiple-choice reading questions.

Compared to a binary two-option format (e.g., true/false, A/B), a multiple-choice technique reduces the likelihood of students arriving at correct answers through random guessing, although it does not eliminate it. Moreover, its utility extends to formative assessment contexts, wherein teachers can promptly assess students' comprehension of the text and discover the reasons behind correct and incorrect answers. The provision of feedback can be closely aligned with students' performance, facilitating targeted interventions to address areas of misunderstanding.

The drawbacks associated with this technique become particularly pronounced in high-stakes summative assessment. In such contexts, the inherent reliance on chance introduces unpredictability, potentially leading to instances where students arrive at the correct answers through random selection or for a wrong reason rather than genuine comprehension. Additionally, students may employ test-wiseness strategies as expedient shortcuts to rapidly and accurately respond to questions without necessarily profoundly engaging with the reading material. These drawbacks can compromise the validity and reliability of the testing and assessment outcomes.

While the ability to answer multiple-choice reading questions can serve as a valuable indicator of specific reading skills, such as basic comprehension and text analysis, it is essential to recognize its inherent limitations in predicting performance in real-world reading contexts. This structured format may not accurately reflect the nuanced and dynamic nature of authentic reading experiences, where students or test takers are required to independently navigate through complex texts, interpret meaning, and conclude without the aid of predefined questions or options.

The following are recommendations when designing a multiple-choice reading test:

1. Select a text appropriate to the proficiency level and interests of the target student group. Align it with the specific context and purpose of the test and assessment.
2. Employ clear and concise language in the reading passages and questions.
3. Avoid questions that rely solely on general knowledge or prior information unrelated to the text. Students can answer the questions without having to read the text.
4. Ensure that each question has only one correct answer.
5. Craft questions that test and assess reading comprehension skills only. Avoid tasks that require students to depend on non-reading abilities, such as mathematical calculations.

Cloze technique

The cloze technique prompts students to fill in a sentence by supplying a missing word. It measures their ability to comprehend interrupted or redundant text, known as the reduced redundancy principle, by restoring the missing words to aid comprehension. To create a cloze task, words are systematically deleted at regular intervals (a pseudo-random procedure) after providing some reading context. Deletions occur every fifth to twelfth (every sixth word is the most common). Completing a cloze test requires students to read a paragraph for overall comprehension, striving to grasp the meanings and concepts conveyed by the text. Students or test takers often transition from lower-level, bottom-up reading to higher-level cognitive processing throughout a cloze task. An extract of a cloze technique can be illustrated as follows.

Completing a cloze test requires (1) _________ to read a paragraph for (2) _________ comprehension, striving to grasp the (3) _________ and concepts conveyed by the (4) _________.

The advantages of this technique include its ease of construction and the ability to create many items based on one text. It has the potential to capture the dynamics of language use in that plausible words (not strictly from the original text) should be permitted as long as they make sense in the gap and do not change the text's original meaning. Tests using the cloze technique can discriminate well between poor and good readers, as this technique assesses reading comprehension holistically and produces good internal consistency. This technique can be hybridized with a multiple-choice technique. However, it is important to note that a multiple-choice cloze test does not measure reading comprehension like the constructed-response cloze test.

The limitations of the cloze technique include requiring students to have essential grammatical and vocabulary knowledge and awareness as these play a critical role in supplying missing words – a test of lexico-grammatical knowledge – an understanding of how vocabulary (lexis) and grammatical structures work together in a language. This task requires students to engage in linguistic analysis when checking supplied answers. Topics can influence students' success; some may have more prior knowledge or experiences than others. A novelty factor may play a significant role in students' performance. Students seeing this technique for the first time tend to perform poorly or spend more time figuring out how to solve the cloze tasks despite having competent reading skills.

Here are some recommendations for constructing a cloze test:

1. Provide instructions to the test takers, specifying the criteria for completing the cloze sentences. For example, indicate whether only one word should be supplied per blank space and whether correct spelling and word forms are essential.
2. Permit standard variations in spellings and word forms in the answers to accommodate different linguistic conventions. For instance, consider accepting both 'colour' and 'color' as correct responses.
3. Consider plausible answers that test takers may provide when evaluating responses. Recognize that there might be multiple correct options for filling in the blank space (e.g. options/choices/alternatives; lifts/elevators).

4. Ensure that the reading passage provided before the cloze sentences is sufficient for understanding the content. Removed words should challenge comprehension while still allowing for meaningful interpretation.
5. Choose appropriate intervals for deleting words from the text (e.g. every *n*th word). This can vary depending on the test's difficulty level and the target students' reading proficiency.
6. Provide sufficient practice opportunities for students to familiarize themselves with the cloze task format and practise their skills before the assessment. If cloze tasks are never part of the classroom activities but are used in summative assessment, their use will be unaligned with the classroom curriculum (see Chapter 1).
7. Review the cloze test items for the target students' clarity, fairness and appropriateness. Ensure the test accurately measures the intended language skills and does not contain biased language or content.

C-test

The C-test operates on the same principle as the cloze technique, utilizing the reduced redundancy principle to assess language proficiency comprehensively. It measures general language proficiency, requiring students or test takers to engage various language components, including lexico-grammatical, discourse and pragmatic knowledge, alongside reading skills (Eckes & Grotjahn 2006).

To construct a C-test, keep the first and last sentences intact. Then, in the second and subsequent sentences, remove the second half of every second word, with the deletion based on the number of letters in the word divided by 2. If a word has an odd number of letters (e.g. 3, 5, 7), delete one additional letter beyond the remaining intact letters (e.g. 'point' becomes 'po_ _ _' and 'process' becomes 'pro _ _ _ _'). An example of a C-test can be illustrated as follows.

Thirdly, akin to the cloze technique, the C-test lacks authenticity in reading assessment, resulting in low public acceptance. While te _ _ creators m_ _ find i _ convenient t _ generate te _ _ items, ma _ _ students fi _ _ the ta _ _ cumbersome, mai _ _ _ because th _ _ are unfam _ _ _ _ _ with th _ _ type o _ assessment. Topic complexity, font sizes and time constraints can further impact student performance.

Answers:

st/ay/t/o/st/ny/nd/sk/nly/ey/is/f

The strengths of the C-test are similar to those of the cloze technique. For example, they can be objectively scored and cost-effective, as a short text can produce many items, producing a high-reliability estimate. Nevertheless, this technique comes with several notable drawbacks. First, proficiency in spelling, particularly in a standardized form of the language, can significantly influence performance. For instance, the spelling difference between 'color' and 'colour' presents a challenge (e.g. 'co_ _ _' versus. 'col_ _ _'). Second, the degree to which C-test performance correlates with overall reading proficiency remains unclear (Eckes & Grotjahn 2006), as the test primarily assesses lower-level skills and problem-solving abilities. Test takers are often required to review their answers, even though the task mainly involves lower-level cognitive processes. Third, akin to the cloze technique, the C-test lacks authenticity in reading assessment, resulting in low public acceptance. While test creators may find it convenient to generate test items, many students find the task cumbersome, mainly because they are unfamiliar with this type of assessment. Topic complexity, font sizes and time constraints can further impact student performance. Last, there is a significant likelihood that some students may opt out of attempting the test altogether.

When crafting a C-test, item writers should adhere to two technical recommendations:

1 Utilize a single underscore for each missing letter (e.g. '_ _ _' for three letters) rather than consecutive underscores without spacing ('____'). In the instructions, clarifying that one underscore represents one missing letter is crucial.
2 Refrain from using dots (.... ... .) as placeholders, as they may obscure the number of letters to be inserted to complete the target word.

Selective gap-filling

While similar to the cloze technique, where words are omitted from a text for students to complete, the gap-filling technique diverges in its word selection process. Unlike the cloze test's pseudo-random method, the gap-filling approach relies on writers' discretion. The choice of omitted words is guided by their judgement of relevance to the test's constructs. This method relies on item writers' linguistic reasoning regarding what knowledge and skills are crucial for students. Item writers may remove content words to assess comprehension of overall meaning, textual coherence and supporting details. In contrast, function words may be omitted to evaluate grammatical sensitivity or lower-level processes.

Instructions: Complete each gap in the paragraph with ONE word only. Ensure you check your spelling.

Understanding word stress in English is similar to noticing your movement when you dance or clap your hands. Stress can be (1) ___________ as the degree of intensity or (2) ___________ placed on a sound. English has (3) ___________ types of stress: primary (strong emphasis), secondary (a less strong emphasis) and zero (unstressed). (4) ___________ a stressed syllable, the vowel (5) ___________ is longer and louder (6) ___________ it is in an (7) ___________ syllable.

Plausible answers:

1. defined/understood; 2. loudness; 3. three; 4. In; 5. sound; 6. than; 7. unstressed

The gap-filling technique offers several advantages over the cloze technique, primarily in its greater flexibility. Target words can be selected and alternative words that meaningfully fit the space can be considered correct answers. Reasons and justifications for selecting words can be documented. Furthermore, scoring can be automated and objective.

Some drawbacks of this technique are as follows. First, there is no definite rule for choosing a word for omission, which novice item writers may find challenging. Second, this technique measures sentence-bound reading skills rather than reading beyond the lines. Third, the scoring reliability depends on whether item writers set out the acceptable answers beforehand (e.g. fixed as in the original text or variable depending on the acceptable, plausible words). The latter is recommended because students need to encode their understanding of the text, which may not be the same as that of the writer.

When constructing a gap-filling task, it is essential to consider several key factors:

1 In the test and assessment specifications, clearly define the selections and specify the required number of content or function words required to complete the answer. It is crucial to maintain a balance between both types of words.

2 Provide clear instructions in the scoring manual or programming for spelling variations in students' answers. To allow students to demonstrate their reading skills effectively, avoid choosing low-frequency words, as students may not have encountered them before and may struggle with spelling.

3. Avoid including giveaway clues that could make the correct answer too obvious. For example, if the word before the deleted word is 'an', students may assume that the missing word starts with a vowel sound.
4. Include comprehensive answer keys to enhance scoring reliability. In Question 1 in the example above, the expected answer is 'defined'. However, students may provide alternative answers, such as 'expressed', 'explained', or 'understood', each completing the gap meaningfully.

Short-answer technique

A short-answer technique can test and assess students' understanding of critical concepts, facts or information presented in the text. Some questions may require students to evaluate information, make judgements or draw conclusions based on the text. Students may also need to synthesize information from different text sections to answer a comprehension question. Therefore, this technique requires students to respond concisely to specific prompts or questions. Unlike multiple-choice questions, short-answer questions require students to answer with brief responses rather than just a single word. The following are examples of short-answer questions.

Instructions: Read the following passage and answer the questions. Write no more than five words in your answer.

Passage

Bilingualism is the ability to speak and understand two languages fluently. There are many benefits beyond simple communication. Research has shown that bilingual individuals often possess cognitive advantages over monolinguals, leading to improved problem-solving skills, enhanced multitasking abilities and greater mental flexibility.

(text continued)

Overall, the benefits of bilingualism are undeniable. Scientific research has shown robust evidence that it offers advantages in cognitive function, academic achievement, cultural awareness and career prospects.

1 What are the benefits of bilingualism beyond communication?

____

2 How does bilingualism affect brain health, according to research?

____

Source: Modified AI text from ChatGPT 3.5

There are several strengths to this technique. First, it helps teachers or assessors understand students' comprehension levels and knowledge application more accurately than multiple-choice questions because they need to construct their answers. Students must analyse information, connect concepts and apply their knowledge to address questions. This process involves the use of critical thinking skills. Second, short-answer questions can reflect real-world scenarios or reading tasks. It has a positive washback because students can apply their reading skills in practical situations. It hence promotes authentic assessment. Third, it offers opportunities for teachers to provide constructive feedback on students' responses, highlighting areas of strength and areas for improvement.

The potential disadvantages of this technique are as follows. First, it is more time-consuming to score the test, especially when there are many students. Teachers may experience delays and fatigue in grading students' responses and providing timely constructive feedback. Second, scoring can be subjective because students' depth or length of responses may vary. Third, guessing correctly cannot be ruled out in short-answer questions. This possibility challenges teachers or assessors to be sure whether students genuinely understand the text or are simply guessing. Finally, this technique can be challenging for students due to language barriers or low proficiency levels. It involves writing skills, which are not the primary target constructs for testing and assessing reading.

Information-transfer technique

This technique is a semi-constructed response technique. It can be seen as a variant of the short-answer technique. This technique tends to be linked to visual representations or mind maps of texts. Test takers are asked to read a text and complete a graph, diagram, chart or table with missing information. The missing information is usually short (e.g. one to three words), but longer texts are possible. Information-transfer techniques are also often used in grammar or vocabulary tests, which may be indirect writing assessments. The following is an example of an information-transfer technique.

> *Instructions*: Read the following passage about climate change and complete the table below. Write ONE to THREE words only for each impact.
>
> Climate change refers to long-term shifts in temperature, precipitation patterns and other climatic variables primarily driven by human activities such as burning fossil fuels and deforestation. These changes significantly impact ecosystems, weather patterns and humanity.
>
> (text continued)

Aspect	*Impact*
Rising temperatures	(1) ____________________
Alteration of precipitation patterns	(2) ____________________
Extreme weather events	(3) ____________________
Social and economic challenges	(4) ____________________

Source: Modified AI text from ChatGPT 3.5

This technique has significant advantages. First, students must use concept-mapping processes to classify or sequence processes or events. It is also suitable for assessing the ability to elicit factual information. Second, it is an authentic and common reading task for students in many academic situations. Third, students' responses can be scored relatively objectively, as information is based on a given text or provided information.

Cautions are needed as this technique has limitations. First, students' performance on information-transfer tasks may rely on writing and critical thinking skills beyond those explicitly being tested. This could confound the testing and assessment of the targeted skills and lead to inaccurate interpretations of students' abilities. Second, students may initially encounter challenges in understanding how to transfer information to a table, diagram or graph. This may require extra processing time as students familiarize themselves with the task format and interpret the provided visual representation before completing it. Third, some students may be more accustomed to this type of task than others, depending on their academic background or prior exposure to similar tests and assessments. For example, science students may be more familiar with graphs or diagrams than students in social sciences. This difference in task familiarity could introduce issues of fairness in the interpretation of results.

The following recommendations provide valuable guidance for enhancing the quality of the information-transfer technique.

1. Ensure that test instructions are explicit, including guidelines on the number of words allowed in each space. Limiting the number of words encourages concise responses and enhances the scoring process.
2. Provide sufficient time for students to complete the task. Rushing through the task can lead to response errors and inaccuracies of students' actual reading abilities.

3. Select texts that describe straightforward processes, sequences or classifications to facilitate comprehension and completion of the graph, diagram or table. Ambiguous texts may impede students' understanding accuracy, resulting in incomplete or incorrect responses.
4. Ensure the graphical text is clear, legible and comprehensible. It should be noted that authentic graphs (e.g. those taken from an academic journal or specialized magazines) may only sometimes be suitable for the test.
5. Avoid requiring students to perform calculations to complete missing gaps in diagrams or tables. The focus of the test should remain on AL reading skills rather than mathematical abilities.

Summary technique

This integrative technique evaluates reading comprehension via writing or speaking. When testing and assessing reading comprehension, the focus is on accurately expressing or paraphrasing the main ideas, important information or specific details from a text. A rating scale can be developed to judge the quality of a summary, aiding in more reliable and effective scoring.

Instructions: Read the following passage about the importance of good communication skills. Summarize the main ideas in no more than 50 words. You should not spend longer than 10 minutes to complete this task.

Good communication skills are invaluable in personal and professional life. They facilitate effective interactions, build trust and foster positive relationships. Clear communication enhances teamwork, problem-solving and conflict resolution. (text continued)

Your summary:

____

____

____

____

____

____

Source: Modified AI text from ChatGPT 3.5

The advantages of this technique include eliminating guessing and resembling an authentic task where individuals synthesize what they have read in their own words or understanding. However, it requires articulating and organizing the primary information cohesively and rhetorically. It may not be suitable for beginners lacking sufficient linguistic resources in the target language.

Suggestions for constructing a summary reading task are as follows:

1. Avoid highly technical or scientific texts, as their specialized content and terminology can hinder summarization.
2. State explicitly in the instruction the expected word count for writing or the time limit for speaking.
3. Provide reasonable time for students to read the text, plan their summary and then produce their summary.

In summary, these testing and assessment techniques have strengths and weaknesses. It is essential not to rely on one technique but to combine different techniques as they can complement one another.

Summary

This chapter has considered critical considerations in designing and using a reading test or assessment, such as reading purposes, reading processes and reading test techniques. It also discusses factors that affect reading comprehension and reading test performance. Much of what is described in this chapter concerns what AL readers need to do successfully when they read and perform reading test tasks in an AL. Despite recognizing that first and AL reading differ, there is an assumption of what reading in an AL involves (as discussed in Figure 5.2). Reading and writing skills are firmly connected, and both require complex linguistic knowledge and cognitive, emotional and social skills (Hinkle 2002; Hyland 2016; Shaw & Weir 2007; Weigle 2002) because reading allows readers to observe writing patterns and styles across various writing purposes and contexts. The next chapter, therefore, discusses testing and assessing writing.

Discussion

1. After studying this chapter, what is involved in AL reading comprehension?
2. Why is it essential to understand the nature of reading comprehension before designing a reading comprehension test?
3. What testing and assessment techniques discussed in this chapter have you used before? What are the strengths and weaknesses that you have learnt?

Further reading

Alderson, C., 2000, *Assessing reading*, Cambridge University Press, Cambridge.

This book comprehensively discusses the framework for assessing reading. It examines the nature of reading, factors affecting reading, a framework for designing reading tests and techniques for determining reading for different test purposes.

Grabe, W., 2009, *Reading in a second language: Moving from theory to practice*, Cambridge University Press, Cambridge.

This book presents the theoretical foundations of reading, variations in reading (e.g. L1 and AL reading) and reading development. Chapter 17 is devoted to assessing reading in standardized and classroom testing contexts.

Grabe, W. & Stoller, J., 2020, *Teaching and researching reading*, 3rd edn, Routledge, New York.

This book provides a comprehensive theoretical and methodological treatment of teaching, researching and assessing reading.

6

Testing and Assessing Writing

Overview

This chapter discusses the theoretical foundations of additional language (AL) writing. It examines various testing and assessment techniques, providing illustrative examples of task formats. It presents different types of rating scales and basic steps for developing them for evaluating writing.

Guided questions

1. What is writing? What influences writing performance?
2. How do you know whether a written text is good or bad?
3. What evaluation criteria should be used when testing and assessing writing?

Introduction

Writing is a productive skill because it is the process of encoding and representing information using the given language symbols and system (e.g. alphabets and letters, word orders, punctuation, syntax). Writing reflects the author's intended meanings and fulfils the author's writing purpose. Like reading and speaking, writing performance is not solely a product of individuals' skills since it can be significantly shaped by various external factors (e.g. topics, the writing context, the level of task demands, complexity and familiarity; Hyland 2016). Both L1 and AL learners tend to learn to write at school or in the classroom. Grabe and Kaplan (1996/2014, p. 61) postulate that 'learning to write requires the manipulation of many complex structural and rhetorical dimensions, with greater complexity occurring in expository/argumentative writing'. Unlike speaking, which requires spontaneous adjustment to speech as speakers interact with their listeners or audience (Hyland 2016; Weigle 2002), writing is often less spontaneous since writers do not know who their real-time readers are nor the extent of these readers' current reactions as they read the text.

This chapter first discusses the theoretical nature of AL writing, purposes of writing and a writing model. Understanding the nature of writing is a prerequisite for designing valid writing tests and assessments. Second, it presents techniques for testing and assessing writing, accompanied by illustrative examples. Finally, this chapter explores the development and use of rating scales for evaluating writing performance.

The nature of AL writing

Figure 6.1 shows some characteristics of successful writers.

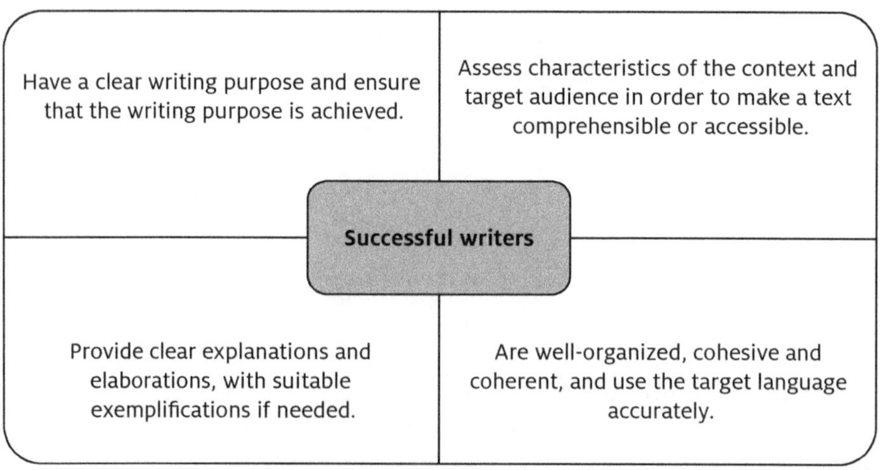

FIGURE 6.1 *Key features of successful writers.*

Purposes of writing

Similar to testing and assessing reading, knowing the purposes of writing is essential. Writing purposes and contexts influence decisions on writing styles (formal/informal) and expected conventions. Writing purposes, for instance, range from personal to academic or professional writing, and they often overlap. They are useful when testing and assessment is needed.

1. *Personal writing* aims to reflect or express feelings, experiences, opinions, beliefs, attitudes or gratitude (e.g. diary, letters, emails, social media). This type of writing can be less formal and language styles can be colloquial.
2. *Elicitation writing* aims to gather or request information that the writer does not have (e.g. asking for directions, services, clarification, assistance or permission). This type of writing requires the writer to provide references or points in which they inquire.
3. *Responsive writing* aims to provide requested information that the writer may be asked to provide (e.g. completing a form, responding to an inquiry, questionnaire or email confirming details). This type of writing can be brief and straight to the point. Some responses may be incomplete sentences or phrases.
4. *Descriptive writing* includes writing to describe actions, events, objects and processes (e.g. report of an event, advertisement, cooking recipes). This type of writing may require some elaborations of the descriptions or processes involved.
5. *Instructive or regulative writing* aims to direct or instruct others to do something (e.g. giving orders, instructions, persuasion or warning). It requires writers to express the meaning clearly and logically, including the consequences of not following the instructions.
6. *Learning to write* aims to translate what writers know about writing into practice. This purpose is similar to learning to read, as discussed in Chapter 5. Since writing is a productive skill, writers need to produce a written output. Learning to write most likely occurs in formal education (e.g. taking a writing class) and is a lifelong journey.
7. *Writing to learn* can be reciprocal to learning to write. Still, the focus is on producing written responses to academic or professional tasks assigned as part of formal education or workplaces. The outcomes are often in academic or specialized texts (e.g. responses to examinations, assignments, portfolios, thesis and dissertations, books and policies).

Models of writing

Several writing models influence how AL writing has been explained (Paltridge et al. 2009; Weigle 2002). For example, Hayes (1996) describes writing as a recursive and non-linear process. Cognitively, writing involves the writers' long-term memory of linguistic, genre, topical and audience knowledge, task schemas and ongoing metacognitive strategies, such as planning, monitoring, correction and revision. Hayes (1996) also incorporates writers' affect and motivation (e.g. predispositions, beliefs and attitudes) into explaining writing processes. In terms of the writing environment, Hayes (1996) describes the task environment in its social and physical aspects. The social environment, which represents the social dimension of writing, includes the role of the audience (readers), the extent of their collaboration (e.g. co-authoring, feedback on writing) with the writers and access to computer technology. The physical environment is related to the medium of writing (e.g. handwriting, typing, texting) and the text that has been written so far.

Grabe and Kaplan's (1996/2014) model considers text construction and approaches to writing processes. The authors consider the environment that includes participants (e.g. writers, readers, collaborators), the setting (e.g. classroom, libraries), the task (e.g. letters, essays), and the topic and provide elaborate examples and explanations of these contextual features (Weigle 2002). According to Grabe and Kaplan (1996/2014), seven communicative components form the basis of writing:

1. *Syntax* represents the linguistic systems of surface structure and underlying interpretation, from word meanings to sentential meanings (e.g. word order, and various phrasings and clause constructions).
2. *Semantics* represents interpretations of textual meanings of objects and events (e.g. from words to phrases, clauses, sentences and paragraphs).
3. *Lexicon* is a mental word list that provides the basic meaning and inference of a given syntactic structure, semantic sense and pragmatic interpretation.
4. *Cohesion* establishes relationships or connections among text phrases, clauses and sentences. Grammatical cohesion includes the use of references (e.g. him, her), substitutions (e.g. use of other words to avoid repetition of words already used), ellipses (e.g. start when ready), and conjunctions (e.g. and, but). Lexical cohesion includes reiteration (e.g. rephrasing) and collocation (e.g. an association of linguistic items, such as oceans, seas and beaches).

5 *Coherence* relates to what the writer tries to say and how the reader comprehends and interprets it. Writers use coherence to help readers build a mental comprehension model and guide them in analysing their intentions.

6 *Functional-use dimensions* relate to how the writers combine the various textual features such as text organization (e.g. rhetorical or logical), styles (e.g. formal/informal, superior/equal) and the use of voice in writing.

7 *Non-linguistic resources* are resources outside the above components, including background, topical or world knowledge, domain-general and -specific content knowledge, knowledge of genres and registers, and situations.

AL writing model

Figure 6.2 presents a simple model of AL writing. Writing involves understanding writing tasks and conditions (e.g. topic and audience). This information is presented in a social environment. As writing has a social function and purpose, it is essential to recognize the sociocognitive nature of AL writing.

First, it is essential to consider the external writing environment and social context. For example, writers need to understand the writing task and conditions, including topics audience, and time availability. Their writing can be affected by the extent to which they have access to external sources for language and content to help them write (e.g. books, articles, access to the internet) and how much feedback they receive externally during their writing. Writers initially process a given writing task and instructions. This initial process requires assessing the current situation and decoding or extracting relevant information (part of strategic competence discussed in Chapter 2).

Second, in Figure 6.2, the oval represents what may occur in the writer's mind. This can be broken down into processes associated with 'internal input' and those with 'internal output':

- *Internal input*: Internal input is a simultaneous, sequential and parallel process of accessing resources, conceptulazing ideas for writing and using metacognitive processes to regulate writing. Writers start to access internal language and knowledge resources as they need them to respond to the writing task requirements. Without these internal resources, they cannot produce their writing. At the same time, they conceptualize, formulate and revise processing (e.g. semantic, syntactic processes), which interacts through metacognitive processing with higher-order processing (e.g. planning, monitoring, evaluating and reflecting).

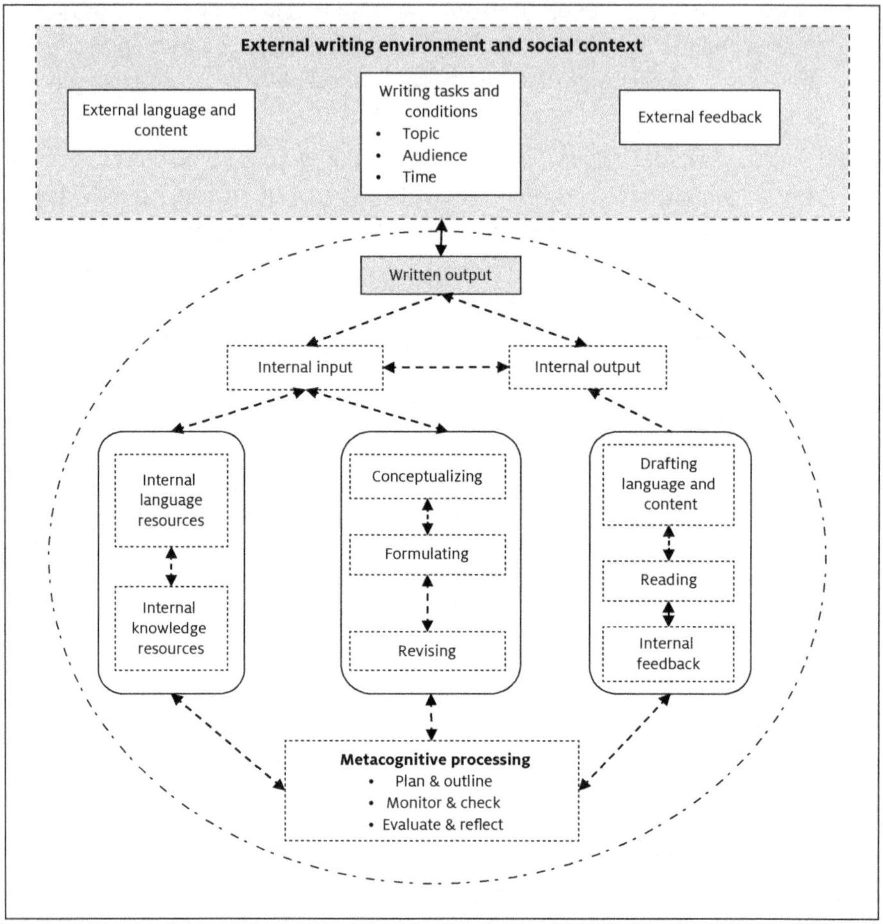

FIGURE 6.2 *AL writing.*

In Figure 6.2, metacognitive processing is hypothesized to mediate all internal and external writing processes. For example, after students have read or understood the task instructions and requirements, they should engage in planning (e.g. brainstorming and outlining what to write). They allocate time for writing, checking, and editing, ensuring they have fulfilled the writing requirements. In classroom assessments, students may receive external feedback on their writing from their teachers or use technology such as Grammarly and generative AI programs. However, some feedback can be internal as students question their writing and assess what they have written by themselves.

- *Internal output*: Internal output is typically non-observable since what they are about to write is still internal. However, earlier forms of their writing or responses (labelled as 'written output' in Figure 6.2) may include an outline of their texts, incomplete, fragmented, emergent working drafts that are read and fed back into the input reception loop directly (illustrated through a double-headed arrow between 'Internal input' and 'Internal output') or into the external context (illustrated through a double-headed arrow between 'External output' and 'External writing environment and social context'. The latter may involve external interactions, such as with co-writers, teachers or supervisors (if any) who provide external feedback. When permissible, writers may also attempt to access external language and content resources required to help them complete their writing in a given social environment.

Finally, writers should aim to check the alignment between their writing responses with the task, instructions and other requirements to ensure they will succeed in their writing. In classroom contexts, students' written responses may still be incomplete or ineffective due to several factors, such as levels of task difficulty and complexity, a lack of motivation or interest and time limitations.

In Figure 6.2, writing processing can be sequential (step-by-step, recursive) at one time; at other times, it can be a parallel process (several processes in the model are orchestrated). Hence, double-headed arrows are used in the figure.

Techniques for testing and assessing writing

This chapter presents techniques for testing and assessing writing, ranging from restricted to constructed-response tasks (see also Chapter 2). These techniques are grouped according to two writing orientations (i.e. linguistic versus communication/situation orientation).

Linguistic-orientation writing tasks

This writing task type focuses on writing-related knowledge, such as syntax, vocabulary and morphology. Linguistic-orientation tasks often utilize selected-response techniques, making them suitable for assessing beginner to pre-intermediate students and younger learners. Some advantages of linguistic-orientation writing tasks are as follows. First, they are helpful in the early learning stage. Students can improve their metalinguistic awareness of writing (e.g. word orders, sentence structures, prepositions and vocabulary use). Therefore, they are suitable for writing scaffolding, as linguistic errors are explicit and controlled. Corrective feedback can be provided to students promptly. In some writing tests, selected-response writing tasks may be used because they are easy to administer and score. A significant limitation of restricted-response techniques is that students' or test takers' performance does not ultimately indicate their natural writing ability since the task condition controls their responses.

Spelling technique

Students may be asked to spell a word they hear (e.g. sophisticated, magnificent). They can be asked to identify a word that is incorrectly spelt in a sentence and to correct it.

Instructions: Each sentence has a word that is incorrectly spelt. Underline the word and write the word with the correct spelling.

1 A speedboat was caught in a whurlpool at Bondi Beach.

2 One cause of menthal health issues is loneliness.

Source: Original

Answers:

1. whirlpool; 2. mental

Ordering technique

Students are asked to order a set of words into a grammatically correct sentence. In this task, all the words provided must be used.

Instructions: Reorder the list of words into a grammatically correct sentence.

1 tree / buying / a / commitment / mature / is / a / big /.

2 the / cat / fly / chased/ the /.

Source: Original

Answers:

1. Buying a mature big tree is a commitment.
2. The cat chased the fly.

Error identification technique

Students are given a series of discrete sentences and asked to identify any linguistic errors that they contain. Test designers can decide whether only one error or more than one will need to be determined by test takers. They can also ask test takers to correct the error(s) they have identified to make the sentence more linguistically appropriate.

Instructions: Identify a language error in each sentence below by choosing A, B, C or D.

1 'Jeff (A) doesn't strong enough to (B) carry this (C) printer the other (D) day.'

2 'Tennis (A) players need to (B) be more cardio-respiratory (C) strength than (D) muscular strength.'

Source: Original

Answers:

1. A; 2. B

Sentence completion technique

Students are given an incomplete sentence or a short text with incomplete sentences, which can be used to assess their writing knowledge. The task is similar to the gap-filling technique discussed in Chapter 5. This type of task may be considered integrative, requiring students to read and understand the ideas presented before completing it. Question 1 employs a multiple-choice technique, whereas question 2 is a short constructed-response task.

Instructions: Complete the sentence by choosing A, B, C or D.

1 'Some people believe that climate change is fake news and argue that ____________________ around the world are natural phenomena.'

A several climate disasters

B climate several disasters

C disasters several climate

D several disasters climate

Source: Adapted from https://en.wikipedia.org/wiki/Climate_change

Instructions: Complete the sentence by writing words that complete the spaces meaningfully.

2 'In recent years, gardening (1) _____ ______ a popular activity for many people. Plant prices (2) _____ ______ from two figures to more than a million. For example, Variegated Monstera or 'Swiss cheese plant' sells for up to $5000. Factors (3) _____ ______ rarity, beauty, breeding and propagation, all potentially (4) _______ a role. The desire to own rare and attractive species is also, consequently, another (5) _____ ______ their prices.

Source: Adapted from https://www.thespruce.com/most-expensive-houseplants-5080132

Answers:

1 A

2 (1) has become; (2) can range; (3) such as; (4) play; (5) factor affecting

Paraphrasing technique

Students are asked to paraphrase a sentence or a short paragraph. This linguistic-orientation task is a constructed response task that requires their newly constructed sentences to be content-accurate (maintaining the original

Instructions: Paraphrase the following sentences while maintaining the original meaning.

1 Several factors play a damaging role in causing climate change, which results in global warming and extreme rises of temperatures faster than the global average.

____

____

____

2 One major factor is humans who burn fossil fuels for energy, resulting in the emission of carbon dioxide and methane.

____

____

____

3 Other human activities such as agriculture, industries and forest destruction are amplifying causes of climate change.

____

____

____

Source: Adapted from https://en.wikipedia.org/wiki/Climate_change

meaning) and grammatically correct. Paraphrasing is an integrated task, as students must read and understand the text before writing.

Dictation technique

The dictation technique is an integrative task because students need to use their listening, reading and writing skills to complete a dictation task. Students can be asked to write what they have heard verbatim. The level of task difficulty may be determined simply by whether the text is read once or twice and whether the reading speed is slow, moderate or fast. Partial dictation, which asks students to write phrases or sentences in specific areas in a given text, is another form of dictation. Additionally, dictation can be valuable for formative assessment because teachers can provide corrective and cognitive feedback that aids in refining writing skills. It can also have a positive washback effect that enhances students' memory retention and boosts fluency and accuracy in information recall.

Instructions: Listen to the following passage and write down what you hear. Pay attention to spelling, punctuation and capitalization. The passage will be read three times. The first time is at a natural speed; the second time is at a slow speed with a ten-second pause at the end of each sentence; and the third time is at a natural speed again.

Time 1: Natural speed reading

'It is important that students create an outline of their essay before commencing their writing. It helps them consider ideas and examples needed to convince their readers. To develop a good outline, students need to understand the nature of the task requirements, such as what they are asked to do, how long they need to write and how much time they are allowed to have.'

Time 2: Slower speed with a ten-second pause after each sentence.

Time 3: Natural speed reading.

Source: Original

Several limitations associated with dictation tasks should be noted. First, they adopt a behaviourist perspective, framing performance solely based on the reproduction of heard information, often penalizing inaccuracies. Consequently, errors are viewed as indications of incompetence rather than development. Additionally, dictation primarily functions as a memory test, focusing on the accuracy of information recall through writing. Even proficient students, including native speakers, may still make mistakes in dictation tests. Second, dictation represents a one-way task for students, potentially leading to disengagement. Third, it may pose an unfair assessment method for individuals with hearing impairments or low literacy levels. Lastly, scoring dictation tests can be intricate and time-consuming, particularly in addressing spelling or punctuation errors.

Recommendations for enhancing linguistic-orientation writing tasks

Some essential recommendations are for enhancing the quality of the above testing and assessment techniques:

1. Defining and choosing linguistic constructs relevant to the target; writing knowledge is essential before creating items or tasks and producing sufficient samples.
2. The tasks remain primarily linguistically oriented, focusing on accuracy and fluency. Students' performance consistency is needed, and many items must be included.
3. It is essential to consider a writing context to ensure that the task is a test or assessment of writing. The task should present relevant and meaningful content. Otherwise, it will be similar to a grammar or vocabulary test.
4. Linguistic-orientation writing tasks can be presented early in a more extensive writing test and assessment. They can serve as warm-up tasks since they are less demanding than communication-oriented ones.

In summary, these techniques are useful for gathering specific information about students' or test takers' linguistic knowledge and skills relevant to writing. Correction of performance and feedback can be specific and effective. They can also help them prepare for more complex writing, such as communication orientation tasks as discussed next.

Communication/situation-orientation writing tasks

This writing task type seeks to replicate real-life language-use scenarios. Communication-oriented tasks usually utilize constructed-response techniques, prompting students to write in response to a given task or prompt. These tasks encompass a variety of formats, ranging from guided questions to facilitate idea formation to more open-ended responses such as essays or narratives. The following presents examples of communication orientation writing tasks.

Free-written recall technique

This task can be considered a variant of the dictation task. Students listen to an audio recording or watch a video recording and write the information to recall what they have understood in their own words. The focus of this type of assessment is on accurate comprehension. Note-taking or pre-performance planning should be allowed to reduce students' cognitive load. The assessment criteria can include content accuracy or relevance, spelling, grammatical accuracy, vocabulary use and mechanics (i.e. punctuation).

> *Instructions*: You will listen to an audio recording about the importance of environmental conservation. You are allowed to take notes while listening. Write a 100-word summary of what you have learnt from the recording. In your summary, include the main ideas, key facts and important information discussed in the recording. Your summary should be content-accurate. You have twenty minutes to complete this task after the recording has ended.

While this task is primarily communication-oriented, it retains a significant linguistic focus on the accuracy of written recollection, as students are not expected to add their opinions about the topic. This task can be helpful in classroom assessment since memorizing or retaining important information is essential to study. Students can practise recalling what they have heard, and they can start with simple videos or audio recordings and then move to more complex and lengthy ones. This technique is useful to help students learn to memorize and retain new information for later use. They will, however, need scaffolding assistance and good feedback on their performance. This task promotes positive washback as students learn to recall information in real-life situations. However, the ability to recall information can be affected by the text topics or text familiarity. It is also important to note that this task tests information retention (like dictation). Success in this task depends on, for example, students' memory strategies, concentration, control of thought, and current physical and mental health. Finally, as this technique constitutes a recall test, students may inevitably infer beyond a given text and include their inferences in their written responses.

Letter or email technique

Students are asked to write a letter or email to address a particular purpose or scenario, which can be about personal or business issues. This integrated task requires students to read the scenario and requirements before writing. This task helps assess students' understanding of letter or email conventions.

A series of questions or descriptions can guide this task and allow students to address it and control their writing. A situation and context should be provided to make this task resemble a real-life scenario. A letter or email task can be tailored to suit various topics, reading levels and learning objectives, making it a flexible technique for testing and assessing writing.

Instructions: Your best friend told you that they are going to visit your hometown. Email them about a tourist attraction in there. Write about 100 words. In your email:

- Tell your friend you are excited to know they plan to visit your hometown.
- Introduce a tourist attraction you will show your friend when they arrive (e.g. What is it called? What is its history? What is unique about it? and What you can do there).
- Close the email by inviting your friend to visit your family home and stay for the night.

The advantages of this task are as follows. First, it requires students to read and understand the situation and requirements before commencing their writing, thereby strengthening their reading skills and promoting active engagement in the task. Second, it can enhance students' critical thinking skills because they need to evaluate the content of their letter or email (e.g. how well they have addressed the task requirements). As this is a meaningful task that students will perform in their personal or professional situations, it can reinforce their learning and retention.

Picture or diagram description technique

This task focuses on students' ability to describe and explain a picture, diagram or graph that has been provided to them. It can be applied in various scenarios, including writing tests and assessments for specific purposes. For example, students are asked to describe a diagram or chart showing statistical trends or changes over one decade. To perform this task, students must extract the main aspects of the pictures or diagrams. There may be information in which they can compare or contrast.

Instructions: Summarize and describe the following diagram. You have twenty minutes to complete this task. Your writing should be clear, present accurate information and be grammatically correct. To complete this task:

1 Examine the diagram to understand its components, labels and any trends or patterns presented.

2 Write *no more than 120 words* summarizing the diagram and highlighting its main features, key data points and notable observations.

3 Mention any trends or patterns in the diagram.

[e.g. Insert the diagram to be used here]

The benefits of this task are as follows. First, it can promote students' ability to express ideas or information concisely. Before writing, they need to analyse the information in the diagram or graph, focusing on identifying key trends, patterns and relationships. Some diagrams or graphs that include comparative data allow students to practise discussing similarities and differences. It should be noted that while describing a picture can be applied across different groups of students, a diagram or graph tends to be used more frequently in sciences than in social sciences. Task unfamiliarity may influence the performance of some student groups. Use culturally neutral scenes to avoid culturally sensitive issues in a picture task. A picture that puts students in a negative frame of mind is unlikely to elicit their optimal performance.

The following are practical guidelines for constructing a picture, diagram or graph writing task:

1 Select a picture, diagram or graph depicting statistical trends or changes over a specified period. Ensure relevance to the learning objectives. The image must be clear and readable.

2 Provide explicit guidelines and instructions on approaching the task, such as what information should be extracted, described or explained.

3 In classroom assessment, students should be prepared to address this task and receive constructive feedback on their performance and be given opportunities to revise their work.

Free-written recall technique

This integrative task can be considered a variant of the dictation task. Students listen to an audio recording or watch a video recording and write the information to recall what they have understood in their own words. The focus of this type of assessment is on accurate comprehension. Note-taking or pre-performance planning should be allowed to reduce students' cognitive load. The assessment criteria can include content accuracy or relevance, spelling, grammatical accuracy, vocabulary use and mechanics (i.e. punctuation).

Instructions: You will listen to an audio recording about the importance of environmental conservation. You are allowed to take notes while listening. Afterwards, write a sixty-word summary of what you have learnt. Include the main ideas, key facts and any important details mentioned in the recording. Your summary should be clear and concise and reflect your understanding of the content. You have ten minutes to complete this task after the recording has ended.

While this task is primarily communication-oriented, it retains a significant linguistic focus on the accuracy of written recollection, as students are not expected to add their opinions about the topic. This task can be useful for classroom assessment, since memorizing or retaining important information is an essential study skill. Students can practise recalling what they have heard, and they can start with simple videos or audio recordings and then move to more complex and lengthy ones. This technique is useful to help students learn to memorize and retain new information for later use. They will, however, need scaffolding assistance and good feedback on their performance. It also promotes positive washback, as students learn to recall information in real-life situations. However, the ability to recall information can be affected by the text topics or text familiarity.

It is also important to note that this task can be considered a test of information retention (like dictation). Success in this task depends on, for example, students' memory strategies, concentration, control of thought, and current physical and mental health. Finally, as this technique constitutes a recall test, students may inevitably infer beyond a given text and include their inferences in their written responses.

Written review technique

This integrated writing task asks students to compose a review of various products, including books, films, programmes or places. This task can be part of classroom assessment or in a non-test condition where students can complete it as part of their portfolio. For instance, they may be tasked with critiquing a recently watched TV documentary, providing details such as its title, a summary, specific issues highlighted and their own reactions. In a testing condition, the task may involve multimodal elements, such as watching a video or listening to an audio recording on a lifestyle topic, followed by writing a response summarizing the content and sharing their viewpoints on the presented issues.

Instructions: You will watch a short video titled 'Exploring Lifestyle Choices in the Modern World'. The content discusses various aspects of lifestyle, including diet, exercise, work–life balance and mental health.

Your task is to summarize the video content and express your opinions about some aspects of the lifestyle discussed. You should support your views with examples. Write no more than 150 words. You have twenty-five minutes to complete this task, including watching the video.

The benefits of this task are as follows. First, it encourages students to activate and use critical thinking and analytical skills because they need to evaluate the content they review. Second, it allows them to structure their written expressions of ideas and opinions. Third, it will enable students to actively engage with multimedia materials that are common in real-life situations. Finally, extending beyond the assessment task (e.g. sharing their views or what they have done with their peers) cultivates their communication skills.

Independent essay technique

This communication orientation task asks students to write an essay about a topic or issue (e.g. a personal, cultural, academic topic). Essay prompts may include structured guidelines, such as the requirement for an introduction, body text and conclusion paragraphs, or specific questions to address within each section. In language proficiency tests, structured outlines may not be provided. Instead, students are presented with a statement or issue and instructed to express their agreement or disagreement, substantiated with relevant examples, knowledge or personal experiences.

Instructions: Deforestation is a significant environmental issue affecting ecosystems worldwide. Write an essay discussing the causes, consequences and potential solutions to deforestation. Support your arguments with relevant examples and evidence. You should write approximately 250 words. You have thirty minutes to complete this task.

An essay task promotes students' ability to analyse the task requirements, essential for successful communication. Students are prompted to address a complex issue relevant to their way of life in an academic essay. Students can learn to articulate their thoughts and opinions clearly and persuasively. It also encourages students to propose a solution to a problem. Nonetheless, one of the most challenging issues in essay tasks is the subjective nature of scoring, which can rely on human judgement (except when an automated scoring system is used). It can also be time-consuming, especially in large-scale testing contexts. Some students may experience test anxiety when writing essays under timed conditions, resulting in poor essays. Some important considerations include:

1. Avoid a topic or statement that may inadvertently favour students from specific linguistic or cultural backgrounds but disadvantage students from other linguistic or cultural backgrounds.
2. Consider accommodations for students with disabilities or those who require accommodations, such as extended time or alternative formats.
3. Develop a careful test and assessment design, including the assessment criteria and rater training.

Integrated academic essay technique

There are different ways to design this integrated essay task (see Chapter 2; Plakans 2022). For example, students are asked to read a short passage about a contemporary topic. They then watch a mini talk from an expert or professor about the same topic. They are next asked to write an essay in response to a statement about the topic by choosing a position. Students must use the information they obtain from the short passage and mini talk in their essay. They should provide other relevant examples, knowledge and experiences to substantiate their position beyond the given passage and talk. The example below shows how students are asked to read two texts and respond to the integrated writing task.

Instructions: Write a 200-word essay to respond to the following texts about climate change. First, read the two passages and use them to help you write about the topic. Second, state whether you agree or disagree that climate change is a severe problem. If you use a text from the passage, cite the author or use quotation marks around a quote if you use a direct quote. Even if you paraphrase the source text, you should acknowledge the source. Support your position with examples. You have forty minutes to complete this task, including reading the two passages.

Passage 1: Professor Johns (2020)

Climate change represents one of the most pressing challenges of our time, demanding urgent action from individuals, communities, and governments worldwide. (text continued)

Passage 2: Dr Joker (2021)

The climate change discourse has been marred by misinformation, exaggeration, and alarmism, obscuring rational debate and policymaking. (text continued)

Source: Modified AI text from ChatGPT 3.5

There are several benefits of an integrated essay task. First, it is an authentic task that tests and assesses multiple language skills, providing more comprehensive evidence of students' language proficiency. It resembles a real-world task in that students must comprehend and communicate information from various sources. To achieve this, students need to synthesize information from multiple sources. This task is flexible for applications in different academic disciplines since instructions and assessment purposes can be specific.

Some significant challenges in adopting this task are as follows. First, it is time-consuming to develop a good task. Developing high-quality integrated essay tasks requires access to diverse and authentic materials, such as academic articles, audio recordings or video clips. Limited access to relevant resources may constrain the design and implementation of integrated tasks. Second, scoring can be highly complex and time-consuming. Raters can find it challenging to separate the quality of students' writing from the source text used, especially when students fail to acknowledge the source text. There is also a need to train and moderate raters in terms of the accuracy and validity of their ratings. Third, for students, being asked to process information from diverse sources simultaneously within a time constraint can impose a significant cognitive load on them. This may subsequently hinder their ability to comprehend and synthesize information effectively. Therefore, training and preparation are essential to help students familiarize themselves with the task. Integrating multiple skills within a single writing task can pose challenges in time management for both students and assessors. Students may not manage their time to sufficiently address the task, while assessors spend too much time reading responses before being able to evaluate them.

Situation-oriented writing technique

Situation-oriented techniques are a specific form of communication-oriented tasks. However, the focus is on an authentic, professional or academic situation or task relevant to test takers or students' current or future careers or studies. Situation-oriented tasks can be thought of as particular purposes, content-based writing tasks (e.g. forms, notes and referral letters that doctors, nurses or health professionals need to complete, an executive summary of a business case, a conference abstract, assignments, a research report, and a thesis or dissertation). Douglas (2000) comprehensively discusses the specific purposes of language assessment tasks. Situation-oriented techniques can be associated with scenario-based language assessment (see Purpura 2024). The real purpose of these writing tasks is to evaluate the adequacy of language use in a work environment, for example.

In summary, while communication/situation-oriented writing tasks are authentic in that they resemble real-life writing, they require extensive work, experience and resources to make them effective and useful. For a large-scale standardized test, test and assessment developers need to consider issues of practicality due to the potential excessive cost and time involved. These tasks have a strong positive washback for classroom language assessments, especially for more advanced proficiency levels. Students will probably transfer these skills in real-life situations because they promote authentic, comprehensive, integrated language use. Communication-oriented writing tasks also promote social language use, scaffolding opportunities and co-construction of language with others, as discussed in Figure 6.2.

Scoring and evaluation of writing responses

Responses to linguistic-orientation techniques, such as restricted-response writing tasks, can be scored quickly and objectively (i.e. they do not rely on scorers' personal judgement). However, responses to constructed-response techniques used in communication-/situation-orientation tasks (e.g. descriptions, essays, reports) are more complicated to score. A significant challenge inherent in constructed-response writing tasks is the subjective nature of performance judgement (see Chapter 3) and the time required to score them, making a practicality issue (see Chapter 4). Without careful consideration and quality control of scoring, writing tests and assessments employing constructed-response tasks may become invalid and unfair.

This section aims to provide an overview of methods for scoring constructed-response tasks (see also Brown 2012; Green 2020; Weigle 2002). It should be noted that the discussion of rating scales is also relevant and useful for testing and assessing speaking (discussed in Chapter 8). This section also recommends issues related to rater training and moderation.

Types of scoring methods

Four methods for scoring written responses are presented in this chapter: checklists, simple rating scales, holistic scales and analytical scales.

Checklists

Checklists are the most straightforward analytic scoring method for constructed-response writing tasks. Scorers are presented with a list of aspects used to judge writing. Checklists reflect a criterion-referenced approach to assessment as they do not focus on how test takers' performance compares to that of others. Figure 6.3 presents an example of a checklist for a short essay.

In Figure 6.3, raters or assessors are to check if the criteria are present (yes) or absent (no). Checklists are helpful for simple tasks, such as paraphrasing, short narrative essays and guided writing tasks. In classroom assessment, this method is convenient and less time-consuming to use. It is, however, essential to be careful when crafting a checklist. In particular, adjectives that describe the subjective quality of writing should be avoided because raters only have a yes–no option. Additionally, adding adjectives such as 'greatly', 'significantly', or 'satisfactorily' will make it more difficult for raters to decide on a dichotomous rating. If that is the case, they will probably be forced to choose the 'no' option due to the effect of adjectives.

No.	Criteria	Yes	No
1.	Addresses the given writing task.		
2.	Fulfils the given writing task requirements.		
3.	Is a well-developed essay of correct length.		
4.	Presents a topic sentence or main idea.		
5.	Includes adequate examples or points to support.		
6.	Is understandable to read.		
7.	Is logical and well-organized.		
8.	Uses appropriate word choices and forms.		
9.	Has accurate sentence structures.		
10.	Uses appropriate language mechanics (e.g. capitalization, full stops, commas, spacing).		
Total counts for yes/no.			
Total score:			

FIGURE 6.3 *A checklist for assessing a writing task.*

Given the simplicity of checklists, they are arguably appropriate for assessing beginner or intermediate learners or new writers. Checklists, therefore, allow test takers or students to learn the basics of writing before advancing to more complex writing tasks, which require more complex scoring. However, one fundamental limitation of a checklist is that it cannot capture each criterion's complexity range. In reality, assessing writing performance requires more than answering a yes–no question. Also, using checklists may not motivate students to spend quality and creative time in their writing responses. High-ability students may not make a great effort in their writing if they are likely to get scores similar to average writers.

Simple rating scale

Rating scales measure the quality of written performance based on established criteria. While it may be possible to create a generic rubric that can be used to judge multiple writing tasks, testing and assessment can be more accurate when rubrics are tailored to fit the constructs underlying a given writing task. The standard criteria used for evaluating written responses include the extent to which a student or test taker has:

- adequately and appropriately addressed the topic or task.
- provided clear descriptions and explanations.
- given suitable examples/details to support a claim.
- written cohesively and coherently.
- correctly and appropriately used the language (grammar, vocabulary, mechanics).

A simple rating scale typically ranks writing performance along a continuum (e.g. very weak, weak, average, good or excellent). It allows assessors to judge writing quality more realistically than a checklist. Figure 6.4 presents an example of a simple rating scale based on the checklist given in Figure 6.3.

Some limitations of the simple rating scale should be noted. For example, while it allows raters to discriminate the level of writing quality and provides valuable feedback for students, raters are prone to either overuse the extremes (e.g. very weak/very good) or choose the middle point. Furthermore, rating behaviours can be affected by the so-called halo effect, in which each aspect may be affected by the rater's overall judgement of a given essay.

Key: 1 = Very weak 2 = Weak 3 = Average 4 = Good 5 = Very good

No.	Criteria	1	2	3	4	5
1.	Addresses the given writing task.					
2.	Fulfils the given writing task requirements.					
3.	A well-developed essay of correct length.					
4.	Presents a topic sentence or main idea.					
5.	Includes adequate examples or supporting points.					
6.	Is understandable to read.					
7.	Is logical and well-organized.					
8.	Uses appropriate word choices and forms.					
9.	Has accurate sentence structures.					
10.	Uses appropriate language mechanics (e.g. capitalization, full stops, commas, spacing).					

FIGURE 6.4 *A simple rating scale.*

Holistic scoring method

Holistic scoring methods seek to determine the quality of a given response. A single, holistic score provides an overall impression of students' performance. Holistic scoring rubrics typically contain several distinct levels that describe written performance. For example, the TOEFL iBT test uses two holistic rubrics for assessing writing (see https://www.ets.org/s/toefl/pdf/toefl_writing_rubrics.pdf). Figure 6.5 presents an example of a holistic rubric rating for an opinion essay. In this rubric, only three levels are considered: superior (3), satisfactory (2) and unsatisfactory (1).

The holistic scoring method has advantages since only one score is assigned to a written response. First, it is practical for large-scale testing or assessment because of the relative ease and fast marking speed. Second, scores can differentiate various levels of performance. Third, the focus on scoring is more on students' strengths rather than their weaknesses.

Point	Description
3: Superior	Essays at this level: • address the task and present relevant information • are persuasive • explain points clearly with credible supporting evidence or relevant examples • contain well-developed and logical ideas • are easy to follow and understand • are of a correct length • may contain minor grammatical or typo errors
2: Satisfactory	Essays at this level: • sufficiently address the task and mostly contain relevant information • attempt to include credible evidence or relevant examples to support points • develop some persuasive ideas with sound logic • have or almost are of a correct length • contain some grammatical and typo errors that do not inhibit intended meanings • require some further revision
1: Unsatisfactory	Essays at this level: • contain no responses or are insufficient to evaluate • do not sufficiently address the task • contain poorly developed ideas or illogical information • do not look like an essay • contain many serious grammatical and typo errors, causing unclear communication • require a significant revision

FIGURE 6.5 *A holistic scoring rubric.*

However, there are some disadvantages to this method. First, scoring can be unreliable if raters do not fully understand the scales and distinctions among different bands or levels. Therefore, rater training is required (e.g. through benchmarking). Second, when two raters are used, two raters can assign different scores to the same writing response. When this happens (i.e. scores differ by more than one point, called scoring discrepancy), a third rater may be appointed. Finally, the feedback on performance that test takers receive is limited to a single score, so weaknesses in written responses will not be specifically identified.

Analytic scale

Analytic scoring refers to a scoring method that is based on the assignment of a score to each assessment criterion (see, e.g. IELTS Writing Task 2 band descriptors, https://www.ielts.org/-/media/pdfs/writing-band-descriptors-task-2.ashx?la=en). Figure 6.6 presents an example of a five-point analytic rubric. In this rubric, three criteria are used (i.e. task fulfilment, cohesion and coherence, and language use).

Analytic scoring rubrics have many advantages. For example, reliability is higher than holistic scoring because various aspects are rated separately. Strengths or weaknesses of students' written responses based on the criteria can also be more apparent, providing valuable diagnostic information or feedback to test students. However, applying the analytic scoring rubrics for rating essays is more time-consuming than the holistic scale. Furthermore, rater training is critical to using the analytic scoring rubric effectively.

Key steps in designing and developing a rating scale

Although an existing scale or rubric can be adopted or adapted in some contexts, a specific scoring rubric may be needed. The following are some critical steps to be followed when developing a rating scale (see Brown 2012; Phakiti & Steinhoff 2023; Weigle 2002). As further presented below, test designers can adopt various scoring tools (e.g. checklists, simple rating scales and holistic or analytic scales):

1. Consider the constructs of writing or learning outcomes relevant to writing to be assessed by the task. This allows rubric developers to match the scoring guidelines with the constructs or learning outcomes of interest. Use the test purpose, types of functions and conditions (e.g. task complexity and demand, levels of students or test takers), and context of assessment to inform what scoring method should be used.
2. Identify and list specific observable writing attributes that should be observed in students' or test takers' responses. For example, identify the characteristics, skills or performance that should be found in the written responses. Common mistakes or errors that are likely to be found should also be listed as they can be used to form part of the lower performance scales. Use responses from a pilot study to help in this step.

Criteria	Very good (5)	Good (4)	Average (3)	Weak (2)	Very weak (1)
Task fulfilment	Successfully fulfils the task requirements; displays excellent depth of task coverage. Presents highly relevant, appropriate and credible information and ideas from various relevant sources and effective examples.	Mainly fulfils the task requirements, mostly with relevant, accurate and appropriate information; may contain minor inaccurate, insufficient or inappropriate support in a few aspects; uses relevant and credible information and examples to make a good case.	Attempts to address the task requirements; some valuable ideas are presented but may not be fully developed; contains some relevant, sound, and appropriate information; some examples are given but can be further substantiated or more effective examples should have been chosen.	Partially or insufficiently addresses the task requirements; underdeveloped or premature ideas presented; shows evidence of limited understanding of the topic; demonstrates little evidence of having read or understood the instructions and task.	No or insufficient responses; too many highly fragmented or unrelated responses; verbatim copy of the test instruction or task.
Cohesion and coherence	Ideas and details are firmly connected and unified; effective and appropriate use of cohesive devices. Ideas are tied together seamlessly; very well-conceived, coherent, logical, well-presented and well-organized.	Appropriately uses a range of cohesive devices; may overuse or underuse some cohesive devices; topic sentences within each paragraph are presented.	Generally, competently uses a range of cohesive devices; some ideas or details are not organized coherently; some cohesive devices are inaccurate or inappropriate and may not be written in paragraphs.	Uses a limited range of cohesive devices; several ideas or details are not organized coherently; some cohesive devices are inaccurate or inappropriate; does not write in paragraphs.	No or insufficient responses to understand; a small paragraph provided; poorly indicates a logical link between ideas; minimal range of cohesive devices.

Criteria	Very good (5)	Good (4)	Average (3)	Weak (2)	Very weak (1)
Language use	Uses accurate, suitable and sufficient language structures and vocabulary with an excellent command of lexical features; exhibits an excellent command of language-use mechanics (e.g. full stops, commas, capitalization); few minor errors.	Mainly uses accurate, suitable and sufficient language structures and vocabulary with a good command of linguistic features; exhibits a good command of language-use mechanics (e.g. full stops, commas, capitalization); a few or occasional, unexpected errors.	Uses a range of structures with limited grammatical or vocabulary accuracy. Grammatical errors tend to be found in more complex or long sentences than short or simple ones; errors can cause some difficulty for the reader. Exhibits a marginal command of language-use mechanics. Many errors are apparent.	It uses only a limited range of grammatical structures and vocabulary, several incomplete sentences are used, grammatical errors can be found throughout the written responses, and a weak command of language use mechanics is observed. Errors are highly noticeable.	No or insufficient responses to be evaluated or understood. Incomplete sentences or phrases; challenging to identify grammatical, vocabulary or mechanic skills.

FIGURE 6.6 *An analytic scoring rubric.*

3. Write observable characteristics that describe each writing construct or learning outcome. For example, define the characteristics of an excellent, good, average and poor response.
4. For holistic rubrics, decide the number of performance levels needed to distinguish written performance (e.g. excellent (6), very good (5), good (4), average (3), weak (2) and very weak (1); accomplished (4), competent (3), developing (2) and beginning (1). Then, write precise and distinctive narratives that feature the attributes or descriptors for each level.
5. For analytic rubrics, decide both the levels of performance (as with holistic rubrics) and the number of criteria to judge. An optimal number of criteria ranges from four to six (Weigle 2002) because a more significant number can overload raters' cognition, resulting in extra time spent on judging performance. Write precise and distinctive narratives for each criterion, indicating all levels, from excellent to poor work. Compare each level of a given criterion and adjust the narratives accordingly.
6. Review the rubrics and seek feedback from colleagues or experts.
7. Conduct a pilot study:
   - **a** to collect responses that exemplify each level. Ensure that responses cover the range of students' or test takers' abilities or proficiency so that each scoring descriptor can be fully used.
   - **b** to use the scoring rubrics to rate responses, observe unforeseen issues in the use of the rubrics, and ask if the full range of performance levels has been exemplified.

   The pilot study's results should be used to assess the rubric's effectiveness and revise it as necessary.
8. Seek feedback from colleagues or experts. Validating a scoring rubric is an ongoing task.

Rater and rater training

In the subjective assessment of skills such as writing and speaking, raters' effect on quality scoring is significant (see Brown 2012; Pill & Smart 2021). For example, raters may be unable to distinguish between written performance at different levels, making scoring unreliable. Some raters may give more attention to one aspect or criterion than others. Also, some raters tend to be consistently lenient or harsh in their scoring, and some raters may have some bias toward a particular topic and may intentionally or unintentionally penalize test takers who disagree with them regardless of the quality of their responses. Pill and Smart (2021, p. 141) present some valuable steps in rater training:

1. Help raters understand the constructs being assessed through the rating scales and the writing features that will not be considered.
2. Describe and explain the scope of each rating criterion as reflected in the descriptors.
3. Give benchmark responses with their ratings as examples to help raters familiarize themselves with the rubrics.
4. Ask raters to practise scoring new responses and align their ratings with benchmark performances and commentary to support appropriate ratings and feedback for further improvement.
5. Repeat Step 4 (if applicable or necessary). Have a straightforward remedial and supportive process for inconsistent, harsh or lenient raters.
6. Promote good scoring habits by visiting the scoring rubrics and developing rating consistency and independence.
7. Allow ample opportunities for raters to ask questions or seek advice.
8. Monitor raters' ratings and rating behaviours during the training and actual rating.

In conclusion, scoring methods must be considered along with writing tasks and techniques when testing and assessing writing.

Summary

This chapter has explored the intricacies of writing and its constructs. It has illustrated the complexity of testing and assessing writing, highlighting the need for assessors to consider factors such as the nature and genre of writing, the proficiency levels of students or test takers, and the specific purposes and contexts in which aspects of writing are being evaluated. Additionally, the chapter has introduced methods for assessing writing, including writing tasks and evaluating written performances. The next chapter discusses testing and assessing listening.

Discussion

1. What are the fundamental processes that define AL writing?
2. What testing and assessment techniques discussed in this chapter have you previously used or completed?
3. Do the writing techniques presented in this chapter offer avenues for your testing and assessment contexts? Why or why not?
4. How can different types of rating scales for evaluating writing be applied in your educational context?

Further reading

Eckes, T., Müller-Karabil, A. & Zimmerman, S., 2017, 'Assessing writing' in *Handbook of second language assessment*, eds D. Tsagari & J. Banerjee, De Gruyter Mouton, Boston and Berlin, pp. 147–64.

This chapter provides an overview of essential issues and considerations in writing assessment (e.g. the quality of assessment tasks, controversial topics such as automated scoring, and tensions between standardized and localized writing assessment).

Shaw, D. & Weir, C. (eds), 2007, *Examining writing*, Cambridge University Press, Cambridge.

This volume comprehensively discusses the theory and methods for assessing writing concerning Cambridge ESOL tests.

Weigle, S., 2002, *Assessing writing*, Cambridge University Press, Cambridge.

This is a must-read book for anyone interested in learning more about writing assessment. It is accessible and, despite being two decades old, its content is still relevant to current contexts.

7

Testing and Assessing Listening

Overview

This chapter presents the nature of additional language (AL) listening skills, including the purposes of listening and theoretical models explaining listening processes and comprehension. It discusses testing and assessment techniques for eliciting listening performance, and stresses the unique considerations that affect the efficacy of listening tests and assessments.

Guided questions

1. What is listening?
2. What contributes to listening comprehension?
3. How can you test or assess people's listening comprehension skills?

Introduction

Listening is a receptive skill that allows people to gain linguistic and non-linguistic information from spoken language. Information from listening can serve as input for various language skills such as reading, writing and speaking. However, the language input for listening is spoken texts. It can be a simultaneous process with other language skills (Field 2008). For example, in a conversation, people use non-linguistic cues (such as speakers' facial expressions, tones and emotions) to help them comprehend what their interlocutor is saying. While waiting to see the doctor, a patient notices an announcement while reading a medical brochure. In a lecture, students listen to their professor's lecture for learning purposes while taking notes and flipping through their textbooks.

This chapter provides essential considerations in testing and assessing AL listening. It clarifies the nature of listening and listening comprehension (e.g. how it takes place, the types of knowledge used and critical factors involved), including discussing models that explain listening processes. It presents techniques and essential considerations for effectively testing and assessing AL listening.

The nature of AL listening

Because of the receptive nature of the skills, listening comprehension shares similar processes to reading (Buck 2001). However, spoken texts for listening are unique in various ways, unlike written texts for reading. It is, therefore, helpful to discuss the nature of spoken texts. Green (2017) explains some key differences between spoken and written texts (Figure 7.1) that can help clarify how listening can differ significantly from reading.

First, according to Figure 7.1, spoken language usually contains redundant information. This can be seen from oral features such as pauses, hesitations, backtracking, fillers, repetition, repairs and corrections. Written language, by contrast, tends to be more precise (except in the case of transcriptions or play scripts for acting, for example). Second, idea units in spoken texts are smaller than written texts. Spoken texts are often incomplete and short sentences contain one or a few idea units at a time. By contrast, written texts can be syntactically rich and contain complex idea units. Third, content words in spoken texts are presented through simple grammatical structures and redundant oral features. Fourth, spoken texts are temporary (they disappear once spoken unless recorded), and speakers use dialects and slang. Finally, spoken texts use prosodic cues (e.g. stress, intonations and pauses), whereas written texts use punctuation, text enhancement and paragraphing to help readers comprehend.

Purposes of listening

It is important to discuss why people listen or why students need to learn to listen appropriately. Understanding listening purposes is essential for successful testing and assessment design. Figure 7.2 illustrates five listening purposes (Buck 2001; Field 2008; Green 2017).

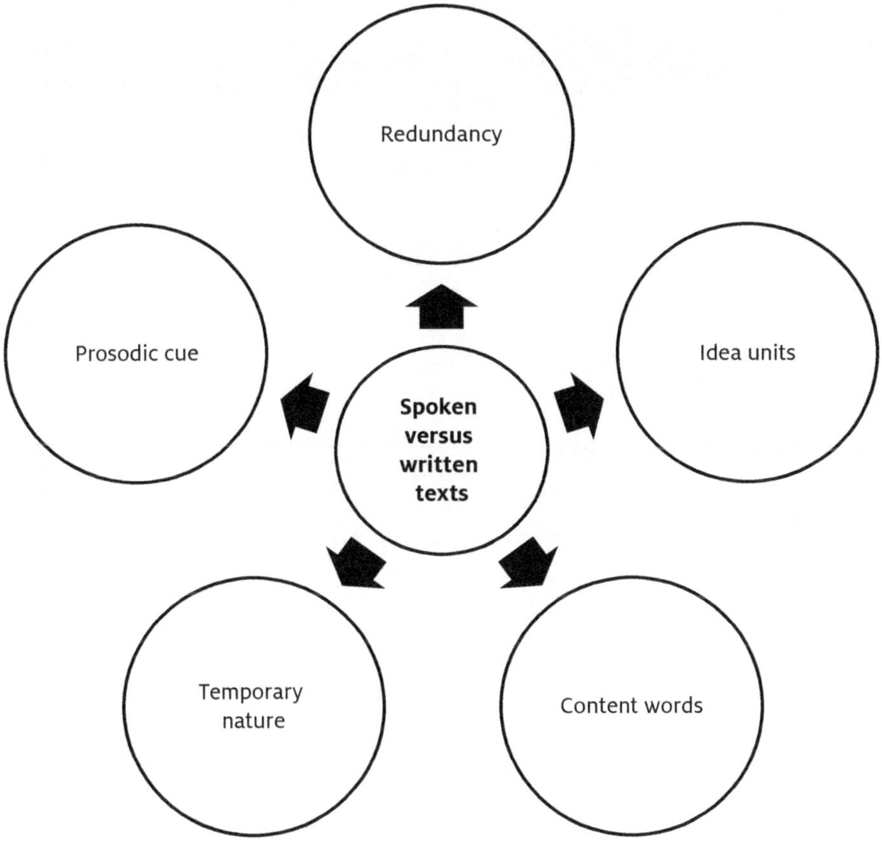

FIGURE 7.1 *Spoken texts versus written texts.*

1. *Listening to search for information* involves gathering information from spoken texts. It requires scanning (identifying specific details) and skimming (grasping general concepts) skills and attention to fulfilling what is being searched for through listening.
2. *Listening for general comprehension* involves grasping the overall meaning or gist without focusing on specific details. For example, people seek to answer, 'What does the speaker want?' and 'How or why did they do that?'
3. *Learning to listen* may appear strange to be considered a listening purpose. However, people learn to listen from birth, so learning to listen can be a natural process in L1. However, in AL contexts, learning to listen can be more explicit. Since input for such a listening purpose is spoken text, it entails grasping and noticing linguistic aspects or features of spoken language (see Figure 7.1) that are symbolic of the intended meaning.

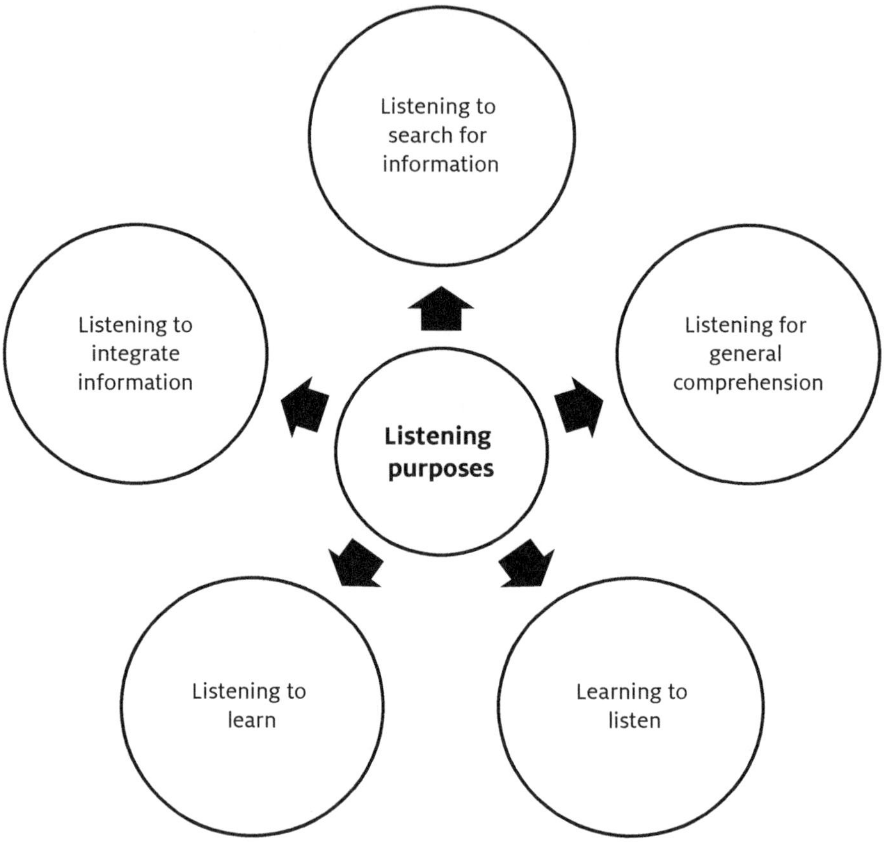

FIGURE 7.2 *Five key listening purposes.*

4 *Listening to learn* serves the purpose of human development. It is prevalent in everyday, academic and professional settings. Information, including declarative (what), procedural (how) and conditional (why) knowledge obtained from listening can be stored in long-term memory and integrated with previously stored knowledge. Therefore, listening to learn involves information processing, such as memory retrieval and critical thinking skills to assess information quality.

5 *Listening to integrate information* requires the various listening purposes discussed above. This purpose is particularly useful when explaining a complex learning or professional situation that requires people to combine information from multiple sources or modes of information. In this case, it goes beyond relying on spoken texts. For example, to complete a written assignment, students must watch a

documentary, read some texts and interview others before they can write their assignments. Information is based on spoken and written sources integrated with their knowledge and beliefs.

Models of listening

This section discusses three listening models for understanding the nature of AL listening (Vandergrift & Goh 2012; Field 2013; Rost 2024). A model of AL reading (Figure 5.1) is also useful for learning about the nature of AL listening, given that they are receptive skills.

Vandergrift and Goh's (2012) model

Vandergrift and Goh (2012) present a cognitive listening model that captures three main phases (illustrated in Figure 7.3). Their model acknowledges the interaction between top-down and bottom-up processes and includes metacognition as a mechanism to control and regulate listening processes. The model starts from the *perception phase*, in which the listener decodes incoming spoken texts and generates phonetic representation. In Figure 7.3, the phase includes bottom-up processes (see Chapter 5), phonetic representation and linguistic knowledge such as lexico-grammatical knowledge. This phase next moves to the *parsing phase*, in which the listener generates a plausible incoming speech stream by activating potential words (e.g. semantic and syntactic parsing of incoming speech). Success levels in the perception and parsing depend on the listener's linguistic knowledge and repertoire. Both phases largely utilize bottom-up processing (see Chapter 5, which discusses it in relation to reading). In the *utilization phase*, the listener uses their prior

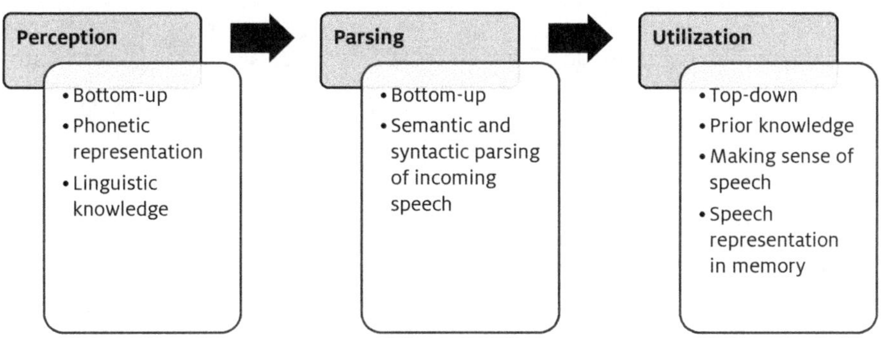

FIGURE 7.3 *Cognitive model of listening (based on Vandergrift & Goh 2012).*

world, pragmatic and discourse knowledge to make meaning and represent perceived speech in memory. Therefore, this phase can be seen to integrate the top-down processes that aid comprehension and understanding.

Field's (2013) five-level listening process

Field (2013), which shares some features of Vandergrift and Goh's model, describes listening as a dynamic process by which the listener formulates a hypothesis or perception about what they have heard. Their initial hypothesis may be revised based on new speech information. Figure 7.4 represents Field's (2013) five listening-process levels.

The first three levels are considered lower-order processes (i.e. fundamental/bottom-up processing), and the last two are considered higher-order processes (i.e. meaning and discourse representation).

1 *Input decoding* refers to the process of accessing speech-like sounds forming the phonological system of the target language. This phase includes phonological processing, phoneme decoding, syllable decoding and acoustic information transforming into groups of syllables.
2 *Lexical search* refers to the process in which the listener matches the sounds with their lexicon (e.g. content and function words), which leads to meaning-making. This phase is also largely bottom-up processing as it focuses on lexical processing, word-level matching to what has been heard and phonological matching.
3 *Parsing* refers to the process of connecting what has been identified from lexical search to plausible upcoming sounds as discussed above (e.g. using intonation contour and emerging syntactic structures, relating lexical material to the context to determine or clarify lexical

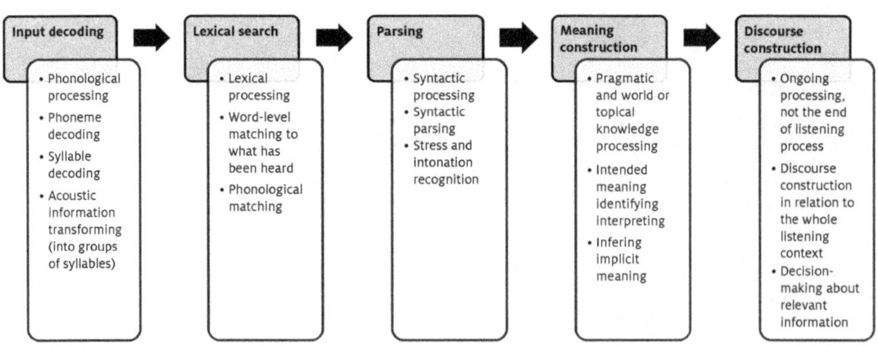

FIGURE 7.4 *Five listening levels.*

meaning, constructing a syntactic pattern concerning pragmatic, background and sociolinguistic knowledge). Instead of waiting for speech to be complete, listeners predict what the speaker will say next using the current speech's lexical and syntactical patterns.

4 *Meaning construction* moves toward a more concrete process in which the listener constructs and interprets the meanings of words or utterances based on their decoding and parsing. To construct meaning, the listener needs to be able to relate received words or utterances to their pragmatic forms and associated world or topical knowledge. They process pragmatic and topical knowledge, identifying and interpreting speakers' intended meaning and inferring implicit messages.
5 *Discourse construction* refers to relating information derived from speech to the listening context or event. This requires the listener to be able to select information to relate to the event or situation, integrate new information or meaning with ongoing discourse construction, monitor the accuracy of new information, and construct hierarchical discourse patterns. This phase is continuing processing as it connects to other phases and should not be considered the end of the listening process.

Field (2013) argues that lower-proficient listeners spend their time dealing with the first three levels and experience a significant cognitive load on their working memory. By contrast, highly proficient listeners can handle the first three levels more smoothly and spend more time on the last two levels. Based on this, testing and assessment listening can emphasize particular phases of listening depending on students' listening proficiency.

Field (2013) also recognizes the importance of strategic competence and listening strategy use, which takes place regarding 'the use of contextual and co-textual "top-down" information to solve local difficulties of comprehension' (p. 108). Strategy use also occurs at various word levels, mainly when the listener is unsure about the accuracy of their understanding. In a language testing and assessment context, strategies include conscious processes that are standard parts of listening, communication strategies used to compensate for lack of knowledge, and test-wiseness strategies used to outsmart testing methods.

Rost's (2024) model of listening

Rost (2024, p. 1) describes listening as 'a dynamic process with contributions from multiple, parallel cognitive operations' with 'four overlapping types of processing in listening: neurological, linguistic, semantic, and pragmatic' (illustrated in Figure 7.5).

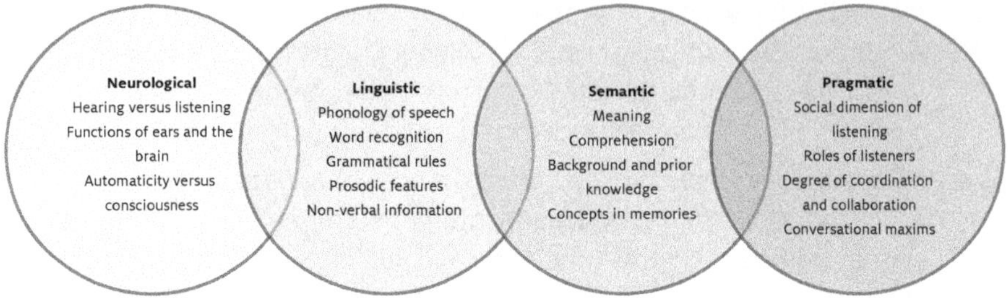

FIGURE 7.5 *Multi-level listening processes.*

1 *Neurological processing* distinguishes hearing (the basic neurological systems and processes involved in hearing) from listening, which requires attention and desire to comprehend or understand texts. To learn about neurological processing, one needs to have some knowledge of the areas and functions of the ears (e.g. the eardrum and auditory nerve) and the brain (e.g. the left hemisphere, left prefrontal cortex for processing information during comprehension, primary auditory cortex for speech perception and secondary auditory cortex for intonation). Another aspect of neurological processing is the distinction between automatic and conscious processing. Consciousness initiates attention, memory and understanding, whereas automaticity is that effortless part that listeners are unaware of (e.g. automatic word recognition and grammatical features). Automatic processing is often the result of learning over a long period.

2 *Linguistic processing* involves decoding the phonology of speech, word recognition, applying grammatical rules and prosodic features, and using non-verbal information available to perceive meanings in speech. Linguistic processing often combines bottom-up and top-down processing for speech perception and comprehension. According to Rost (2024), the first type of linguistic processing concerns how people perceive speech (e.g. ellipsis – omissions of presumed information) and phonological reduction. Several factors can influence speech perception. For example, sound frequency (in hertz), tone, speech duration and intensity (in decibels). The second type is related to how people identify the units of spoken language that aid their perception. Features of spoken language include, for example:

- The frequent use of additives (e.g. and, then, but).
- Ellipsis (e.g. 'Moment please' = 'Give me just a moment please')
- Fillers (e.g. um, like, okay, now, you know)
- References (e.g. that student yesterday)

The third type concerns how people use prosodic features to process speech (e.g. rhythm, stress and intonation). The fourth type is related to how people recognize words in speech. The concept of words in written forms differs from that in spoken form. In spoken language, words are described in the phonological hierarchy as smaller units to more complete structures (e.g. syllable, phrase, utterance). This requires people to recognize word boundaries in speech. The fifth type is about how people use their phonotactic knowledge (knowledge that certain sounds are allowable in speech) and knowledge of speech variations (e.g. assimilation – e.g. last year → pronounced as 'last jear') and elision (e.g. left turn → pronounced as 'lef turn') to perceive speech (see, e.g. https://www.eslbase.com/tefl-a-z/connected-speech).

The sixth type concerns how people use syntactic parsing or mapping to process incoming speech. Parsing refers to speech streams that listeners predict as incoming information (e.g. formulaic expressions and familiar word orders to process incoming speech). The final type concerns how people use non-linguistic elements to process or confirm speech (e.g. body movement, eye contact).

3 *Semantic processing* is best described as encoding words or phrases' meaning that leads to comprehension. Rost (2024) pointed out that comprehension is the number one priority of listening. Comprehension involves listeners relating speech information to existing information they may have, as well as their backgrounds, prior knowledge and concepts in their memories. As Rost (2024) noted, it is not the words but concepts that build comprehension. This, thus, leads to the second concept of semantic processing, which is concerned with the role that schemata or existing knowledge (e.g. topical or world knowledge) or previous experiences play in understanding. Activating appropriate schemata during speech perception assists in understanding the incoming audio text. Furthermore, the degree of semantic processing depends on the extent of shared common ground between the listener and the speaker.

Semantic processing requires that the listener infers the speaker's intended meaning or intention. This can be achieved through the use of spoken discourse structure or priming. Integration is related to how visual cues or signals (e.g. gestures, lip movements) help the listener process incoming speech. Rost (2024) pointed out that inferencing is a problem-solving process that requires inductive and deductive reasoning for meaningful conclusions to be reached. As the listener is also likely to lose some focus attention or start to feel tired, resulting in semantic processing breakdown, compensatory strategies may be used (e.g. an approximation strategy such as using a concept that the speaker is likely to intend to say, and incompletion strategy such as waiting for new information to clarify the incomplete information).

4 *Pragmatic processing* relates to pragmatic competence (i.e. listening in [social] context). It is associated with the social dimension of hearing: the listener attempts to understand the speaker's intended meaning in the given context. Meaning is co-constructed during this pragmatic process. Rost (2024) suggests that the extent of pragmatic processing depends on the listener's role in the specific context (e.g. participant, addressee, auditor or overhearer). For example, listeners as participants are directly spoken to and [may] have the same speaking rights as the speaker. Listeners as addressees are directly communicated to but do not have equal speaking rights with the speaker (e.g. students versus teachers). Listeners as auditors are directly spoken to but have limited rights to respond (e.g. listeners of announcements and advertisements). Listeners, as overhearers, are not directly spoken to and have no rights or are not expected to respond. Understanding the roles of listeners has implications for listening test and assessment design. For example, students or test takers are often assumed to be auditors or overhearers in many listening test tasks (e.g. when they listen to a conversation, an advertisement or a lecture). Still, they may have a participant role in a roleplay speaking or interview task.

According to Rost (2024), pragmatic processing requires both the speaker's and the listener's intentions to interact, resulting in discourse meaning in context. In this way, the listener acts as an interpreter, requiring coordination and collaboration with the speaker. Another important concept of pragmatic processing is conversational maxims (Grice 1975), which include four basic principles that ensure successful interaction between the speaker and the listener:

1 The maxim of quantity is concerned with giving sufficient information. Violation of this maxim includes giving too much information.

2 *The maxim of quality* concerns the reliability, truth or validity of information. Violation of this maxim includes providing information that lacks accuracy or evidence that contradicts reality.

3 *The maxim of relevance* is concerned with related information. Violation of this maxim includes giving responses unrelated to questions that have been asked.

4 *The maxim of manner* is concerned with brevity and order. Violation of this maxim includes giving information that is vague, irrelevant or ambiguous.

According to Rost (2024), affective involvement or emotional engagement during pragmatic processing is critical in raising or lowering anxiety or confidence in listening. For example, anxiety or apprehension can be linked to poor listening, perceived social distance reduces the listener's willingness to communicate, and backchannelling by the speaker (e.g. I see, that's right) can lead to the listener having empathy for the speaker.

In summary, the discussion of the three models has implications for describing the nature of AL listening in which at least two languages are assumed to be involved. Similar to AL reading comprehension presented in Figure 5.2, AL listening requires individuals to engage in internal processes such as the bottom-up and top-down processes. It also involves information processing in the working and long-term memory. Buck (2001), Flowerdew and Miller (2005) and Green (2017) provide comprehensive discussions of AL listening models.

Techniques for testing and assessing listening

Listening constructs

In order to address a specific listening purpose, some listening comprehension skills and abilities are necessary. The following are examples of listening constructs that are used in testing and assessing listening.

1. The ability to identify the gist or general information from spoken texts (e.g. central topics, problems, purposes, main points).
2. The ability to determine a speaker's attitude or intention towards a listener or a topic.
3. The ability to correctly guess the meanings of unfamiliar words using context clues.
4. The ability to identify and recall specific information (e.g. people, places, times, years, causes and effects).
5. The ability to infer implicit meaning or purposes and draw correct conclusions from spoken texts.
6. The ability to integrate added information with existing knowledge.

It is important to stress that listening is the most challenging construct to test or assess (Field 2013) because it is a silent, internal skill for processing coded speech waves. Consequently, the extent to which people understand speech and process online information is challenging to observe.

In a listening test and assessment situation, students or test takers receive information from test instructions, spoken or audio-visual texts and listening tasks through initial decoding. In test-taking, spoken or audio-visual streams continuously enter test takers' reception and perception. The decoding processes continue throughout the lower-level processing (word and meaning recognition) to the higher-level processing (e.g. prediction and use of prior knowledge) mediated via metacognitive processing. Internal processes lead to output encodings, such as current comprehension of spoken texts, which may be integrated into an upcoming speech. The level of listening comprehension is internal, so, to test and assess it, language testers and assessors need to ask questions or give them prompts to extract it.

Techniques used to test and assess AL listening can be similar to those in reading comprehension. Both reading and listening test tasks are designed to capture various levels of literal and inferential comprehension. In a listening test and assessment, students or test takers listen to speech instead of reading texts (He & Jiang 2020). Success in a listening test and assessment depends on the choices of test and assessment techniques used. Some techniques can be discrete (e.g. true–false), multiple-choice, matching and short answers. Unlike productive language skills, there are fewer techniques that only aim to assess listening constructs. Often, reading ability is an enabling skill in a listening test or assessment because students or test takers need to read questions and provide responses. Writing skills are also required when they need to write answers rather than choosing available options.

Therefore, it is essential to acknowledge that listening test and assessment performance depend on other language skills, which may be an irrelevant variance if they are not defined as part of the listening constructs. Listening skills are integrative to speaking tasks in communicative language testing and assessment. Buck (2001), Geranpayeh (2013) and Green (2017), for example, provide a discussion of techniques for assessing listening.

Classification of techniques

Similar to what has been discussed in the previous chapters, techniques for testing and assessing listening can be placed along a continuum of linguistic-oriented and comprehension-based approaches. On the one end, a linguistic-oriented technique focuses on the language components of listening (e.g. vocabulary knowledge and sound discrimination). This is a weak form of testing and assessing listening as it focuses on students' or test-takers' linguistic knowledge associated with listening rather than on applications of listening skills in authentic communicative situations. This approach is, however, beneficial for classroom assessment as it provides valuable diagnostic information to help students overcome weaknesses in their listening skills.

However, this approach can be limited as people find it challenging to put what they know into use (e.g. when listening to an actual conversation).

On the other end, a comprehension-based technique focuses on understanding spoken texts (e.g. understanding the gist or main ideas, speakers' purposes, idiom expressions, extracting details, making inferences and deducing the meaning of unfamiliar lexical items from the context). Similar to reading comprehension skills, this approach helps identify how people can obtain meaning and comprehension based on speech from a communicative activity. Nonetheless, students or test takers are usually seen as speech recipients overhearing a conversation or talk and using their imagination to visualize the scene. A more authentic approach to testing and assessing listening is an integrative (e.g. dictation and interview technique) and integrated (e.g. listening to write or combine with other language skills) one. Some techniques for testing and assessing listening are presented as follows.

Two-choice technique

This technique can be illustrated in a homophone discrimination task, which can test students' phonological knowledge of word sounds in contexts. For example, students need to choose the word they hear from a spoken text. In this test, students are given a pair of homophones and asked to select the word they hear in a given context. They listen to sentences containing the target homophones and select the correct word. This task has some elements of communicative language use in that a sentence allows them to connect the correct word in context.

Instructions: Listen to the following sentences, each of which has a word missing. The options for the missing words contain a pair of words that have similar sounds; these will be spelled out to you. Choose A or B to complete the sentence meaningfully.

1 Students hear: 'She has planted a beautiful ____ in her mum's garden.'

A vine

B wine

2 Students hear: 'I would like to have a slice of ____ with my soup.'

A meet

B meat

Source: Original

Answers:

1. A; 2. B

This technique tends to be linguistically oriented because it assesses students' or test-takers' word recognition and grammatical features. Test takers need to comprehend incoming spoken texts to supply the correct answer. As discussed in Chapter 5, the two-option technique is prone to guessing. It may not be reliable for inferring listening skills, especially when the number of questions is small or moderate.

Matching technique

This technique can be used to assess listening comprehension in that it requires little writing or reading. For example, students or test takers can match a spoken description they hear with a picture that best describes it. They may listen to a series of events and asked to put a number in chronological order on the pictures. This technique is similar to a multiple-choice technique in a reading comprehension test, but students or test takers choose pictures instead of reading available written choices.

Instructions: Match a description you hear with a corresponding picture. After listening to a description, select the corresponding picture (A, B or C).

1 Students hear: 'You now have five seconds to look at the pictures before you hear the description. [wait for five seconds] In this scene, there is a sandy beach with many palm trees. A few people are relaxing on beach towels.'

  A Picture A (a city with tall skyscrapers).

  B Picture B (a mountain with red, yellow and orange trees and a blue sky).

  C Picture C (a tropical beach with palm trees, sand and people who are sunbathing).

Source: Original

This technique is useful for young learners and adults at the beginner level. For young learners, drawings can be used. The complexity of the pictures, spoken description and length of the description can increase the task difficulty level. This task can be problematic in assessing listening comprehension, especially when the provided pictures contain rich information and some pictures in the options share similar scenes.

There are important recommendations for designing effective picture-matching tasks. First, allowing students or test takers some initial time to look at the pictures is important. Second, for this task to work effectively, the spoken text should contain relevant examples and vocabulary, and include the features of spoken texts discussed earlier in this chapter. Third, depending on the test-takers' proficiency level, playing the recording twice may be more appropriate for beginners due to their slow listening process. Fourth, avoid providing many matching items or pictures in one question because students must also look at the available options as they listen to the spoken text.

Multiple-choice technique

A multiple-choice question for listening comprehension typically contains a comprehension question and written options. Students or test takers listen to a spoken or multimedia text (e.g. a talk or conversation between two speakers). They may be asked to read a comprehension question using the options available. Then, they choose the best answer that corresponds to the spoken texts. In some contexts, questions may not be written on the test for students or test takers but will be read to them after completing the speech. The reason for this option is to assess more listening skills and increase the difficulty level.

Instructions: Listen to the following conversation between a professor and a student (Sam) about feedback on his essay. Then, answer the questions choosing A, B, C or D.

[Students hear a conversation]

1 According to the conversation, what aspect of Sam's academic essay does the professor suggest needs further improvement?

A The discussion on consumer behaviour.

B The economic factors influencing sustainability.

C The transitions between paragraphs.

D The use of case studies and examples.

Source: Original

According to Buck (2001), multiple-choice questions have the potential to measure various subskills, such as understanding explicit literal meaning, making pragmatic inferences, and understanding implicit meaning or speech acts. An advantage of this technique is that it does not require test takers to construct their responses to the questions but to choose the best option. Field (2013, p. 128) points out that this technique can be used to 'tap into various levels of processing identified in the [his] listening model'. For example, *meaning construction* can be assessed by asking inferences and pragmatic interpretation questions, and discourse construction can be assessed by asking about the main idea or speaker's purposes.

Although this technique can minimize the impact of irrelevant language skills such as spelling, typing and writing that confound test-takers' performance, it requires reading comprehension skills since they need to understand both the question and options to respond to the task successfully. Whether a multiple-choice technique is suitable for assessing listening is debatable. For example, the format is considered artificial and invalid for assessing comprehension (Weir 1990, 2005). Field (2013) pointed out that multiple-choice listening tasks impose heavy cognitive demands on test takers. For example, to complete a multiple-choice question, test takers not only look out for positive evidence to answer the questions but also negative evidence to disconfirm other options. Such cognitive processes go beyond non-test listening situations.

Some recommendations for constructing a multiple-choice test for listening comprehension are as follows:

1. Ensure test questions follow the audio or video recording order. Otherwise, test takers may risk searching for answers that have yet to arrive or have already passed.
2. It is essential to leave sufficient time for test takers to answer the questions. Since they can only briefly retain information during test-taking, they have to answer the questions as they listen. Do not ask, for example, two questions based on spoken texts that are too close to each other because while test takers are answering the first question they can miss the answer to the second.
3. Questions and options must be precise because it is not a reading test. Test takers may choose incorrect answers due to incomprehensible questions and options rather than what they have understood in the recording (Field 2013).
4. Plan to construct the test earlier by developing test and assessment specifications. This technique requires much time to develop, as the test must be created (item writing, revision, pilot), and high-level professional training for item writers is required.

Gap-filling technique

This technique is similar to that used in reading tests, in which students or test takers extract information from written texts to fill in missing gaps in a written text. In a listening test, this can be achieved from spoken texts. A text with missing gaps is given to test takers to fill in, which should be taken verbatim from the recording. Tasks such as table, chart, diagram, map or note completion are examples of information-transfer tasks using the gap-filling technique. Students or test takers are typically asked to supply up to a few words in information-transfer tasks. This activity is close to real-life activities (such as form filling via phone and note-taking during meetings or lectures; Field 2013).

Field (2013) pointed out that this technique tends to assess lower-level processing of listening rather than higher-level processing. This technique, nonetheless, can be cognitively demanding (much more than real-life listening) in that it requires careful reading both before and during listening. Students or test takers rely heavily on linguistic search (Field 2013). Lower-ability test takers are likely to produce ungrammatical answers.

Instructions: Listen to the speech about the different kinds of ecosystems in the world. Fill in the missing information in the table provided. Write no more than TWO words in the space provided.

[Students hear the audio recording only once.]

Ecosystem type	Components	Characteristics
Forest	Trees, (1) ____________	High biodiversity
Desert	Sand, cacti	(2) ____________
Ocean	(3)____________, marine life	Large bodies of water
Grassland	Grass, herbivores	(4) ____________

Source: Original

Some valuable recommendations are as follows:

1 Explicitly specify the number of words to be filled in per gap. Inform students or test takers that exact words from the recording should be used.
2 The speaker should sound natural and be intelligible, and background noise should be minimized.
3 The recording may be played only once in a proficiency test. Still, depending on students' proficiency levels, in classroom contexts the

recording may be played more than once with sufficient time spacing between the first and second plays. During the first play, students can fill in the gaps and, during the second play, they can check and confirm their answers or pay attention to answers they might have missed during the first play.

Short-answers technique

The short-answers technique is similar to the one used in testing and assessing reading. This technique asks students or test takers to supply information by themselves. It is a limited constructed-response technique. Questions can be similar to those used in multiple-choice comprehension questions (e.g. main points, details and inferences). This technique somewhat eliminates the guessing factor inherent to the multiple-choice or true–false techniques. This technique depends on both reading and writing skills.

Instructions: Listen to the following podcast about Australia's current public housing crisis and answer the following questions. Your answers must come from the podcast you listen to. Your answer should not be more than five words. [The podcast is played to the students twice.]

1 Identify ONE of the main challenges facing public housing in Australia.

____

2 Indicate ONE impact of the shortage of public housing units on low-income individuals and families.

____

3 Give ONE example of the issues with the quality of public housing units.

____

4 Name ONE marginalized group who often faces barriers to accessing public housing in Australia.

____

5 Write ONE initiative that has been proposed to improve the public housing system.

____

Source: Original

Some practical recommendations for increasing the effectiveness of this technique are as follows:

1 Specify the maximum number of words in the answer (e.g. no more than three words).
2 Questions should be sequenced with the order of the speech information.
3 The answers should derive from the audio text, so explicitly instruct students or test takers on this requirement.
4 Decide in the scoring method and whether spelling errors are considered correct.

Factors affecting listening test efficacy that must be considered

As discussed in earlier chapters, test performance results are produced from an interaction among test takers' characteristics, processes and test method facets, including test administration, scoring and random errors (Bachman & Palmer 1996, 2010). The previous sections in this chapter have also introduced several factors that can influence listening processes. This section presents major factors affecting listening comprehension performance.

Personal characteristics

According to Elliott (2013), for instance, student or test-taker characteristics which influence listening test performance can be grouped into (1) physical/ physiological, (2) psychological and (3) experiential characteristics. Physical/ physiological characteristics include age, gender, health and physicality. Psychological characteristics include (1) cognitive characteristics, such as working and long-term memory, cognitive style, cognitive development and attention span, and (2) affective characteristics, such as personality, motivation and emotion. Experiential characteristics include education, test preparedness, test experience and world or topical knowledge.

Spoken and audio-visual characteristics

Spoken input plays a critical role in listening and listening comprehension success. Voice quality, speech rate and pitch range variations can influence students' or test takers' comprehension levels (Field 2013). Students need to process speakers' voices while attempting to comprehend the information. The following aspects of spoken and audio-visual features should be considered (Buck 2001; Field 2013).

Topics

When choosing spoken texts, selecting texts on suitable topics is essential. While many topics can be authentic, they may not be ideal for testing and assessment because they can trigger anxiety or apprehension in test takers, resulting in poorer performance. Taboo topics include alcohol, death, crime, gambling, historical references, racism and sexism (see Elliott 2013). Since listening performance is strongly influenced by test takers' motivation, emotion and memory, the spoken topic should be interesting and relevant to social contexts.

Original or scripted input

Test and assessment designers should aim for authentic listening input when possible (Ockey & Wagner 2018; Rossi & Brunfaut 2021). Authentic texts are those appearing in a natural, social or real-world setting (e.g. actual conversations, documentaries, TV programmes, lectures). However, authentic texts can range from an informal, poorly structured dialogue to a formal, highly structured monologue. Additionally, the usability of authentic texts depends on speakers' voice quality, precision and speech rate (Field 2013). Therefore, using an original spoken text is often challenging for test designers. Furthermore, spoken texts need to be graded for language learners to make speech more accessible to the level of the learners being tested.

There are several ways to use and adapt authentic texts for listening tests. According to Field (2013), the transcripts of authentic materials can be re-recorded using studio actors. This procedure can also ensure the clarity of audio delivery (e.g. by minimizing background noise, redundancy and speaker overlap). It is essential to avoid using written texts to create spoken texts for listening tests (see Green 2017).

Speaker voice

Speakers in authentic communicative situations vary widely. Therefore, speaker variation is vital in choosing and preparing audio scripts (Kang & Moran 2018). In particular, test designers need to consider and decide on speakers' accents and gender balance. That is, when possible, both male and female voices should be used. Since not all native and non-native speakers are good speakers, test designers must choose and train them strategically. It is important to note that test difficulty may be affected by the speakers' voices, as some are more difficult to process (e.g. depending on familiarity) than others. It is necessary to allow test takers to familiarize themselves with the speakers' voices and accents before they are asked to complete test tasks. When deciding on speakers and voices, there is a trade-off between authenticity (by bringing a great range of speakers into the audio script) and fairness (some test takers unfamiliar with some accents may be disadvantaged). In testing and assessment, the intelligibility of speakers' voices is essential to ensure a valid and fair listening test.

Speech rate

Speech rates also affect test takers' success in a listening test. Slower speech can aid comprehension, but it may not be natural or authentic for some listening test purposes. Speech rates can be measured by calculating words per minute. For example, according to Buck (2001), the average word-per-minute rate for conversations is 210, whereas that for a lecture is 140. This measure is limited in that some words are longer than others, some types of speaking can vary in length, and some people speak faster. Nonetheless, test designers need to consider speech rates in their listening test, attempting to balance naturalness and the reality of test-taking. For many second language listeners, their listening processes may be limited to the first three levels in Field's (2013) listening model, so a fast speech rate means they will encounter too much cognitive overload and cannot comprehend the texts or complete the test tasks.

Visual input

As discussed earlier, listening is also multimodal in that listeners can use visual cues to aid their comprehension (e.g. compensating for some linguistic limitations). Visual cues include speakers' facial expressions, eye contact, intonation, tone of voice and settings). Depending on the practicality of test delivery and the specific testing context, visual inputs may or may not be available for test takers. Suppose visual inputs are not available in a listening test. In that case, it can be expected that test takers will be required to visualize and imagine the scene in which the speakers are talking.

Therefore, test instructions must provide sufficient contexts for the test takers (e.g. settings and relationships between the speakers). Visual input (interactive and non-interactive) is possible in a computer-based test. One possible interactive visual input is a video of two speakers interacting or a speaker giving a talk. Non-interactive visual input could be a picture, graph or diagram. Given the current advanced state of technology, it is now possible to include visual inputs in a listening test (see Ockey & Wagner 2018). It is important to note that there is controversy regarding whether to include visual inputs in a listening test. For example, some visual inputs (e.g. content input) can aid comprehension, whereas some visual inputs (e.g. some graphics or characteristics of the speakers) may inhibit comprehension. This is particularly true when different listeners interpret facial expressions differently, resulting in other responses to the test task (Ockey & Wagner 2018).

Length of speech or script

Listening can be demanding on test-takers' memory capacity, especially for lower-ability test takers. Spoken text lengths must be considered, and decisions on how long a script should be are critical in test design. Speech characteristics (e.g. speech rate, density and modification of information), speech organization (e.g. step-by-step speech or speech with cross-references) and speech types (e.g. transactional/non-reciprocal versus interactional/reciprocal) influence the nature of speech lengths.

In essence, the longer the audio script, the more demanding and complex is the test that test takers are asked to complete because they need to attempt to construct not only meaning and discourse but also retain information as long as possible, while at the same time working on answers to test questions. Test takers are most likely to read test questions and options or construct their answers while listening in a listening test. Therefore, a long script can also reduce their confidence and motivation to complete the test.

In conjunction with speech length, test designers must first consider the number of questions for assessing listening according to the audio script. Second, they need to consider the nature of idea units in the script. Idea units are related to the content of the script. The script will probably be extended if the content is linguistically demanding (e.g. it gives aspects of law) and highly abstract (e.g. philosophy, cultural beliefs). As a rule of thumb, a script should be at most three minutes long for a complex listening task, and it is essential to allow test takers to take notes while listening.

Single, double or triple play

Test designers must consider whether test takers are to hear the recording only once, twice or thrice. The issue of playing the recording once or twice is controversial (Field 2013). Well-known large-scale proficiency tests such as IELTS and TOEFL allow test takers to hear the recording only once, but this is different for all listening tests. Test designers must rationalize their decision on the number of plays about test purposes, target test takers and test consequences. For example, the test developers may base their decision on real-life listening because the listener cannot hear the exact spoken text twice (e.g. radio, news, TV programmes). Furthermore, a proficiency test aims to place test takers into various proficiency levels; highly proficient listeners may be able to listen just once and complete the listening task successfully, whereas other less proficient learners may not.

Test designers may decide to play the spoken text twice, arguing, for example, that in a real-world listening situation, visual cues are available for the listeners to aid their comprehension. Listeners may be able to ask for repetition or clarification if they are listeners as participants. In a listening test, they may need more information or opportunity. Therefore, a double play can compensate for the lack of such opportunity (Field 2013). The first play allows test takers to establish general comprehension and locate information required to answer test questions or tasks. The second play will enable them to confirm or revise their comprehension and answers. Double play allows test takers to move from decoding and parsing to meaning and discourse construction and have greater confidence in their listening success. This decision is, therefore, justifiable as appropriate. Nonetheless, the double play also means a longer listening test. It may lead to considerations of test practicality (especially with cost and the time required to develop, administer and score the test).

Test administration

Test administration plays a significant role in listening test performance, whether the test is paper- or computer-assisted, with or without a human proctor. In a listening test, inconsistency of test administration across different test rooms will lead to unfair test performance. If the audio recording is to be played, it is crucial that all test takers can hear the recording. Test administration may be effective in a computer- or internet-based test if a listening test is administered in a computer lab. However, practicality is always a constraint. For example, during the Covid-19 pandemic, travel restrictions were imposed, and test takers needed to take the test from home. A home listening test edition has several challenges in administration, especially in terms of test fairness (e.g. access to high-quality internet), test security and test-takers' confidence and worries in completing the test on their own (e.g. lack of administrative support in a high-stakes test). In classroom listening assessment, administration can vary and differ from class to class since testing and assessment can be for formative and/or summative decision-making.

Summary

This chapter has explored theoretical and methodological principles for testing and assessing listening. Understanding these principles is beneficial for listening test and assessment design. Understanding the purposes and types of listening is essential to developing an appropriate listening test or assessment task. This is especially important because test developers model their tests using real-life listening situations. Listening and subsequent actions, such as verbal responses, are affected by genres and types of listening. Green (2017, p. 1) points out that language testers and assessors should be able to answer the following questions before they start to develop a listening test and assessment:

1. How do the spoken and written forms of the language differ?
2. How does listening input vary?
3. What does the listening process involve?
4. How does listening differ from context to context and from listener to listener?
5. What makes listening difficult?

The next chapter presents testing and assessing speaking, which is often linked to listening skills or abilities discussed in this chapter.

Discussion

1. What are listening skills and purposes focused on in the learning outcomes in your teaching and assessment contexts?
2. How does the nature of spoken texts help you understand the nature of listening comprehension?
3. What have you learnt about the nature of listening according to the three models presented in this chapter?
4. Consider one of the testing and assessment techniques in this chapter. Can you create a listening task using this technique?
5. Discuss factors that affect listening test performance. Why can't we ignore them in language testing and assessment?

Further reading

Brunfaut, T., 2017, 'Assessing listening' in *Handbook of second language assessment*, eds D. Tsagari & J. Banerjee, De Gruyter Mouton, Boston and Berlin, pp. 97–112.

This chapter provides a fundamental discussion of what listening is and how it can be assessed. The author addresses several vital factors affecting listening assessment.

Buck, G., 2001, *Assessing listening*, Cambridge University Press, Cambridge.

This is a must-read book on assessing listening. It comprehensively presents and addresses both fundamental and critical issues in determining listening.

Geranpayeh, A. & Taylor, L. (eds), 2013, *Examining listening: Research and practice in assessing second language listening*, Cambridge University Press, Cambridge.

This edited volume is highly recommended. It addresses various aspects of listening test validity, using several Cambridge listening tests to illustrate issues.

Green, R., 2017, *Designing listening tests: A practical approach*, Palgrave, Macmillan, London.

This book is an accessible resource for considering and developing a listening test. It discusses several critical considerations in designing a listening test, including test specifications and techniques, and provides examples of test tasks.

8

Testing and Assessing Speaking

Overview

This chapter presents the nature of speaking, its purposes and models for explaining speaking processes and performance. It also presents and considers several testing and assessment techniques for speaking and scoring methods.

Guided questions

1. What is speaking ability?
2. Why do we need to know people's speaking ability?
3. What are important considerations when testing and assessing speaking skills?

Introduction

Green (2020) pointed out that speaking is a productive and interactive language skill that requires spontaneous production and exchange of language, ideas and interactions. Unlike writing, many speaking situations occur in real-time, so skilful speakers learn to automatize linguistic processes and adapt to a specific situation, including a change of topic and audience. Therefore, the choice of language use in speaking can be affected by the characteristics of a particular context (Luoma 2004).

Look at the following conversation between Jing and Jon.

Jon: 'Who do you think is the NBA GOAT?'
Jing: 'NBA what?'

In this example, Jing knew the NBA stands for National Basketball Association (in North America), but she could not associate it with a goat (an animal), and so became confused. Note that Jing did not see the spelling of GOAT. Her response was then 'NBA what?' Here is the next part of their conversation.

Jon: 'GOAT – greatest of all time. When someone is referred to as the GOAT, it means they are the best at something.'
Jing: 'Right … Hmm … Michael Jordan? Slam dunk!! Yes!'

This conversation was chosen because it exemplifies what may be involved in a communicative language activity, such as a conversation (e.g. questions and answers, turn-taking) and what may eventually influence a person's communicative language success. This excerpt captures several features of speech discussed in Chapter 7 (e.g. redundancy and idea units). In the excerpt, speaking is less structured, emergent, evolving and dynamic as the topic changes during the spoken interaction.

This chapter builds on Chapter 7, which discussed the nature of spoken language or discourse that listeners need to process and comprehend and Chapter 6, which outlines how to evaluate productive skills. This chapter aims to explain the nature of speaking, purposes of speaking and models explaining speaking. It also focuses on techniques and methods for testing and assessing speaking. This chapter discusses examples of rubrics for evaluating speaking performance and key considerations when scoring and evaluating speaking.

The nature of speaking

Understanding the various theoretical perspectives on additional language (AL) speaking skills can broaden our knowledge of AL speaking constructs to be tested and assessed.

What makes a person a successful speaker?

Successful speakers may share some of the characteristics presented in Figure 8.1.

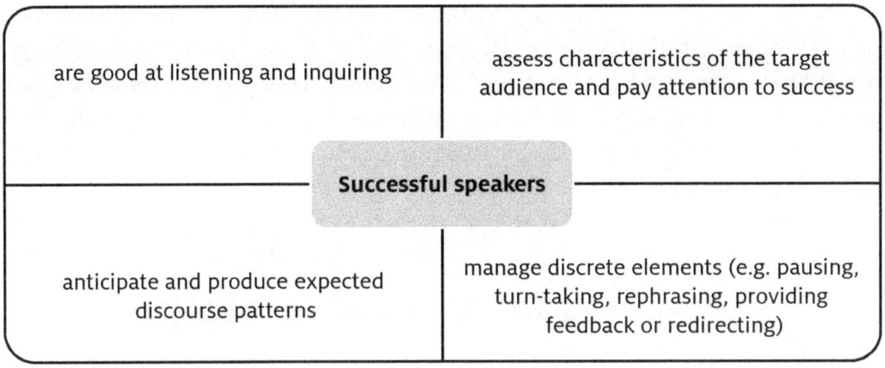

FIGURE 8.1 *Characteristics of a successful speaker.*

First, successful speakers need to be good listeners. They listen to understand the gist and the purposes of other speakers (i.e. they aim to understand their interlocutors). For example, they cannot respond accurately and appropriately without good listening skills. When they feel they do not understand something, they also can inquire, ask for clarification or confirm their understanding rather than pretend they know.

Second, successful speakers need to understand the background of their audience. They evaluate or observe their audience's or interlocutors' characteristics. In a two-way conversation, this is important because not adjusting their speech, word choices or speed to suit their audience can result in communication breakdown or lack of engagement. Successful speakers can dynamically opt to use plain, non-technical language when talking to people unfamiliar with the topic under discussion. They also tend to cluster ideas into small units, cohesively link them and use some repetition strategy. This is important to ensure comprehensibility. Successful speakers not only listen attentively but also monitor responses to know whether they are successful in delivering their speech. This can be seen through the audience's engagement, facial expressions and nodding frequency. This may also be achieved by using phrases such as 'You know what I mean?', 'Right?' and 'Okay?', as well as taking note of their interlocutors' feedback, such as 'hm?', 'Aha!', and 'Yes/yeah' (see interactional competence below).

Third, successful speakers predict and produce discourse patterns that their interlocutors anticipate. Compared to linguistic features such as grammar and phonology, discourse is a chunk of spoken language that makes up intended meanings. Listeners need to be assisted with what speakers are attempting to convey. Speakers can do this by, for example, making a topic or direction of the speech clear, using discourse markers (e.g. and, but and then, as discussed in Chapter 7).

Fourth, successful speakers manage discrete elements as they speak or interact with their audience. This can be observed when they pause (to allow their interlocutors to process information), take turns (to enable their interlocutors to respond or react), rephrase (to allow or ensure mutual comprehension is taking place), provide feedback (to confirm understanding), and redirect (to offer an alternative explanation).

Purposes and types of speaking

In a spoken discourse, there can be various purposes (see also Luoma 2004). The following are some of the common speaking purposes:

1. *Speaking to inform*: This broad speaking purpose occurs frequently in everyday communication (e.g. how to cook a dish, make something or write about something).
2. *Speaking to persuade*: To convince someone, people need to choose speech and vocabulary appropriate to the target listener. The speaker must present information logically and observe the listener's reactions.
3. *Speaking to establish and maintain a friendship or relationship*: Talking and social interaction can help you get to know someone and establish trust. You should have pragmatic and cross-cultural communication skills to develop a successful friendship.
4. *Speaking to learn*: Speaking is essential to learning new knowledge or language. People need to seek information and help from others. They need to seek confirmation or directions for their study. They learn to use various strategies to help them improve their speaking skills as they learn other skills, such as self-monitoring, self-correction and social strategies.

Models of speaking

Bachman and Palmer's (2010) model of reciprocal communicative language ability illustrates what is involved in an interaction between two or more people. Levelt's (1989) speaking theory is intended to explain first-language speaking but has been influential in explaining AL speaking (Field 2011; Fulcher 2003/2014; Luoma 2004). This chapter explores Levelt's (1989) model. There are three main processing components (e.g. conceptualizer, formulator and articulator), plus a speech-comprehension system in Levelt's (1989) model. The different components receive and produce particular kinds of information,

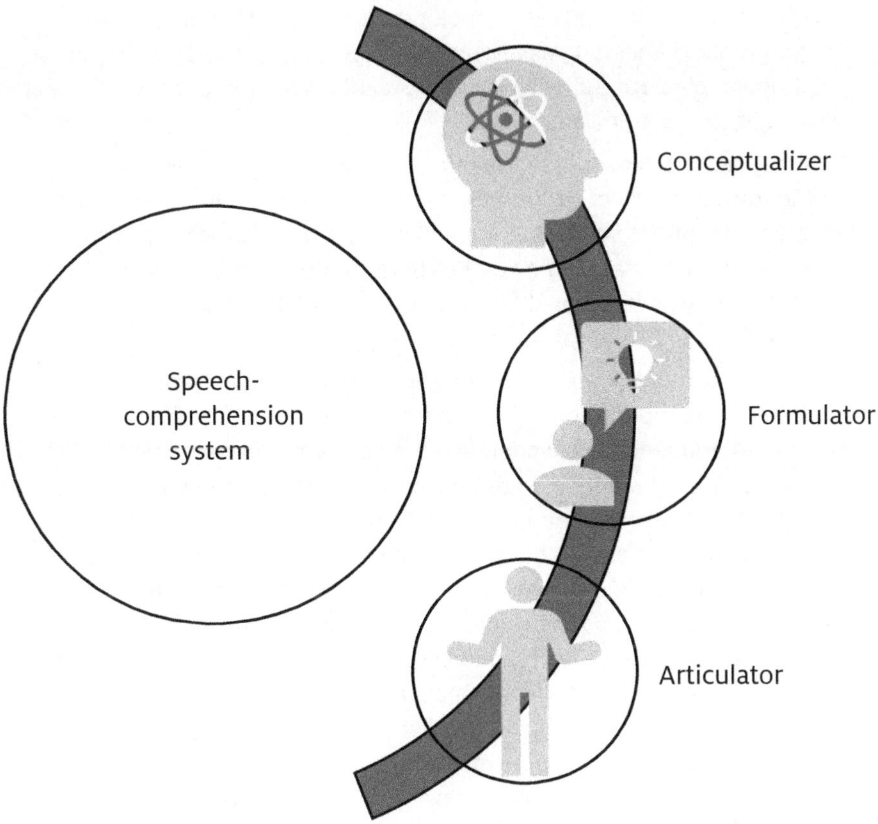

FIGURE 8.2 *Componential model of the speaker as an information processor.*

and the output of one element can become the input for another. Figure 8.2 depicts the interactions among these components.

1 *Conceptualizer*: This initial stage requires the speaker to conceive and select relevant information to use while speaking, order information and keep track of what has been said. Within this component, attention and monitoring are constant activities. The speaker needs to access procedural knowledge (how-knowledge) and declarative knowledge (what-knowledge), which are available in the long-term memory. The conceptualizer must produce messages that meet language-specific conditions for the formulator to accept them as input.
2 *Formulator*: This component accepts the messages from the conceptualizer and transforms them into a linguistic structure. The first step involves grammatical encoding (e.g. meaning, syntax, utterance).

The second step involves phonological encoding that builds the grammatical encoding as a whole, leading to the so-called internal phonetic plan/output (i.e. internal speech). This internal speech is next served to the articulator.

3 *Articulator*: This executes the phonetic plan or output derived from the formulator by making the speech overt or aloud through motor execution/effectors. As there could be delays in speech articulation, some internal speech may be temporarily stored in the 'Articulatory Buffer' (Levelt 1989, p. 12). The output of the articulator is overt speech (or speech that others can hear).

4 *Speech-comprehension system*: This system is interconnected with the three components. First, it monitors the conceptualizer to keep track of sequences of what has been said, what is being said and how it is being said. Second, in the formulator, internal speech is monitored and corrected/revised (consciously, subconsciously, automatically) before it is sent out to the articulator. This system is, thus, related to self-monitoring or personal audition processing (currently known to be part of metacognitive processing). Third, in the articulator, the overt speech is also monitored. In addition to the external hearer, audience or interlocutors, the speakers must hear and process their overt speech/voice. The speakers listen to their overt speech for its phonological, morphological, syntactical and semantic accuracy. A clear example of the output of this system is self-correction/self-repair due to a slip of the tongue, poorly expressed speech or poor word choice. This system also allows the speaker to input from the environment to the following process: correct or adjust speech.

It is important to note that, first, Levelt (1989) discusses input information and output representation in terms of an algorithm (if-then procedure), suggesting that the model is mainly sequential. However, human information processing can occur in parallel (Anderson 2000). Second, as this model was designed to explain first-language speaking, the verbatim application of this model for AL speaking is limited, especially in the light of the current need for multilingual-multimodal models of AL speaking. Third, affect and cognition are treated as separate systems, so in cognitive models affect was not often included in explaining information processing holistically. Finally, the social dimension of speaking was not focused. In real-life language use, an interlocutor significantly contributes to a person's speaking performance (e.g. in a speaking test, an interlocutor or an assigned partner in a paired speaking task contributes to meaning construction. Kramsch (1986) argues that successful communication requires the collaborative efforts of people as they aim to meet each other's expectations.

A model of AL speaking

Figure 8.3 is modelled from Figure 5.2 to provide a visualization of AL speaking to illustrate what is involved when people talk. This sociocognitive model recognizes the social context in shaping language use and processing (see Chapter 2). Since various theoretical components were explained in Figure 5.2, only some theoretical concepts related to speaking are discussed.

In Figure 8.3, the environment or social context may include a combination of interlocutors or audience, topics, purposes of speaking, types of speaking, tasks and unique tasks, and social constraints. The environment serves

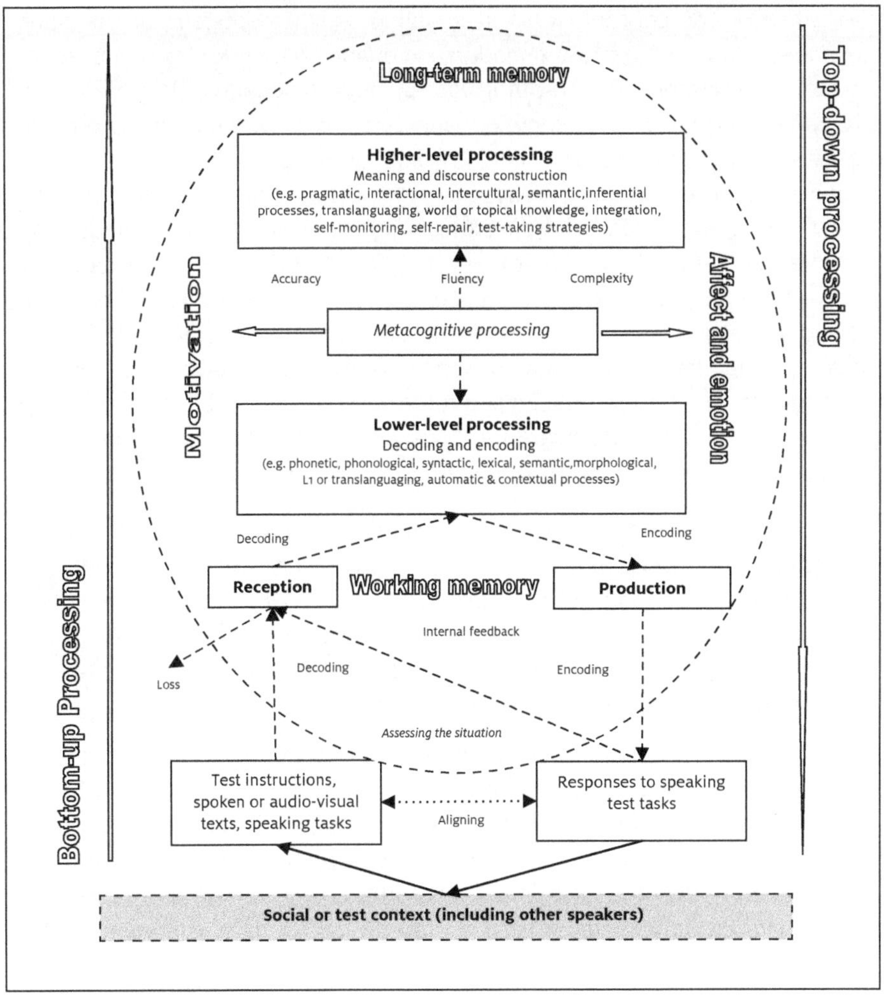

FIGURE 8.3 *A sociocognitive model of AL speaking.*

to provide input (e.g. audio-visual-sensual information) into the speaker's cognitive system (input reception via the so-called receptors (e.g. ears, nose, eyes, touch). The input is then processed using the conceptualizer discussed above.

It is important to note that speech is an invisible language-coded sound wave present in real-time (except when texts are accompanied). Incomprehensible, inaccessible or unimportant information can be lost or ignored. Input that can be retained next enters (decoded) the working and long-term memories, which require neurological and linguistic processes, such as activating linguistic and topical knowledge, memorizing, recalling, comprehending and attending. These processes may range from automatic to highly conscious. The speaker's affect plays a significant role in speech processing due to confidence or affective schemata towards content, topic or situation. Next, responses or reactions (e.g. speech and gestures) are encoded and pushed back into the environment through the effectors (e.g. mouth, vocals, body language). The interaction between what is inside (e.g. knowledge and competence) and what is outside (e.g. interaction and co-construction) is fluid (Fulcher 2003/2014).

Therefore, speaking test and assessment performance is context-specific and can be achieved individually, in pairs or in groups. In the case of individual performance, the student or test taker may respond directly to the test task (e.g. read sentences aloud). In the case of pair or group speaking tests, the social dimension of speaking needs to be recognized because individual speaking is affected by the characteristics of the interlocutors (interviewer, speaking partner), speaking tasks and raters.

Some of the terms associated with lower-level processing in Figure 8.3, not discussed elsewhere in the book, are explained as follows:

- *Phonetic and phonological processing* is related to pronunciation (the sound system). Pronunciation conveys grammatical meaning or the speaker's intention (Kang & Ginther 2018). Pronunciation includes segmental (vowel and consonant sounds, individual words) and suprasegmental (or prosody such as stress, intonation and rhythm) elements of a word or phrase.
- *Syntactic processing* (forms and structures of spoken discourse, but also meanings associated with a given language) is significant in that the speaker needs to be able to convey lexical, phonological and morphosyntactic meanings in their speech. It is also connected to pragmatics (Chapter 2) in that syntactical meaning needs to follow expected conventions and to be appropriate, meaningful and acceptable in a given context.
- *Lexical processing* is related to knowledge of words and strings of words, such as collocations, and how to use them in speaking.

Knowing a word is critical when speaking. It entails predicting the probability of encountering the word when spoken, the syntactic behaviours associated with the word, the associations between the word and other words, and the different meanings associated with the word.

- *Semantic processing* is related to lexical processing. It refers to interpreting and understanding the meaning in words, phrases and utterances or sentences, for instance, in a given context or situation.
- *Morphological processing* is associated with the term 'morpheme' – the smallest meaning unit of the language. It helps break down words or sentences into the smallest meaningful unit, for example, by interpreting the roots, prefixes, suffixes and inflections of words, phrases and utterances or sentences that convey meaning in context.

In Figure 8.3, three aspects involved in metacognitive and higher-level processing should be noted.

- *Accuracy* focuses on speakers' ability to control the correctness and appropriateness of their language use. This can be evident from the extent of their grammatical, vocabulary and pronunciation accuracy expected in a given language.
- *Fluency* refers to the concept of rapid or timely speech. Speakers are fluent when they produce speech at a natural pace without obvious hesitations or long pauses. Fluency can be seen in smooth, eloquent and effortless speech. Fluency can be a challenging expectation for many AL speakers because they need to be able to convert their thoughts into comprehensible sounds, follow conceptualizing, formulate and articulate patterns, and deal with more than one language.
- *Complexity* refers to the extent of the task demand that requires resources, time and effort to speak or complete a speaking task. Complexity can be internal and external. Internal complexity involves a speaker's linguistic knowledge for addressing a speaking task (i.e. linguistic complexity) and cognitive preparedness, such as perceived difficulty levels due to a lack of task familiarity (i.e. cognitive complexity). External complexity is related to the effort, attention and time the speaker needs to complete a speaking task (i.e. task complexity). Test and assessment conditions (e.g. access to resources for use, amount of planning time and time allowance to complete) can increase task complexity.

In summary, speaking is a productive skill that requires not only linguistic and cognitive processing but also depends on a social aspect of communication available within a given social or environmental context (see Chapter 2 on AL proficiency).

Techniques for testing and assessing speaking

The design of a speaking test and assessment follows what was discussed in Chapter 3. As discussed earlier in this chapter, speaking can be one-way (e.g. monologue, reading aloud) and two-way (e.g. conversation). This section presents six one-way and two-way techniques that can be considered for testing and assessing speaking: reading aloud, description and narration, information exchange, role-play, interview and integrated speaking (see also Brown & Abeywickrama 2010; Fulcher 2003/2014; Hughes & Hughes 2020; Luoma (2004).

Reading aloud technique

This technique is a linguistic-orientation and restricted-response technique. It helps test and assess students' or test takers' pronunciation and intelligibility levels (see Kang & Ginther 2018). This technique is flexible for a computer-assisted speaking test as an automated speech-scoring system can evaluate it. It can be applied in a face-to-face speaking test with a human administrator. Several commercial computer-based tests, such as Pearson Test of English Academic, Duolingo and TOEFL Essentials, use this technique. There are variants to reading aloud techniques, including (1) listening and repeating a phrase or sentence (imitation task), and (2) reading a sentence or paragraph aloud (pronunciation task). While students or test takers may comprehend while reading aloud, the intended purpose of this technique is not to evaluate their text comprehension level. It mainly assesses how well they pronounce and articulate the sound in connected speech.

> *Instructions*: Read the following text aloud. You have forty seconds to practise and forty seconds to read the text aloud after your practice time has finished. You will be assessed in terms of your oral fluency, intelligibility and pronunciation.
>
> 'One of the major issues facing public housing in Australia is the shortage of available units. With an increasing population and rising property prices, many low-income individuals and families struggle to secure affordable housing options. This shortage has led to long waiting lists for public housing, leaving many vulnerable individuals without a stable place to call home.'
>
> *Source*: Modified AI text from ChatGPT 3.5

In this technique, students or test takers are generally asked to read a sentence or a short text that can vary in sentence structure and language complexity in a read-aloud task. Typically, to capture a full range of stress, intonation and rhythm, two or more lengthy sentences with meaningful ideas (e.g. approximately fifty words) are more valuable than a single short sentence (e.g. ten–fifteen words). However, test designers can tailor sentences for their specific test takers (e.g. based on proficiency levels or whether it is a proficiency or an achievement test). Some limitations of this technique include a lack of authenticity (i.e. people are not asked to read aloud to others). The ability to read aloud successfully does not equate to the speaker's ability to speak meaningfully and successfully, although pronunciation plays an integral part.

The following are some valuable recommendations for using this technique.

1. Make the test instructions, general information and judging criteria available for test takers beforehand so they can practise reading aloud. Examples should be provided so they are familiar with the task; this can reduce administrative time, too. In a computer-based test, test takers must be familiar with the test interface (e.g. instructions, text sizes, remaining time) and what they must do before and after reading each item aloud.
2. Choose texts that are meaningful to students or test takers. Avoid specialized or professional words unless the test is for specific purposes.
3. For each item to be read aloud, test takers should be given a reasonable amount of time to practise before they read it aloud. Ideally, the time spent practising and reading for scoring should be similar. Pearson Test of English Academic gives forty seconds for test takers to prepare and read each item aloud.
4. The speed at which a student or test taker reads should not unduly influence speaking scoring. Encouraging students or test takers to read fast does not encourage intelligibility, nor does quick speech imply fluency. Instead, it adds a level of anxiety and makes the test more demanding than it should be. Their speech may be recorded for scoring or verification purposes in a non-computer-assisted test.
5. Use a rating scale for judging pronunciation, fluency and intelligibility. These criteria are commonly used to judge this task.

Description and narration technique

A description and narration technique prompts students or test takers to speak by describing the picture or sequences of images or events. A picture task asks test takers to tell what is in the provided picture, narrate a picture-cued sequence of events and give a direction based on a given map. Test takers must use their vocabulary and syntactic knowledge (e.g. appropriate tenses and subject–verb agreements) to construct their speech.

Instructions: You will see three pictures that depict different activities. Describe each picture, including the people, objects, places and actions. You will be assessed in terms of your clarity and sufficiency in the content description, as well as your grammatical accuracy and pronunciation. You have one minute to prepare your description and narration. You have one minute to describe each picture.

1 A picture of friends working in a vegetable garden.

2 A picture of a kitchen in a restaurant.

3 A picture of students using computers to do a group project.

Source: Original

While this task can elicit students' or test takers' constructed speaking, it can be challenging for them. For example, they may not interpret the actions or descriptions of the same pictures in the same way. Their perceptions or interpretations of the picture may not be aligned with those of the test designers. Some photos may be culturally specific and challenging to some students or test takers. It is challenging to find the right pictures, especially for a picture-cued sequence speaking task. For this speaking technique, it is essential to specify how long students or test takers are given to prepare their responses and how long they have to complete their speech after they start. Students should be given time to plan and organize their speech (e.g. 'You have one minute to look at each picture and prepare your speech, and you have one minute to describe each picture'). They should be given the assessment criteria to know what they will be assessed against.

Information-exchange technique

This technique allows students or test takers to interact with each other using the target language. The task can be tailored to suit students' or test takers' level or learning outcomes. There are several ways to create a task using an information-exchange technique. For example, a pair of students or test takers are given different, complementary information. Each is to ask and answer questions of each other in an organized manner. That is, they need to exchange information. This is also known as a jigsaw puzzle task. The task may be the same map where the pair can ask for directions from one place to the target place. It is important to develop two separate information sheets that synchronize each other well in terms of information supply. Pilot them before use. Another example of an information-exchange task is to ask the pair to ask each other about an assigned topic (e.g. traditional celebrations and fashion). Given the advancement of generative artificial intelligence (AI), it is possible that a computer-assisted speaking task can also be developed. The computer program can be used as a speaking partner. This type of speaking task is known as a semi-speaking task. Instructions can be provided in writing and read to students or test takers.

Instructions: You will be given information about how to cook a simple dish. Use the information you are given to explain to your partner, such as essential ingredients, how to prepare the dish and what secret tips to apply. Your partner will listen attentively to your explanations and ask questions for clarification. Both have *three minutes* to prepare to describe their dish on their own. Once three minutes is over, the first student will start talking about their dish. You have *two minutes* to complete your task. Once your time has finished, the other one will take turns. You will be assessed in terms of task fulfilment, pronunciation and fluency, language use, vocabulary range and interactional skills.

This constructed-response task is practical in eliciting various areas of students' and test takers' speaking skills, including non-verbal communication. It, however, can cause test anxiety because of the time pressure to complete the task and a lack of interest in the task. Students' and test takers' may not be familiar with the task or the content of the task. There may be an issue with students' or test takers' incompatibility. With different proficiency levels, the other may feel superior or inferior to the partner. This affects confidence and performance. It is also time-consuming to complete for students and to score by teachers or assessors.

Two practical recommendations when using this task include:

1. Students or test takers need to clearly understand their respective roles and the tasks they must complete. If the task is a summative assessment, students should have opportunities to practise it in the classroom.
2. Provide clear instructions and the task objectives to students or test takers. They should have an opportunity to ask for clarification.

Role-play technique

This is a communication- or task-oriented technique. A role-play technique asks students or test takers to imagine that they are someone in a particular context who needs to speak or achieve something through speaking or interacting with others (e.g. suppose you are a customer, waiter/waitress or doctor). This technique is suitable for assessing specific-purpose language use. Interactions with other speakers allow them to improvise an unanticipated response, making their speaking interaction more natural to the level of their current ability. Although a topic or situation is controlled in a speaking task, students or test takers have more freedom or creativity to produce their linguistic output and exhibit a range of language use, including linguistic resources, fluency, accuracy, complexity and appropriateness.

Instructions: You are the store manager responsible for handling customer complaints and assisting them in resolving their issues. You are meeting with a complaining customer who received a broken product but had an unpleasant experience dealing with the online customer service. As the manager, you are to gather information about the issue. You aim to understand the nature of the service the customer received, analyse the problem with the product and come up with a satisfactory solution to address the issue.

In this task, you will be assessed in terms of task fulfilment, language use, and social skills.

Source: Original

Role-plays can be achieved one-to-one with an interviewer or assessor or in a pair or a group of three to four students assigned different roles in a given scenario. To successfully perform a role-play task, sufficient information and expectations, including a final goal of a communicative task, should be provided to students or test takers. If two students perform the task in pairs, typically, they will have separate information sheets or booklets that give them a different role and contextual information on which to base their speech. Clear information is essential because test takers may need to become more familiar with the roles they are asked to take on.

In a paired task, it is important to know that achieving suitable pairings of students and test takers may be challenging. High-ability students and test takers tend to be more dominant in role-play tasks than low-ability ones, which can lead to their unfair judgement. Furthermore, students and test takers may see a role-play task as a competition and compete with each other rather than collaborate or co-construct their communicative interactions. Acting ability can produce construct-irrelevant variance affecting performance. Students and test takers with acting talent are likely to appear more natural than those without. Therefore, raters need to be vigilant about the impact of acting ability on their judgement. Success in a role-play task can be affected by reading ability. If written instructions (rather than oral) are provided, language use needs to be precise and clear, and the choice of vocabulary needs to be suitable for students or test takers. If they do not understand what they are supposed to do, they will not perform well in their role-play task.

Interview technique

This oral interview technique is most suitable for communication or situation-oriented speaking tests. An interview technique typically requires an interviewer (i.e. interlocutor, teacher) to elicit speaking performance from test takers (i.e. interviewees). It can be carried out face to face or online. Usually, an unequal power relationship between the interviewer and interviewee is assumed in a speaking test because the interviewer has some authority over the test takers, who are in charge of what they ask and the steps to follow to complete the test. Given this, this technique can be intimidating for students or test takers. Therefore, interviewers need to be mindful of the effect of this power relationship on students or test takers.

Typical steps in an interview task

An interview technique (of ten minutes duration) can follow the four stages (see Brown & Abeywickrama 2010, pp. 207–8):

1 Warm-up (approximately one–two minutes) to help the students or test takers settle down (e.g. lower their test anxiety, and understand what they will be asked to do. This step includes greetings and self-introduction. Students or test takers' speaking performance is not judged in this stage.

2 Level check (approximately two minutes) to estimate the students' or test taker's speaking ability level preliminarily. Have a set of pre-planned questions (typically general communication questions, including close-ended and open-ended questions on their background, recent trips, exciting news, hobbies, etc.). Pre-planned questions should allow the interviewer to elicit students' or test takers' grammatical accuracy (e.g. appropriate use of tenses, subject–verb agreements, etc.), use of vocabulary, pronunciation and its clarity, level of fluency and social language skills (e.g. politeness, pragmatic skills). Linguistic performance is usually scored. This stage allows the interviewer to choose or adjust what will be asked in the next stage.

3 Probe (approximately four minutes) to allow the students or test takers to engage in an extended interaction with the interviewer. Questions are generally open-ended and topic-based. Students and test takers may be asked to express their opinions about some issues and provide their thoughts on and possible solutions to these issues. They may be asked to talk about their study or current employment. Questions in this stage should be easy for students or test takers as they may have little to say. In particular, questions on unfamiliar topics should be avoided. This section is the primary source of evidence for scoring students or test takers.

4 Wind down (approximately one–two minutes) to close the interview test. The interviewer can ask how the test takers and students feel, inform them when they will know the result and ask if they have further questions before they leave.

Source: Original

The interviewer follows a set of test instructions and questions. Depending on what speaking abilities are required to be tested, an interview test length can vary. Still, an extended interview test is exhausting for both the interviewer and the students and test takers, and can be impractical. A ten-minute interview may be sufficient to gather evidence of speaking ability. An interview may or may not be recorded depending on the test context. A variant of this is to do a pair interview (two-on-one interview) as it can reduce the time required. Test techniques such as role-play or information exchange can be integrated into the interview format. However, this variant poses an additional challenge regarding pairing and fairness (e.g. high-ability students and test takers can dominate and make low-ability ones under-perform).

Some practical considerations for using an interview technique effectively are as follows:

1 Provide test information, including scoring criteria, to students or test takers in advance so they are well-prepared for the test.

2 Strictly follow the administrative procedures to maintain consistency across students or test takers and achieve timely test completion.

3 Use a well-defined scoring rubric to ensure consistency and accuracy of speaking evaluation.

Integrated technique

The underlying principles of this technique are similar to those discussed about integrated writing tasks in Chapter 6, except the target outcome is spoken language. An integrated speaking task requires students or test takers to use multiple language skills to complete the task. An integrated speaking task can be designed for a unique or specific-purpose language task rather than a task based on speaking in everyday situations. Students and test takers may be asked to watch a video, listen to an audio recording or read a text about a topic. Then, in their speaking, they use the information from the source to produce their speech, together with their thoughts or viewpoints about the issues or topics. Therefore, this task requires students and test takers to analyse and synthesize information. In this task, it is natural for students or test takers to use fillers, pauses or self-repairs during their speech as they articulate their thoughts. An integrated task can be designed as a scenario-based assessment (Purpura 2024). Students or test takers are asked to watch a video, answer comprehension questions and then present their opinions about a topic or issue.

Instructions: You are to watch a video about wildlife conservation (three minutes long) and answer some short-answer questions about factual information presented in the video. You can take notes during the video. Then, you will be asked your opinions about the importance of wildlife conservation and your insights from the video. After answering the comprehension questions, you will be prompted to plan your answers to the interview questions. In the interview, you will be asked the same questions.

1 Watch a video about wildlife conservation and the government's effort to address threats to wildlife generally and endangered species. The government's current conservation projects and how they are hoped to save wildlife from extinction are discussed. The current significant challenges are discussed and how they may be overcome.

2 Comprehension questions

   1 What is the current concern about the wildlife situation?

   2 What wildlife species are listed as endangered?

   3 What are two significant threats mentioned in the video?

   4 Name one current conservation project.

   5 Where does it take place?

   6 What does the project aim to accomplish?

3 Interview questions

Whenever possible, combine information from the video with your opinions, but acknowledge the source such as 'Based on the video, … '.

1 Tell us your opinions about the importance of wildlife for human society.
2 How does wildlife impact the ecosystem and biodiversity?
3 What is one of the significant threats to their livelihood?
4 What do you think you can do to help save them?
5 How would you promote awareness of wildlife conservation projects to people around you?

Source: Original

In recent years, computer-assisted language testing and assessment (CALTA) has gained popularity in delivering speaking tests and assessments. In the case of an integrated speaking task, CALTA can be applied. When students or test takers are asked to respond to a speaking prompt and record their responses on the computer, the test is considered semi-direct testing (see Chapter 3). The distinction between direct and semi-direct testing is linked to the presence or absence of human interlocutors in real-time. Understanding the difference between direct, semi-direct and indirect testing can be helpful for people new to language testing and assessment. It should be noted that speaking to a human requires different mental processes from speaking to a computer. In the example above, the task can be computerized and sequenced. Students and test takers can respond to the comprehension questions directly by typing and corresponding to the robot partner using a microphone. The speech and responses will also be recorded.

In an integrated speaking task, the language proficiency level of students or test takers will probably influence performance success in this technique. Individual test takers are commonly asked to complete an integrated speaking task independently. However, speaking tests that require students or test takers to work in pairs or groups to complete integrated speaking tasks are possible. Integrated speaking tests can be practical in classroom assessment as topics can be related to the learning activities, and there is less time constraint for students to complete.

The following are some practical suggestions when using this technique.

1 It is essential to allocate time for students or test takers to plan before they start speaking. They should be allowed to take notes as they watch a video, listen to an audio text or read the written text to help them organize their speech. Permission to do this is accepted, as people usually take notes in non-test speaking contexts. For example, after watching the video, they have two minutes to gather their thoughts and prepare their speech to respond to the task using what they have heard and read.

2 Provide some guidance on how students or test takers may structure their responses and give an explicit prompt to what they need to address in their speech (e.g. 'Do you agree or disagree with the speaker? Why or why not?' Use the information from the speaker to illustrate your position and agreement or disagreement).
3 In the instructions, indicate clearly how long students or test takers are given to complete their speech (e.g. 'You have two minutes to speak'). A visible clock or countdown timer should be provided.
4 Topics and text complexity influence students' or test takers' level of comprehension and integration. Therefore, test designers should be careful with topic choices and the level of language complexity used.
5 Rubrics must be explicitly developed for assessing integrated speaking performance (e.g. https://www.ets.org/s/toefl/pdf/toefl_speaking_rubrics.pdf). Criteria such as task fulfilment and accuracy in the use and integration of resources should be considered.
6 Failure to complete this task may not imply that students or test takers are not good speakers, as performance can be affected by a given topic or task complexity. They may not be familiar with the task, or their performance may be affected by problems or issues in the above points.

Relevant issues to speaking test techniques

Appropriate test and assessment techniques for speaking need to be considered in the light of several factors. First, it is essential to use the theory of speaking and real-life language use or task situations (e.g. proficiency or specific-purpose tests) or the learning outcomes and classroom activities (e.g. achievement tests) to inform speaking test and assessment design. The selected test and assessment technique and task should align with the target constructs or learning outcomes. Different test techniques and diverse speaking tasks may be combined to assess different speaking constructs.

Second, success in a selected speaking technique may rely on other language skills (e.g. listening and reading). If students or test takers are asked to listen to audio texts or interact with different speakers, their speaking performance success will depend on their listening skills. In some techniques, they may be asked to read aloud or exchange information from provided handouts or tests to assess their pronunciation and fluency. In this case, their speaking performances also depend on their reading skills.

Third, task difficulty can be associated with test techniques. Although task difficulty is defined by the level of cognitive demand to complete (i.e. the same task may be perceived as easy or difficult depending on the student or test taker), the level of task difficulty can vary for students or test takers (e.g. reading aloud versus integrated speaking tasks). Subsequently, ordering test tasks and techniques from less to more complex is essential to facilitate students' and test takers' task engagement and speaking performances. Finally, students or test takers may be asked to complete speaking tasks individually, in pairs or a group, meaning performance in individual, pair or group tasks must be judged differently.

Administration

One of the most challenging aspects in testing and assessing speaking is test administration, which faces several issues of test practicality. If not fully considered, delivering a speaking test and assessment is unlikely to be successful. First, compared to tests and assessments of other language skills, such as listening, reading and writing, which can be administered in a test room where all students or test takers can be together, a speaking test will probably require individual or one-on-one test administration. Therefore, test designers need to plan (1) how a given speaking test will be administered (e.g. physical environments, individual or pair tasks), (2) how and where other students and test takers can wait before completing their speaking test, and (3) how their speaking performance will be recorded and stored. Furthermore, training interviewers or interlocutors on administering the speaking test is critical, as variation in administration should be minimal across students and test takers.

In CALTA, test designers need to consider whether the speaking test can be administered in a computer lab or whether a home edition is viable. A computer-based speaking test has some challenges that differ from a face-to-face speaking test (e.g. the identification check, moderation of dishonest behaviour, test interactiveness and performance recording). In a computer-based speaking test, students or test takers may get distracted by other students or test takers while taking it, so it is essential to manage this issue effectively.

Factors affecting speaking test performance

Several factors affect speaking, and test designers need to consider test-specific and other factors that shape speaking test performance. Hence, validation of speaking test and assessment tasks is required. These factors include the nature of the speaking test constructs, the alignment between test tasks and test constructs, the impacts of construct-irrelevant variance, types of speaking tasks, delivery modes (e.g. face-to-face, online, computer-based), and types of scoring (holistic, analytic, human scoring and machine scoring).

Scoring

Similar to assessing writing, assessing speaking, especially in constructed-response tasks, is considered subjective because it requires raters' judgements on performance. In scoring speaking performance, at least two key issues must be considered. The first is constructing and using a scoring rubric or rating scale. In assessing speaking, holistic and analytic rubrics are commonly used. The second is ensuring rater reliability through training and moderation. This is also true for automated speech scoring because test developers need to train and calibrate the program with unbiased speech data to score reliably and validly. A language teacher may be the sole assessor of their students' speaking performance. Hence, reliability from designing to scoring is critical for their speaking tests to be useful.

As with the writing assessment, scoring speaking tests is challenging and complex (see Chapter 6). First, criteria or standards for judging speaking performance must be developed (discussed below). They need to be suitable for the test and assessment tasks used, and, therefore, it is not easy to adopt an existing scoring rubric as there may be a mismatch between the rubric, test tasks and students' or test takers' level or context. As in a writing assessment, holistic scoring is more practical than analytic scoring in a large-scale speaking test. However, analytic scoring helps identify specific strengths and weaknesses of students' and test takers' speaking. Training and moderation are also required to address test reliability, validity and fairness.

Advancements in automated speech-scoring technology (e.g. artificial intelligence, natural language processing) have made it possible to use software to rate speaking performance more quickly and reliably (see Zechner & Evanini 2020, who comprehensively discuss this technology). Although a hybrid approach using both human raters and automated speech scoring is possible, test developers tend to use automated speech-scoring systems solely to mark speaking performance based on evidence of scoring reliability and validity and the need for test practicality.

However, this decision has pros and cons, and much empirical research is needed regarding its effectiveness and possible misuse (Zhang, Bridgeman &

Davis 2020). For instance, first, automated speech scoring may not cover all the speaking constructs of interest (e.g. speaking abilities valued by human raters may not be given credit by the software). Second, what automated speech scoring can assess well (e.g. pronunciation) must be accommodated in the test design. This may imply that tests are not construct-driven (e.g. one that evaluates the ability to speak meaningfully to communicate with others). Lastly, automated speech-scoring systems are viable only when sufficient and sustainable financial and technical support exists. Underfunded educational institutes are likely to be unable even to consider this technology. Therefore, test designers need to maintain a fine line between wholeheartedly embracing automated speech-scoring software and being overly sceptical in using it for rating speaking.

Rating scales and scoring rubrics

In this chapter, types of scoring rubrics will not be discussed in detail (see Chapter 6). It may be said that scoring rubrics or rating scales represent the underlying speaking constructs of interest used to assess students' and test takers' speaking performances (Fulcher 2003/2014, 2012b). Therefore, scoring rubrics may include criteria such as task fulfilment, accuracy, fluency, intelligibility, interaction, appropriacy, vocabulary range and flexibility. It should be noted that no more than six criteria should be included in a speaking rubric because they can influence scoring consistency over time and impose a cognitive demand on raters' cognition.

Different scoring rubrics should be developed for assessing individual, paired and group tasks since they differ in social collaboration and co-construction of meaning. Before its actual use, test designers must carefully develop and validate a scoring rubric specifically for their test or adapt an existing rubric to fit their test task. The following presents examples of scoring rubrics for assessing speaking test performance, from a simple checklist and rating scale to holistic and analytic rubrics.

Simple checklist

A simple checklist is used to identify the presence or absence of particular criteria in students' and test takers' speaking performances. It is a criterion-referenced approach since it rates whether the students and test takers have met specific requirements. Figure 8.4 is an example of a simple checklist. One limitation of a checklist is its crude, either–or judgement of speaking performance. It is, therefore, useful for beginner or intermediate levels and formative assessment.

No.	Criteria	Yes	No
1.	Address the task/question sufficiently.		
2.	Complete the task/question within the time allowed.		
3.	Produce logical speech with accurate facts or suitable examples to support.		
4.	Use effective discourse markers, signposting or transitions.		
5.	Use language appropriate to their audience.		
6.	Use an appropriate speaking style for the task.		
7.	Use grammatically correct language structures.		
8.	Produce intelligible speech with clear pronunciation and appropriate volume.		
9.	Use appropriate gestures and body language, including good eye contact.		
10.	Overall performance is satisfactory.		
Overall score:			

FIGURE 8.4 *A checklist for assessing speaking performance.*

Simple rating scale

Figure 8.5 is an example of a simple rating scale. It is an extension of Figure 8.4. As can be seen, this offers a more refined evaluation of a speaking performance, and the ratings can be transformed into points for each student and test taker. It provides more helpful feedback for student and test takers regarding their strengths and weaknesses. However, compared to the simple checklist, this rating scale requires more time to complete.

Holistic rubric

Holistic rubrics are used to provide a single score on speaking test performance. As discussed in Chapter 6, holistic scoring is practical when there are many students and test takers to be rated, but it does not provide feedback for specific areas of speaking performance. Figure 8.6 is an example of a holistic scoring rubric for rating a read-aloud task. In this example, the description for each level is distinctive in describing students' and test takers' read-aloud

No.	Criteria	Very weak	Weak	Average	Good	Very good
1.	Address the task/question sufficiently.					
2.	Complete the task/question within the time allowed.					
3.	Produce logical speech with accurate facts or suitable examples to support them.					
4.	Use effective discourse markers, signposting or transitions.					
5.	Use language appropriate to their audience.					
6.	Use an appropriate speaking style for the task.					
7.	Use grammatically correct language structures.					
8.	Produce intelligible speech with clear pronunciation and appropriate volume.					
9.	Use appropriate gestures and body language, including good eye contact.					
10.	Overall speaking performance.					
Overall score:						
Other comments:						

FIGURE 8.5 *A simple rating scale for assessing speaking performance.*

Point	Description
4 (Very good)	Performance at this level: • Overall pronunciation is highly intelligible. • The speaker has minor errors in pronunciation. • Speech is smooth and almost at a natural pace without obvious hesitations or long pauses. • Vowel and consonant sounds and individual words are clearly articulated. • Stress, intonation and rhythm are clearly, naturally and correctly enunciated.
3 (Good)	Performance at this level: • Overall pronunciation is intelligible. • The speaker has some occasional errors in pronunciation. • Speech is relatively smooth and at a natural pace, with a few occasional hesitations or pauses. • Vowel and consonant sounds and individual words are articulated quite well, with some occasional inaccuracy. • Stress, intonation and rhythm are quite naturally enunciated, but with some mistakes or errors.
2 (Average)	Performance at this level: • Overall pronunciation is occasionally unintelligible. • The speaker has some consistent errors in pronunciation. • Speech does not flow at a natural pace, with some noticeable hesitations, fast speed and pauses. • Some vowel and consonant sounds and individual words are not well articulated, and there is some noticeable inaccuracy. • Stress, intonation and rhythm are often incorrectly enunciated.
1 (Poor)	Performance at this level: • Overall pronunciation is largely unintelligible. • The speaker has many consistent errors in pronunciation. • Speech does not flow at a natural pace, with many noticeable hesitations, fast speed and pauses. • Many vowel and consonant sounds and individual words are not well articulated, and there is some clearly noticeable inaccuracy. • Stress, intonation and rhythm are largely unacceptable.
0 (Very poor)	Performance at this level: • Overall pronunciation is serious. • Speech is largely fragmented. • Tasks were partially completed or minimally completed. • Insufficient to evaluate.

FIGURE 8.6 *A holistic scoring for a read-aloud performance.*

performance. It should be noted that the words 'native-like' or 'equivalent to that of a native speaker' and 'first-language accent' are purposefully avoided since the focus should be on intelligibility rather than nativeness performance.

Analytic rubric

Analytic rubrics use a scoring grid; raters must assign scores to different aspects of speech, such as task fulfilment, pronunciation, accuracy, fluency and complexity. Analytic rubrics are more reliable than holistic rubrics because raters have a specific set of criteria to focus on for each particular aspect, and an overall score can be calculated as an aggregation of scores across all criteria. Students and test takers will know their strengths and weaknesses from the scores reported. However, analytic scoring is more time-consuming and complex, requiring more comprehensive rater training and moderation. The IELTS speaking rubrics can be adapted to produce a customized analytic rubric (https://www.ielts.org/-/media/pdfs/speaking-band-descriptors.ashx).

Figure 8.7 is an example of a 5-point analytic rubric for scoring a speaking task. The criteria include task fulfilment, accuracy, fluency and interaction.

Rater training

Research suggests that many factors affect raters' scoring behaviours; for example, topics, attitudes about a specific topic, motivation and fatigue (see, e.g. Brown 2012; McNamara et al. 2019; see Chapter 6). In high-stakes and large-scale speaking tests, sufficient, high-quality training and moderation of raters' scoring are required to maintain their scoring consistency and accuracy. Test developers or authorities can decide whether some may not continue rating or need re-training. Experts commonly use pre-scored performances in rater training, so a rater's scores can be compared with the experts. In rater training, raters must understand how to use a rubric and each criterion (see also automated speech scoring above).

Inaccurate scoring in speaking tests and assessments can have long-term consequences on students and test takers. Reliability and teacher training on scoring is critical. Teachers may be provided with initial rater training, followed by independent ratings of some test samples. Their literacy in scoring consistency and accuracy should be part of their pre- or in-service training. During their professional career, scoring skills can be enhanced by peer/expert mentoring and assessment experiences and by learning qualitative methods that help clarify the scoring processes.

Criteria	Very good (5)	Good (4)	Average (3)	Weak (2)	Very weak (1)
Task fulfilment	Successfully fulfils the task requirements; excellent topic management; displays an excellent depth of task coverage.	Mainly fulfils the task requirements and has good topic management, primarily with relevant, accurate and appropriate information.	Attempts to address the task requirements; some good topic management; some valuable ideas are presented with relevant, sound and appropriate information.	Partially or insufficiently addresses the task requirements; under-developed or premature ideas presented.	No or insufficient responses; too many highly fragmented or unrelated responses; does not fit the Weak criterion.
Accuracy	Grammatically and lexically correct speech with excellent control; appears natural and flexible; appropriate for intended meaning.	Mainly produces grammatically and lexically correct speech with reasonable control; appears quite natural and flexible; usually appropriate for the intended meaning.	Produces a mix of grammatically, lexically correct and incorrect speech with some control; often appears to struggle to formulate speech; occasionally inappropriate for the intended meaning.	Largely grammatically and lexically incorrect speech with poor control, leading to misunderstanding; usually appears to struggle to formulate speech; few appropriate, but occasionally inappropriate for the intended meaning.	Basic formulaic expressions; numerous grammatical and lexical errors; no or insufficient responses; does not fit the Weak criterion.

Criteria	Very good (5)	Good (4)	Average (3)	Weak (2)	Very weak (1)
Fluency	Highly fluent, intelligible, flexible, coherent, and sustainable speech; minor errors in pronunciation; smooth and almost at a natural pace without obvious hesitations or long pauses.	Fluent, intelligible, flexible, coherent, and sustainable speech; some occasional errors in pronunciation; relatively smooth and at a natural pace with a few occasional hesitations or long pauses.	Quite fluent, with occasional unintelligible, inflexible, incoherent, and unsustainable speech; some consistent errors in pronunciation; may not flow at a natural pace with some noticeable hesitations, fast speed, and long pauses.	Generally disfluent, unintelligible, inflexible, incoherent, and unsustainable speech; inconsistent pronunciation errors; does not flow at a natural pace with many noticeable hesitations, fast speed, and long pauses.	No or insufficient responses to evaluate; disfluent, unintelligible, inflexible, incoherent and unsustainable speech; does not fit the Weak criterion.
Interaction	Highly, consistently and appropriately interactive; smooth and fluid interaction, with excellent turn-taking management; strong evidence of sensitivity to situations or listeners; strong evidence of interactive listening; effectively utilizing breakdown repairs and nonverbal behaviours.	Mostly interactive and appropriate, with good turn-taking management; good evidence of sensitivity to situations or listeners; good use of interactive listening; utilizing breakdown repairs and nonverbal behaviours.	Occasionally interactive and appropriate, with some good turn-taking management; generally sensitive to situations or listeners; some evidence of interactive listening; partially utilizing breakdown repairs and nonverbal behaviours.	Mostly non-interactive and inappropriate interaction, with some poor turn-taking management; some evidence of insensitivity to situations or listeners, little evidence of interactive listening; minimally utilizing breakdown repairs and nonverbal behaviours.	No or insufficient responses to evaluate; no or little evidence of turn-taking skills and non-verbal behaviours; noticeable lack of interactive listening or engagement; does not fit the Weak criterion.

FIGURE 8.7 *An analytic scoring for an interview performance.*

Summary

Speaking ability is multifaceted and requires the speaker to understand and internalize the target language. It requires the ability to command and articulate the language structure, lexical range and formulaic expressions (Fulcher 2003/2014). The speaker must pronounce the target language words intelligibly and produce meaningful sounds and utterances. Speaking also requires people to focus on pronunciation, comprehension, memory, attention, and control of thoughts and environments. This chapter has presented and discussed the nature of speaking, given some theoretical explanations, and introduced several methods and considerations for effective testing and assessing speaking. It has also discussed scoring methods for evaluating speaking test and assessment performance.

Discussion

1. What are the differences between purposes of speaking and purposes of speaking assessment?
2. Explain the features of Levelt's (1989) componential model of the speaker as an information processor.
3. If you were to design a speaking test and could only allow ten minutes for each student or test taker to complete it, what testing and assessment techniques (presented in this chapter) would you choose? What task(s) would be used? How would you design, pilot, administer and score the test?
4. Why is scoring critical for effective testing and assessment of speaking?
5. Discuss the advantages and disadvantages of holistic and analytic rubrics.

Further reading

Fulcher, G., 2003/2014, *Assessing second language speaking*, New York and London, Routledge.

This book provides a comprehensive account of the history of speaking assessment and methods for assessing and scoring speaking test performance.

Luoma S., 2004, *Assessing speaking*, Cambridge, Cambridge University Press.

This is an often-referenced book for testing and assessing speaking. It comprehensively relates theory to test design and use.

Salaberry, M.R. & Burch, A.R. (eds), 2021, *Assessing speaking in context: Expanding the construct and its applications,* Bristol, Multilingual Matters.

This book presents contemporary issues in assessing speaking. It addresses topics of interactional competence in a speaking test.

Taylor, L. (ed.), 2011, *Examining speaking*, Cambridge, Cambridge University Press.

This volume provides excellent examples of the critical processes and considerations involved in developing, validating and using speaking tests.

9

Test and Assessment Analysis

Overview

This chapter introduces basic test and assessment analysis and discusses quantitative and qualitative analyses that help enhance the quality of language tests and assessments.

Guided questions

1. Why do we need to analyse language test and assessment data?
2. What can be used to demonstrate the suitability of a language test and assessment?

Introduction

This book has so far discussed approaches and methods in language testing and assessment. Test and assessment analysis is critical in educational or social settings and serves dual purposes. First, it facilitates student learning and achievement by aligning educational activities with learning objectives. It enables students to meet their educational goals. Second, it becomes crucial in high-stakes environments where decisions based on assessment outcomes are impactful and often irreversible, affecting students' academic and professional futures (Phakiti & Leung 2024).

In language education, the significance of test and assessment analysis is underscored by its ability to influence both short-term educational strategies and long-term decisions. For instance, formative assessments are designed to provide immediate feedback to students, helping them understand their learning progress and identify areas that need improvement. This ongoing evaluation process is vital for adjusting teaching methods and learning activities to suit students' educational needs. Conversely, summative assessments often come as high-stakes tests and can dictate crucial academic and professional opportunities. According to Green (2020), these assessments are typically used to make significant decisions – from academic placements to job qualifications – which underscores their importance in educational and professional settings. Accordingly, to ensure that both types of assessments effectively serve their intended purposes, they must be well-crafted and accurately reflect the curriculum and the skills students are expected to acquire. This alignment, as discussed in Chapter 1, helps make the assessments fair, relevant and beneficial to students' real-world applications and needs (Green 2020; Kunnan 2018).

Test and assessment analysis is a strategy to understand students' or test takers' responses and preparedness for successful test or assessment tasks. Via test and assessment analysis, we can, for instance, gain an understanding of the:

1. correctness or appropriateness of students' or test takers' answers or responses.
2. errors or mistakes that students or test takers make when responding to questions or tasks.
3. differences or variations between students' or test takers' performance or responses across various questions or tasks with varying difficulties or demands.
4. the extent to which students or test takers consistently respond to questions or tasks.
5. internal and external factors that influence students' or test-takers' performances.
6. types of feedback to improve the test or assessment quality.

As can be seen from sample yields, when evaluating a language test and assessment, questions often arise regarding its reliability, appropriateness of difficulty levels and fairness for all test takers. Basic test and assessment analysis knowledge is instrumental in addressing these inquiries.

This chapter delves into practical test and assessment analysis that can enhance the quality of language testing and assessment practices. It presents a practical guide for checking and improving test and assessment practice. Exploring item analyses of restricted-response techniques offers valuable insights for readers new to language testing and assessment. This chapter explains the concepts of reliability analysis, which ensures the consistency and dependability of tests and assessments. It also discusses some qualitative analysis of test and assessment data.

Quantitative analysis

This section presents data analysis for language test and assessment validation research. It begins with quantitative data analysis, followed by qualitative analysis. Quantification uses numbers to represent students' or test takers' achievement scores, grades or proficiency levels. For example, writing scores (see Chapter 6) are used to represent how well students can write in an argumentative essay task:

- 6 (Excellent) = fluent expression; ideas clearly stated/supported; succinct; well-organized; logical sequencing; cohesive.
- 3 (Average) = non-fluent; ideas confused or disconnected; lacks logical sequencing and development.
- 1 (Poor) = does not communicate; weak organization of essays; not enough to evaluate.

It should be noted that statistical analysis can be performed using statistical software. Teachers and test and assessment designers will rarely calculate statistics by hand.

Descriptive statistics

Descriptive statistics are ways to understand test scores derived from language tests and assessments. Calculations such as average scores and percentages of performance help gain a holistic view of students' or test takers' performance. Table 9.1 presents the scores of 15 EAL (English as an additional language) students in Australia based on three parallel test forms. Each test had a maximum score of 100.

The number of raw test scores in Table 9.1 can be challenging to understand, as it shows how students performed on each test and how each student performed across the three tests. Therefore, having a single value or score that is the most typical of all test scores is more practical. The following calculations will help explain the test scores in Table 9.1.

TABLE 9.1 Students' Test Scores (*N* = 15)

Students	Gender	Test 1	Test 2	Test 3	Individual mean
1. Peng	Female	78.00	64.00	58.00	66.66
2. Wei	Male	80.00	70.00	68.00	72.66
3. Chai	Female	77.00	78.00	72.00	75.66
4. Kim	Male	77.00	78.00	82.00	79.00
5. Ray	Male	79.00	69.00	65.00	71.00
6. Lan	Other	79.00	68.00	80.00	75.66
7. Yan	Male	72.00	65.00	76.00	71.00
8. Susan	Female	75.00	79.00	72.00	75.33
9. Yo	Other	66.00	72.00	72.0	70.00
10. Qian	Female	71.00	74.00	83.00	76.00
11. Monika	Female	64.00	74.00	68.00	68.66
12. Chatchai	Male	72.00	63.00	68.00	67.66
13. Fang	Other	73.00	88.00	89.00	83.33
14. Mohamad	Male	69.00	68.00	83.00	73.33
15. Ni	Female	77.00	69.00	68.00	71.33
Minimum		64.00	63.00	58.00	66.66
Maximum		80.00	88.00	89.00	83.33
Mean		73.93	71.93	73.60	73.15
Median		75.00	70.00	72.00	77.66
Mode		77.00	68[a].00	68[a].00	71.00
Standard deviation		4.91	6.72	8.37	4.46

Note: [a] Multiple modes exist. The smallest value is shown.

Mean

The mean is the sum of all scores divided by the number of scores, commonly known as the average score. In Table 9.1, the mean scores for Tests 1 to 3 are 73.93, 71.93 and 73.60, respectively. Mean scores that may not represent a group of students or test takers are often affected by rare but extreme scores – known as outliers (i.e. unusually low or high scores) – which need to be checked and removed from the calculation.

Median

The median score is the middle score in a score set arranged from the lowest to the highest. If there is an odd number of scores, the median is the score in the middle, but two scores in the middle are averaged if there is an even number. In the latter case, the median score may not exist in the score set. Test 1 can be arranged as follows (64, 66, 69, 71, 72, 72, 73, 75, 77, 77, 77, 78, 79, 79, 80). The median score is 75 (which is close to the mean score (73.93). It is not a standard measure for statistical calculations.

Mode

The mode is the most frequent score in the dataset. The modes for Tests 1 and 3 are 77 and 68, respectively, but there are three modes (multimodal) in Test 3 (i.e. 68, 74 and 78).

In classroom assessment, the mean score is commonly provided as numerical feedback for students to compare their scores with (average, below average or above average). Knowing the mean score can be informative and help them understand their performance relative to their peers. However, when there is a need to perform inferential statistics such as correlations, the median and mode provide additional information that the mean cannot do. For example, when the mean, median and mode values are similar, the score dataset is likely to be normally distributed – a statistical assumption for many standard statistical tests such as correlation (for identifying a relationship) and regression analysis (for predicting outcomes).

The standard deviation

The standard deviation (SD) provides valuable information about score variability in the dataset. Unlike the range, which is a subtraction between the highest and lowest scores (a rough measure of the spread of the scores), SD uses all test scores in its computation and provides the approximate standard distance of test scores from the mean (above and below). The standard deviation tells us whether the test scores are homogeneous or heterogeneous. If, for example, the standard deviation is zero, there is no variation in the dataset, meaning that all students or test takers have obtained the same score. On the contrary, the larger the standard deviation, the more heterogeneous the score set is. In Table 9.1, Test 1 data (SD = 4.91) are, for example, more homogeneous than Test 3 data (SD = 8.37). The standard deviation indicates the average value of points from which the test scores can be placed around the mean score. Because the standard deviation is usually discussed as a normal dataset distribution, we now explain what a normal distribution is.

The normal distribution

The normal distribution is a bell-shaped distribution of test scores. Figure 9.1 presents a hypothetical normal distribution (Mean = 70, SD = 15). The dashed line in the middle represents the mean, and the shaded grey area indicates

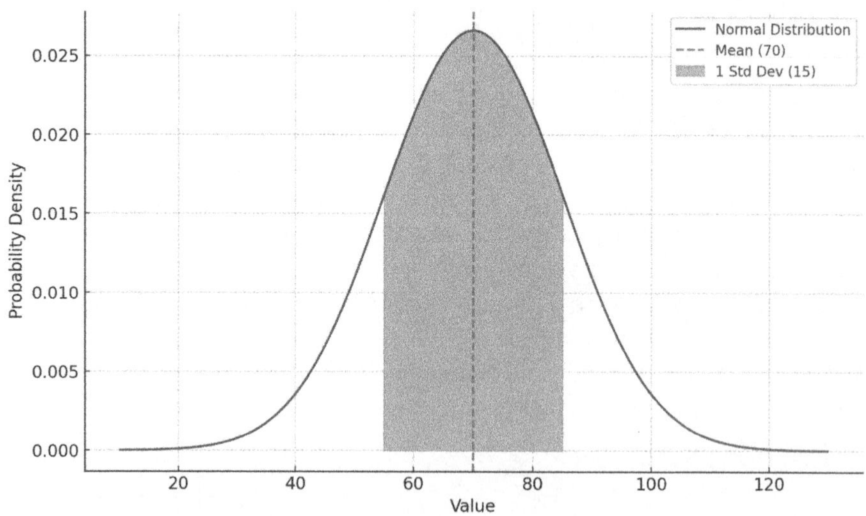

FIGURE 9.1 *A normal distribution based on a hypothetical dataset.*

one standard deviation around the mean. Generally, a test score is plotted along a continuum from the lowest (left) to the highest (right). The figure is symmetric about its mean, showing that scores near the mean are more frequent in occurrence than data far from the mean. In the normal distribution, approximately 68 per cent of the test scores will fall within ±1 standard deviation (between 55 and 85 in Figure 9.1), about 95 per cent within two standard deviations (between 40 and 100), and about 99.7 per cent within three standard deviations (between 25 and 115).

It should be noted that the normal distribution is a statistical assumption for statistical tests such as Pearson correlations, *t*-tests and analysis of variance (ANOVA) in quantitative research (they will be briefly described further below). The concept of normal distribution has influenced the norm-referenced approach discussed in Chapter 2.

Figure 9.2 is an example of the distribution of Test 1 in Table 9.1. In Figure 9.2, the bars indicate the score ranges with frequency counts of different test scores. The normal distribution line was drawn in the middle of the diagram. Figure 9.2 does not show that the dataset (N = 15) is normally distributed since there are missing scores within the normal curve, and more students were placed at the right end of the graph.

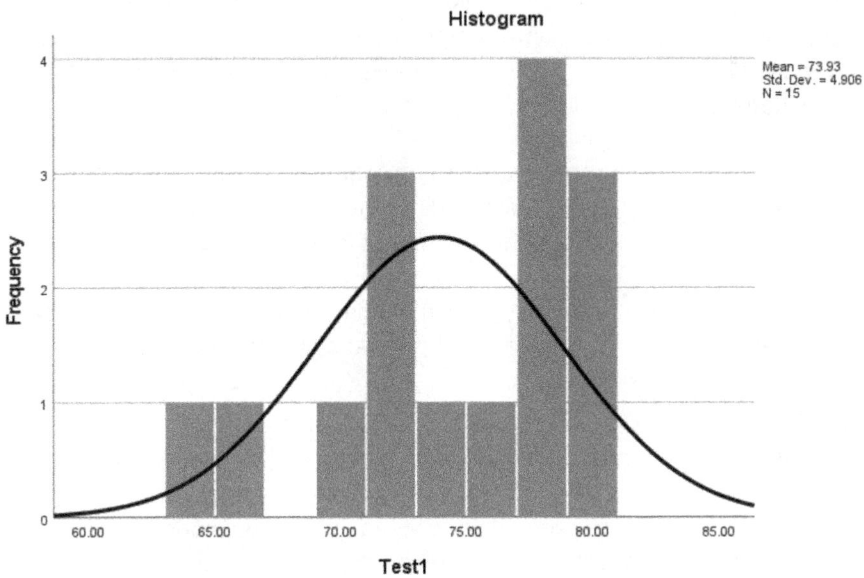

FIGURE 9.2 *Distribution of Test 1 scores (Mean = 73.93, SD = 4.91,* N *= 15).*

Inferential statistics

Inferential statistics are crucial in validating language tests and assessments by examining relationships and differences between variables. Statistical software is widely used for data analysis, including SPSS (Statistical Package for the Social Sciences), *R*, Stata and Excel. They are used to answer validation questions such as relationships between scores from different tests and differences between different groups of students or test takers. Inferential statistics utilize the concept of probability for the findings to occur by chance, typically denoted as the *p*-value. A *p*-value of 0.05 indicates a 5 per cent chance of being wrong in the conclusion about the finding (e.g. a relationship or difference). Statistical significance revolves around accepting a minimal chance of error, typically denoted as a Type I error. This error represents the risk of incorrectly rejecting a null hypothesis (e.g. no relationship, no difference) when it is, in fact, valid. Researchers acknowledge this risk and often set a conventional threshold (such as a *p*-value of less than 0.05 or 0.01) to determine if the observed results can be considered statistically significant, suggesting that the findings are unlikely to have occurred by chance alone. Establishing statistical significance is critical for analysts as it helps validate the reliability and validity of the test or assessment. It ascertains that the results are not merely due to random variations or measurement errors.

This section overviews commonly used inferential statistics in test and assessment analysis. This chapter presents only statistical tests that require test data to be normally distributed (see above) (see Roever & Phakiti 2018 for various statistical tests in detail).

1 *Pearson product-moment correlation* examines linear relationships between two variables, such as different test scores and scores from two raters. By linear, we mean whether and to what extent one score increases, the other will increase (positive correlation) or decrease (negative correlation). Through correlational analysis, we can determine whether one variable has a significant relationship and, if so, how strongly they are related.

2 *Regression analysis* is an extension of correlation analysis that determines whether a variable, such as test performance, can be significantly predicted from the value of another variable (e.g. other test scores). Simple regression focuses on the prediction of one variable on the other variable. Multiple regression investigates the relative predictions of two or more variables on another variable (e.g. IELTS and TOEFL scores are used to predict students' and test takers' academic assignment performance at university).

3 *T-test* allows investigators to determine whether the difference in the means of the two datasets is statistically significant. A paired-samples *t*-test examines whether two mean scores from the same group of participants differ significantly (e.g. comparing Forms A and B scores). An independent-samples t-test investigates whether the mean scores between two groups of students or test takers are significantly different (e.g. male and female comparison).

4 *Analyses of Variance (ANOVA)* provide answers similar to the *t*-tests above but are used when at least three datasets are to be compared. A within-group ANOVA serves a similar analysis to a paired-samples *t*-test (e.g. comparing three test scores of the same students). A between-groups ANOVA is similar to an independent-sample *t*-test (e.g. comparing test performances between beginner, intermediate and advanced students).

5 *Factor analysis* is valuable for examining the underlying language factors influencing test performance. Expanding on correlational analysis, it aids in streamlining assessments by identifying redundant items unrelated to the broader factors affecting performance. By pinpointing items that do not align with these factors, factor analysis helps refine and optimize test instruments.

In summary, descriptive and inferential statistics play an important role in test and assessment analysis as they allow us to go beyond raw test scores, which can be less comprehensible when it comes to understanding commonalities or patterns of performance.

Item analysis of restricted-response techniques

In many language testing and assessment situations, including classroom contexts, restricted-response techniques yield a dichotomous score (i.e. 0 or 1) aggregated into a total score. We do not often use a total score to know how the test questions or task perform to elicit relevant abilities or skills unless we are interested in understanding group differences or correlations between different test sections or tests. It is more useful to analyse the quality of test items or questions, prompting confirmation of their effectiveness or needs to improve or refine them. Item analysis informs test and assessment designers of the quality characteristics of questions/tasks (see Lynch 2002; Green 2013). It should be stressed that item-level analysis can be performed using software such as Excel and SPSS. Hand calculation is labour-intensive and prone to human error. The manual calculation provided is for conceptually illustrative purposes.

The most basic item-level analysis is investigating the *mean score* of item performance. If the mean score is high, it suggests that a given item or task is easy for students or test takers. However, the mean score does not provide precise information on how students' or test takers' performance is captured. Three valuable item analyses are introduced as follows.

Item difficulty index

An item difficulty index indicates the proportion of students answering a question correctly (i.e. the number of students who answer the item correctly divided by the number of all people).

Step 1: Count the number of test takers who get each item correct.
Step 2: Divide this number by the total number of students (i.e. the mean).

The higher the value, the easier the test item. The item difficulty value ranges between 0 and 1 and can be interpreted as the percentage of correction. The higher the value, the easier the item is indicated to be. For example, Question 1 has an item difficulty index of 0.80, meaning 80 per cent of the students can answer it correctly. In contrast, Question 10 has an item difficulty index of 0.50, meaning 50 per cent of the students can answer it correctly. Based on the analysis, Question 1 is much easier than Question 10. Ideally, when developing items for use, an item difficulty index between 0.4 and 0.60 is ideal because questions will be challenging enough for students to complete.

Item discrimination

Item discrimination indicates the extent to which students' total scores are associated with their scores on a given question. Do students who receive a low total score also get the item wrong? An item discrimination index is known as a point-biserial correlation (item-to-total).

Step 1: Students are grouped into, for example, top, middle, and bottom thirds (i.e. about 33 per cent).
Step 2: The item difficulty for each group is calculated.
Step 3: The item difficulty of the bottom-third group is subtracted from that of the top-third group. This results in an item discrimination index.

For example, suppose in Question 1, the item difficulty value of the top 33 per cent group is 0.95 (i.e. 19 points (based on 20 students) ÷ 20) and the item difficulty value of the bottom 33 per cent group is 0.44 (i.e. 8 points (based on 18 students) ÷ 18). In that case, the item discrimination index (similar to the point-biserial correlation) is 0.51 (i.e. 0.95 – 0.44). As a rule of thumb, a value above 0.40 indicates that item discrimination is reasonable (in good order) for discriminating different ability levels.

Distractor analysis

Distractor analysis examines the reliability of the options in multiple-choice questions. A good distractor is determined by an observation that it tends to be chosen more frequently by students who achieve low scores than those who achieve high scores. The analysis, therefore, involves identifying and examining the overall scores of all students who choose each distractor. Information from distractor analysis tells test and assessment designers the distribution of students of different ability groups across all answer choices. If any ability groups do not choose some distractors, a revision of those distractors is considered. The point-biserial index for distractor analysis should be at least 0.25 (as compared to 0.40 for the discrimination index).

In analysing restricted-response test questions such as multiple-choice questions, Rasch Item Response Theory (IRT), which can be performed using IRT software, helps determine the difficulty of each question and the ability level required to answer it correctly. Here, IRT analysis will be used. IRT examines how students with different ability levels perform on each question. It assumes that each test item has a unique difficulty level, and that students' responses depend on both their ability and the difficulty of the items. It can then estimate the difficulty of each question and the student's ability level. It can also provide information about how well the questions discriminate between students of different ability levels and identify questions that are too easy or too difficult relative to their ability level. Questions 54 and 55 are examples of multiple-choice questions in a reading test for Thai students to illustrate distractor analysis (Phakiti 2003).

54. Which of the following weather conditions in the north is not mentioned?
    (a) cloudy (b) heavy rain
    (c) sunny (d) thunder showers

55. Which province is not mentioned in the passage?
    (a) Chiang Mai (b) Chonburi
    (c) Phuket (d) Saraburi

Source: Phakiti (2003)

Item 54					
Categories	a	b	c*	d	missing
Count	59	8	416	102	1
Per cent (%)	10.1	1.4	71.1	17.4	
Pt-Biserial	–.01	–.04	**.20**	–.22	

Item 55					
Categories	a	b	c	d*	missing
Count	62	195	33	295	1
Per cent (%)	10.6	33.3	5.6	50.4	
Pt-Biserial	–.17	–.34	–.14	**.49**	

FIGURE 9.3 *Rasch Item Response Theory (IRT) distractor analysis (N = 586, Phakiti 2003).*

Figure 9.3 shows an example of IRT distractor analysis (only distractor analysis results provided) that compares two test items (Items 54 and 55).

In Figure 9.3, the correct alternative is labelled with an asterisk (*). Count refers to the number of students and test takers who chose each alternative. In Item 54, 416 students (71 per cent) chose Option c. Only eight students chose Option b (1.4 per cent). The analysis shows that some distractors might not attract students with weaker abilities, which will prompt an investigation of the options for further evaluation and revision. The point-biserial index for Item 54 was 0.20, which was below 0.25. This suggests that the distractors did not perform at the expected standard. In contrast, Item 55 shows better distributions of students and test takers choosing different options (Option c may be investigated further to evaluate why only 33 students (5.6 per cent) chose it). The point-biserial value of 0.49 suggests the item has a good distractor index, implying that students and test takers with low scores tend to choose those distractors.

In summary, the usefulness of these item analyses depends on the nature of students or test takers. The greater the variation of ability level within a group and the larger the sample size, the more accurate and valuable the analysis will be. It should be noted that there are other complex item and test analyses used in the field that are not explained in this chapter (e.g. many-faceted Rasch), Generalizability theory (G-theory) and DIF analysis (see Phakiti 2023 and further reading at the end of this chapter).

Reliability estimates

Chapter 4 discussed the concept of test and assessment reliability. This section discusses how it is operationalized in test and assessment analysis. In quantitative analysis, a reliability coefficient is used to define the level of test reliability. It ranges between 0 (0 per cent reliable) and 1 (100 per cent reliable). The higher the test reliability coefficient, the smaller the error in a test score. However, a reliability coefficient of 1 (perfect reliability) is rare (see Chapter 2 on factors affecting test and assessment performance; Bachman & Palmer 1996). This section presents methods for investigating reliability estimates of (1) objective and (2) subjective scores.

Reliability of objective scores

This section presents five reliability analyses that can be performed on objective scores (see Chapter 2 for explanations of objective scoring).

Test-retest reliability

Test-retest reliability is related to the idea that a test should be stable in eliciting a language construct of interest. Conceptually, a test taken by the same students today, yesterday or tomorrow should yield similar results. This concept can be challenging to realize in reality since students learn from taking a test, and if they retake it, they are likely to perform better, meaning that the reliability of the test cannot be that stable. Suppose Tests 1 and 2 in Table 9.1 were the same test taken twice by the same students (noting the small sample size of 15), the same student did not obtain the same or similar score. It suggests that the test-retest reliability is low. This concept, however, is unrealistic in that students can never take the same test twice as each time they complete it, they will learn something and try to improve their performance. There is also a memory factor that will affect the second performance. Language tests and assessments differ from other scales, such as those for measuring weights and heights, which will be more or less stable (today, yesterday and tomorrow, our weights or heights should be similar or the same).

Split-half reliability

Given the difficulty of administering the same test twice, the concept of split-half reliability was developed. To calculate this, a test is only administered once, and the test scores are split into two halves, based on, for instance, odd- and even-numbered questions. For example, if ten questions assess the ability to extract factual and specific information from texts, scores for questions 1, 3, 5, 7 and 9 form the first set of scores, and scores for questions 2, 4, 6, 8 and 10 form the second set. A correlation coefficient for the two sets can be calculated. Theoretically, this method aims to determine the internal consistency level of a given test. It, therefore, assumes that for a given test, each student or test taker should perform consistently well or poorly throughout. When their performance is split into two halves, there should be a strong correlation between the scores in those two halves. This correlation is then inferred to represent the whole test reliability estimate. A formula that is used to adjust the split-half correlation is known as the Spearman–Brown prophecy (see Brown 2005), which can also be computed in statistical software, including the SPSS program (see Roever & Phakiti 2018 for how to compute it in SPSS).

While split-half reliability seems appealing initially, this estimate is overly optimistic. For example, in any language test, not all the questions are designed to be equally difficult, and different questions may be designed to measure different language skills. Therefore, splitting test items into two halves for calculation can be theoretically problematic. Furthermore, this reliability method may be more applicable for some test techniques (e.g. true–false, multiple-choice) than others (e.g. cloze, gap-filling).

Cronbach's alpha

Cronbach's alpha coefficient (α) is an alternative to the split-half method and has been used commonly for examining the internal consistency of language tests and Likert-scale questionnaires. Cronbach's alpha can be calculated by hand using a formula, but statistical software is widely used and recommended as results are more accurate than those computed by hand. Generally speaking, Cronbach's alpha coefficient (ranging between 0 and 1) can be used to determine whether the test questions consistently elicit students' and test takers' responses. When the coefficient is strong (e.g. above 0.70), it suggests a good internal consistency of the test. Cronbach's alpha is not without its caveats. For example, its reliability estimate is affected by the number of questions in the test and the sample size. It also has stringent statistical assumptions (e.g. the scores must be continuous and normally distributed, and the errors for the test questions should not correlate; see McNeish 2018), which causes difficulty in analysing language test data.

Alternate or parallel-forms reliability

This reliability analysis helps establish criterion-related validity (e.g. concurrent validity; see Chapter 4). When test and assessment developers have designed a test and assessment specification, they should be able to develop various test forms – known as parallel forms, equivalent forms or alternate forms. Methodologically, the same test takers complete both forms (Forms A and B). A correlation coefficient between their two test scores is next computed (note that the sample size should be large). A strong correlation suggests that both forms assess the same language constructs consistently. However, it is essential to note that it is not straightforward to be sure whether two test forms are equal in terms of difficulty and the cognitive and linguistic processes required to complete by simply showing a strong correlation between them.

Kuder–Richardson 20 and 21 reliability estimates

The Kuder–Richardson (KR) 20 and 21 coefficients are commonly used for language test and assessment reliability analysis. The score can range from 0 to 1. KR21 is relatively easy to calculate by hand (see Brown 2005; Douglas 2010). Brown (2005) notes that KR21 is prone to underestimating the reliability of a test and that KR20 is a more robust and realistic estimate of test reliability than KR21 (see Brown 2005, p. 181). These analyses can be performed in statistical software using responses from students or test takers.

Standard error of measurement

As discussed in Chapter 4 and the section above, the reliability estimate of a given test and assessment provides information about how much error variance is present in a test and assessment score (see Chapter 2). It is now appropriate to discuss the concept of the standard error of measurement (SEM). SEM is based on classical test theory and norm-referenced testing. It can be used to determine the range of possible scores a given student or test taker may fall into if they repeat the same test. The analysis here focuses on the whole test rather than an item.

For example, hypothetically, when the reliability estimate of a given test is 1, there is no measurement error. This means that the same student will probably obtain the same score when taking the same test for the second time in the same conditions. It means that there is no range score for students and test takers. However, a reliability estimate is neither 1 nor 0 in reality.

Theoretically, SEM determines a 68 per cent confidence band in which 68 per cent of the test scores will fall within ±1 standard deviation. So, if Mary takes the same test twice, 68 per cent of the time, her scores will be within a particular range.

SEM can be calculated by hand as follows:

$$SD^*\sqrt{[1 - \text{reliability estimate}]}$$

Where SD = a standard deviation of the whole test scores.

For example, if a test has a reliability coefficient of 0.85 and SD is 1.3, the SEM of this test can be computed as:

$SEM = 1.3^*\sqrt{[1–0.85]}$
$SEM = 1.3^*\sqrt{.15}$
$SEM = 1.3^*0.387$
$SEM = 0.50$

The addition and subtraction of the SEM score can create a possible range of a students' or test taker's score. For example, if Mary scores 4 out of 10 (4 ± 0.5), her possible score can be between 4.5 and 5.5 (68 per cent of the time).

Reliability of subjective scores

As discussed in Chapters 6 and 8, a rater makes subjective judgements on students' and test takers' performances in performance assessments, such as writing and speaking. Hence, the consistency of the raters' scoring needs to be examined. A reliability estimate of subjective scoring would tell us the extent of their scoring consistency and whether their scores are similar to those of other raters. The following reliability analyses are based on classical test theory (CTT) that are commonly used. It should also be noted that performing reliability analysis (even if it is not the best) is better than not performing it at all.

Intra-rater reliability

The underlying concept of intra-rater reliability is similar to internal consistency reliability in objective scoring. If the same raters score the same responses on different days, will they give the same or similar score? Table 9.2 is used to illustrate a rater's scoring consistency. Next, a correlation coefficient of the two test scores is computed (note: a small sample size is used in this illustration). Typically, a strong correlation coefficient implies that raters are

TABLE 9.2 Sample Scores of a Writing Test Based on One Rater (5-Point Holistic Scoring)

Test taker ID	Time	Time 2
1	3	3
2	1	4
3	2	2
4	5	4
5	5	3
6	4	1
7	3	3
8	3	3
9	1	1
10	5	5
11	3	3
12	3	4
13	4	4
14	1	3
15	2	2
16	2	3
17	2	4
18	5	3
19	4	3
20	5	4

consistent in their scoring. A correlation coefficient of at least 0.70 is desirable for intra-rater reliability. In Table 9.2, a Pearson correlation was found to be 0.35 ($p = 0.129$), suggesting that this rater was not highly consistent in rating the same performance twice. Note that the coefficient was, for illustration purposes, based on a small sample ($n = 20$).

TABLE 9.3 Scores of a Writing Test Based on Two Raters (5-Point Holistic Scoring)

Test taker ID	Rater 1	Rater 2	Exact agreement	Adjacent agreement
1	3	4	0	1
2	2	2	1	1
3	2	2	1	1
4	5	4	0	1
5	5	5	1	1
6	4	3	0	1
7	3	3	1	1
8	3	3	1	1
9	2	2	1	1
10	5	5	1	1
11	3	3	1	1
12	3	2	0	1
13	2	5	0	0
14	1	1	1	1
15	4	3	0	1
16	5	4	1	1
17	3	3	1	1
18	4	3	0	1
19	5	5	1	1
20	1	2	0	1
Total			12/20 = 60%	19/20 = 95%

Inter-rater reliability

Inter-rater reliability is similar to intra-rater reliability, but instead of obtaining the scores from the same rater twice, two or more raters are asked to rate the same responses. To compute inter-rater reliability, the scores given by each rater are put in two columns (see Table 9.3), and a correlation coefficient is calculated. A correlation coefficient of at least 0.70 is desirable for inter-rater reliability. Based on Table 9.3, the Pearson correlation coefficient was 0.726 ($p < 0.001$). The coefficient suggests that the two raters scored similarly in the same essay.

Agreement in percentages

A simple method, such as calculating a percentage agreement between two raters, can be considered if the sample size is small. Table 9.3 includes the percentage agreement calculation.

- *Exact agreement* refers to absolute agreement between two raters' scores. To calculate an exact agreement, 1 is given when the two raters assign the same score and 0 when they assign a different score. In Table 9.3, it was found that the exact agreement was 60 per cent.
- *Adjacent agreement* refers to a relative agreement between two raters whose scores differ by no more than 1 point (meaning that one is also given when the two raters assign a 1-point difference). Adjacent agreement, therefore, includes exact agreement data in its calculation. In Table 9.3, the adjacent agreement was 95 per cent.

It is important to note that agreements in such calculations are affected by the rating scales (e.g. the number of score points; fewer points result in a higher chance for agreement, e.g. a 4-point scale has a higher chance of having an agreed score than a 6-point scale) and sample size. Caution, therefore, is needed when using rater agreement to represent inter-rater reliability. Owing to their weaknesses, both exact and adjacent agreements are not used in standardized tests and assessments. However, it is better to investigate rater agreements than not check them. For classroom assessment with a small sample size of students, agreement indices between teachers are useful to warrant some decision-making.

Cohen's kappa

Cohen's kappa is a more robust method for evaluating inter-rater agreements, especially with a large sample size. It considers the agreement observed between two raters while accounting for the agreement that can be expected to occur by chance alone. Table 9.4 presents a cross-tabulation of the scores

TABLE 9.4 Cross-Tabulation of the Scores for the Two Raters (5-Point Holistic Scoring)

		Rater 2					Total
		1.00	2.00	3.00	4.00	5.00	
Rater 1	1.00	1	1	0	0	0	2
	2.00	0	3	0	0	1	4
	3.00	0	1	4	1	0	6
	4.00	0	0	3	0	0	3
	5.00	0	0	0	2	3	5
Total		1	5	7	3	4	20

for Raters 1 and 2. The kappa coefficient was found to be 0.414. Note again that Cohen's kappa can be calculated using statistical software.

The following are general interpretations of kappa's coefficients (see Roever & Phakiti 2018): 0.00–0.20 (weak), 0.21–0.40 (fair), 0.41–0.60 (moderate), 0.61–0.80 (strong) and 0.81—1.00 (very strong). A Cohen's kappa value of 0.414 indicates fair to moderate agreement between the two raters. This means that while there is some agreement between the raters, achieving higher consistency in their ratings can be possible.

Analysis of differential item functioning

Differential item functioning (DIF) refers to a testing or assessment situation in which some grouping characteristics of students or test takers (e.g. gender, age, disability, ethnicity, nationalities, social class, religion) who are at the same ability or skill level can cause a relative disadvantage in completing test questions or tasks. This analysis was introduced briefly in Chapter 4. It is important not to confuse DIF with item discrimination, in which different ability levels are expected to be more or less successful in completing test items or tasks. Readers new to this area will probably run into publications discussing DIF analysis, so this section only introduces some basic concepts.

DIF can be observed when, for example, two students or test takers who are at the same level but belong to a different grouping characteristic (e.g.

gender) do not have an equal chance or likelihood of being successful in a given test question or task. Unlike DIF, differential test functioning (DTF) refers to bias at an item/task group level. DIF examines an item level, whereas DTF examines a group of items that measure the same or relevant test constructs. Despite the distinction, the analysis procedures are similar. The differential functioning of an entire test can also be investigated.

DIF analysis with dichotomous and polytomous items or tasks is relatively straightforward, as scoring is objective. When scoring is subjective, raters, for example, can exhibit bias or influence differential performance, and this can be best addressed in a multifaceted IRT. DIF suggests that bias exists within a given test or assessment (e.g. item, task or test level). Hence, DIF is considered a threat to test and assessment quality because some groups of students or test takers are not fairly assessed. DIF analysis is critical as it addresses not only issues of test fairness but also those of test validity (e.g. when people of the same ability level do not have an equal chance of being successful, test scores cannot be reliable and valid) and impact. Although DIF is usually considered in test design (e.g. choosing topics, ensuring task familiarity), a statistical analysis (DIF analysis) is conducted after a test is given to students and test takers.

Researchers commonly consider concrete grouping characteristics of students and test takers and use them to compare performance in test items or tasks. Apart from concrete grouping factors, test validators can also use latent groupings (trait characteristics) in DIF analysis (e.g. computer skills, anxiety, mental health). Test validators may consider a mixed model of DIF analysis in which both concrete and latent groupings are considered. A DIF conceptual approach is simple in that a focal group is expected to be disadvantaged. In contrast, a reference group is expected or known to have an advantage in answering a question or task. However, statistical DIF methods are sophisticated as test validators use statistics such as regression and IRT analyses. If the effect size is moderate or large, they need to take action to ensure equality in performance. DIF and DTF results help researchers address the question of construct relevance and construct-underrepresentation, as discussed in Chapter 4.

It is important to note that since the validity of the decision on a differential item or test functioning is critical, this method requires a large sample size because a small sample size produces a heightened chance of statistical errors. DIF results also depend on who participates in the data collection phase (i.e. the group representatives). Often, it is not practical to adopt such a statistical method for classroom assessment. Hence, a qualitative method and careful considerations in test or assessment design and test content analysis are more achievable. To learn more, see Jiao and Chen (2014).

In summary, it should be noted that test developers, especially in large-scale standardized testing, are likely to perform more sophisticated rater analysis in standardized large-scale tests with a high-stakes decision on students and test takers, such as many-faceted Rasch analysis for rater analysis (see Aryadoust, Ng & Sayama 2021). This analysis is robust, particularly in contexts in which multiple sources of variability need to be considered simultaneously. It helps test developers understand the nuances of the rating process and make informed decisions about improving the reliability and validity of ratings. This level of analysis is beyond the scope of this chapter (see 'Further reading').

Qualitative data analysis

In language testing and assessment, qualitative data such as actual test or assessment responses, interview scripts and performance observations can be useful in learning about the quality of a language test or assessment. Diverse ways, such as reflections, diaries, open questionnaires, interviews and psycholinguistic methods (e.g. eye-tracking and priming), can also be used to collect qualitative information from students or test takers.

For example, in a cognitive interview, students can be asked how they completed the test (e.g. how they derived the answer). The following is an excerpt from Phakiti (2024) in which a student (Liang) was asked what he did in an independent writing task.

> After reading the questions, I just started to think about what I'm going to say, to choose, to think of the ideas I want to say, because I, yeah, I started to think about my own opinion, about the importance of the sporting facilities and at the same time to think of some ideas to support both sides in terms of health. And you'll need to analyse things from different perspectives. And you cannot just say, 'I don't like something or favour something.' You need to analyse and evaluate both sides.

However, Liang approached the integrated writing task quite similarly to the independent writing task. It appears that Liang also attempted to understand the task and requirements, but more by conceptualizing ideas than reading the source texts.

> So, after reading the questions, I started reading the passage to get the main idea. Then, I tried to use the ideas from that passage to support the things I wanted to write.

These are just examples of what we can learn about students' and test takers' test-taking processes and determine whether they engage in the test or assessment tasks as we expect them to. In these excerpts, it appears that Liang engaged in the test tasks. This information is useful for test analysis and quality.

There are various ways to analyse qualitative data, depending on the questions we want to answer. Therefore, learning about qualitative research methodology (e.g. purposive sampling methods and inductive approach) is important before analysing qualitative data (see Miles, Huberman & Saldaña 2014). It should be noted that much qualitative data is subjective in that it requires interpretations and involves personal viewpoints. This method is compatible with classroom language testing and assessment as teachers and students share their socio-cultural and trustworthiness perspectives (see Chapter 4).

Owing to the introductory nature of this book, this chapter illustrates thematic analysis as practical methods that help language teachers, testers and assessors to organize and interpret qualitative data (e.g. interviews, observations, and verbal and written reports) to improve and validate their language tests and assessments. Thematic analysis can address various evaluative questions about, for example, evidence of test and assessment content, test-taking processes, and perceived test and assessment usefulness and impact.

Thematic analysis

Braun and Clarke (2006, 2019) propose a systematic thematic qualitative data analysis framework. A theme can be understood as a concept relevant to a research question about language testing and assessment. It can describe the patterns or features of, for instance, test-taking and assessment-completion behaviours. Various types of themes and thematic analysis can be performed (Braun & Clarke 2006), for example, by developing codes from data (inductive thematic analysis), using theory to analyse data (theoretical thematic analysis), analysing surface meaning (semantic themes) and focusing on underlying assumptions or concepts (latent themes). Intra- and inter-coder reliability (similar to those in rater reliability discussed above) is vital for categorizing and grouping data consistently and accurately. Two or more coders may code the same data to check consistency in coding.

Braun and Clarke's (2006) thematic analysis includes:

1. familiarizing with the data through data transcription and multiple readings of the transcripts.
2. generating initial codes (e.g. semantic and latent codes).
3. searching for themes and extracts and choosing the relevant themes.
4. refining codes for a coding scheme containing significant themes and sub-themes.
5. mapping and relating themes, for example, through visual representations.
6. interpreting themes, including comparing patterns in themes among groups of participants.

Example 1 of thematic analysis

Twenty test takers were interviewed to understand their experiences and perceptions of the usefulness and impact of an English proficiency test they had taken. The data was then analysed thematically following the steps discussed above. Four common themes were identified among the interviewees regarding their experiences and perceived test usefulness.

Themes about students' and test takers' experiences and perceived usefulness of the test

1. *Challenges in test-taking preparation*: Many students (n = 15) reported facing challenges in preparing for the English test, including understanding task requirements and expected responses, finding relevant study materials and managing time effectively during test-taking. Some test takers (n = 8) expressed concerns about the difficulty level of the test and the need for intensive preparation to achieve desired scores.
2. *Experienced stress and anxiety*: A significant number of test takers (n = 17) expressed experiencing stress and anxiety during the English test, which they perceived to be a substantial factor impacting their performance. Their anxiety came from the fact that they were not familiar with the new test tasks. Test takers (n = 12) highlighted their pressure to perform well in the test due to its implications for academic and career aspirations. Some test takers (n = 8) also emphasized the importance of their abilities to manage test-related stress through adequate preparation and coping strategies effectively.
3. *Perceived usefulness of the test for academic studies*: Almost all the students and test takers (n = 19) highlighted the importance of the test

scores that would help them gain admission to educational institutions, especially in English-speaking countries. Many participants (*n* = 11) viewed the test as a reliable measure of their English language proficiency, essential for success in academic settings. However, seven students and test takers were unsure because they were unfamiliar with the topics used in the test. Some test takers (*n* = 7) noted that achieving high scores on the test might open up opportunities for scholarships and academic advancement. In contrast, others (*n* = 5) thought scholarships could not be decided merely from the test performance.

4 *Impact on future communication skills in English*: Several positive impacts were found. For example, students and test takers (*n* = 13) acknowledged the positive role of test scores in enhancing their confidence and proficiency in communicating in English, both academically and professionally. Many test tasks included real-life language scenarios that could be learned from, especially from pragmatic and social skills. These opportunities helped to increase their confidence. Several test takers (*n* = 9) believed that performing well on the English test improved their chances of securing employment. Some students and test takers (*n* = 6) mentioned that the English test experience helped them develop effective communication strategies and adapt to diverse linguistic contexts.

Summary: The thematic analysis reflects the multifaceted nature of students' and test takers' experiences and perceptions regarding the English proficiency test, encompassing both the challenges and opportunities associated with this test in the context of academic studies and future communication in English.

Example 2 of thematic analysis

Two raters who were employed to score internet-based integrated writing responses were interviewed after they completed their rating (data from Phakiti 2024). The focus of the interview was on issues they faced during their rating. Six themes emerged from their interviews.

Six themes on issues related to the raters' rating processes and performances

1 *Time management*: Both raters expressed concerns about the additional time required to familiarize themselves with the source material and assess its integration into the essay. Rater 1 mentioned the potential impact of this requirement on raters' workload, considering the number of tasks they must evaluate per day.

2 *Complexity of essay evaluation*: Rater 2 highlighted the challenges of distinguishing between memorized content, paraphrasing and verbatim copying from the source text. Both raters emphasized the need to be familiar with the source material to assess its usage in the essay accurately.

3 *Experienced impact on rater bias*: Rater 1 raised concerns about the possibility of rater bias influencing the assessment of students' and test takers' essays, especially regarding candidates' opinions on contentious topics that the raters might personally disagree with. Both raters noted that introducing the Turnitin program for assessing source material before their rating would be problematic because it would introduce potentially additional subjectivity or intermediary influence into the evaluation process. They felt they would be harsher in their ratings when they saw that students and test takers used source texts verbatim or without acknowledging them. This could affect their focus on other good aspects of students' and test takers' written responses.

4 *Clarity of assessment criteria related to essay content*: Rater 1 expressed occasional uncertainty about the ideal balance between candidate-generated content and content derived from the source material. Both raters highlighted the need for clear guidelines on referencing requirements and the extent to which content from the source material should be incorporated into the response.

5 *Rater workload and efficiency*: Both raters discussed the future challenges of evaluating multiple test tasks with different source texts, emphasizing the increased workload and time required to familiarize with a given integrated prompt and source texts. Concerns were raised about maintaining the balance between assessment speed and accuracy, mainly when dealing with tasks of different prompts.

6 *Standardization of scoring*: Rater 2 compared the evaluation process to standardized tests such as the IELTS independent essay task, highlighting differences in workload and standardized evaluation criteria between the two assessment tasks (independent versus integrated tasks). The latter tended to be less standardized.

Summary: This thematic analysis reveals six critical issues regarding the challenges and considerations of evaluating integrated writing essay tests. These include time management problems, assessment complexity, potential bias, clarity of assessment criteria, examiner workload and standardization of evaluation practices.

Qualitative data analysis software

Various qualitative data analysis software has been developed to assist in qualitative data analysis and management. Many programs help organize and manage multiple data sets (e.g. interviews, images, documents) for a single analysis, identify suggested themes and patterns, and display data visually (e.g. hierarchical structures of themes). For example, NUD*IST (for Mac), NVivo (for PC) and MAXQDA (for Mac and PC) can generate automated codes and multilevel coding systems based on the given data files.

As with quantitative analysis that employs software, caution must be taken when using qualitative software in data analysis. While the software may suggest themes or codes, it does not understand the research context or the meanings people make to communicate in a given data collection. Therefore, the data analysts are responsible for making informed decisions regarding coding and interpreting the data based on their analytical skills and knowledge. That is, one should not be tempted to say, for example, 'NVivo is used for qualitative data analysis and suggests five levels of test takers' processes', just as they would not say 'SPSS is used for quantitative data analysis and suggests a near statistical significance' in their report.

Additionally, as with other statistical programs, language teachers, testers or assessors need to know what qualitative software is most appropriate for the kind of data analysis required for their project, whether specific software is acceptable for use by other researchers, and whether qualitative software can be used at all for a particular data analysis approach. Finally, researchers should have sufficient time to learn and train themselves to use specific qualitative software to maximize its capacity to assist in their qualitative data analysis.

Summary

This chapter has explored the multifaceted world of test and assessment analysis methods in language testing and assessment. It discussed and exemplified applications of quantitative and qualitative data analysis methods, accompanied by practical examples, for language test and assessment research. The next chapter will conclude this book by discussing challenges and opportunities in language testing and assessment.

Discussion

1 What is a quantitative analysis of language test and assessment data? How does it differ from qualitative analysis?

2 What quantitative and qualitative analysis techniques introduced in this chapter could be relevant to your current testing and assessment situations? Why do you think so?

3 What quantitative or qualitative analysis techniques do you consider less likely for you to need to know or use? Why?

4 Have the various data analysis approaches presented in this chapter enhanced your understanding of how to ensure the quality of tests and assessments? Articulate your answer.

Further reading

Aryadoust, V. & Raquel, M. (eds), 2019, *Quantitative data analysis for language assessment volume 1: Fundamental techniques*, Routledge, Abingdon and New York.

This book outlines various practical statistical analysis techniques for validating language tests and assessments. These include item analysis, generalizability analysis, unidimensional Rasch analysis, differential item functioning analysis, many-faceted Rasch analysis and standard techniques such as ANOVA, linear regression and exploratory factor analysis.

Aryadoust, V. & Raquel, M. (eds), 2019, *Quantitative data analysis for language assessment volume 2: Advanced methods*, Routledge, Abingdon and New York.

This book provides advanced methods for Rasch analysis, multilevel analysis, structural equation modelling and data-mining techniques. These sophisticated approaches offer deeper insights and enhanced capabilities for analysing language testing and assessment data.

Bachman, L.F., 2004, *Statistical analyses for language assessment*, Cambridge, Cambridge University Press.

This book elucidates fundamental concepts and approaches to statistical methods for language testing and assessment research. It caters to individuals seeking to understand statistical inferences and decisions with the underlying formulae of specific statistical analysis techniques.

Creswell, J.W. & Plano Clark, V.L., 2018, *Designing and conducting mixed methods research*, 3rd edn, SAGE, Los Angeles, London, New Delhi, Singapore and Washington DC.

This book offers detailed guidance on designing various types of mixed methods research and systematically analysing mixed data. It provides step-by-step instructions and numerous examples applicable to test and assessment analysis.

Douglas, D., 2010, *Understanding language testing*, Hodder Education, London.

Chapter 5 of the book expands on the application of numbers in language testing, offering further examples and delving into descriptive statistics, a concept introduced in the current chapter. Additionally, it presents other statistical methods, such as correlations and *t*-tests, which were not addressed in the current chapter.

Flick, U., 2018, *An introduction to qualitative research*, 6th edn, SAGE, Los Angeles, London and New Delhi.

This updated edition builds upon its previous comprehensive versions, which extensively covered qualitative research design and analysis. It is particularly recommended for readers who are new to qualitative research methodologies.

Green, R., 2013, *Statistical analyses for language testers*, Palgrave Macmillan, Basingstoke.

This volume is tailored for readers new to statistics and its application in language testing. It covers descriptive and inferential statistics and various item-level analysis techniques, such as item difficulty, discrimination and distractor analysis.

Miles, M.B., Huberman, A.M. & Saldaña, J., 2014, *Qualitative data analysis: A methods sourcebook*, 3rd edn, SAGE, Los Angeles, London and New Delhi.

This book has been regarded as the bible of qualitative data analysis. It provides a complete picture of qualitative research from design to analysis and reports.

Roever, C. & Phakiti, A., 2018, *Quantitative methods for second language research: A problem-solving approach*, Routledge, New York and London.

The book extensively explores quantitative methods in language research. Many standard approaches and statistical tests are presented with practical illustrations of how to perform them in SPSS.

10

Challenges and Opportunities

Overview

This final chapter concludes this book by discussing challenges and opportunities in language testing and assessment. It showcases the challenges of applying computer-assisted language testing and assessment (CALTA) in terms of testing and assessment qualities and then discusses future opportunities in this field.

Guided questions

1. Which language testing and assessment topics in this book particularly intrigue you, and why?
2. What are some key challenges encountered in language testing and assessment?
3. How does computer technology attract the interest of both language assessors and teachers?

Introduction

Throughout this book, we have explored language testing and assessment by examining the key considerations, foundational principles, methodologies and critical issues in designing, implementing and utilizing language tests and assessments. We have covered a wide range of topics, such as the purposes of language testing and assessment, alignments between teaching and assessment, theoretical frameworks for understanding additional language (AL) proficiency and skills, standards for evaluating the qualities of language testing and assessment, testing and assessment techniques for assessing specific language skills, and methods for analysing language testing and assessment data.

Davidson and Lynch (2002) emphasize that while accessible instructions and guidelines for developing language tests and assessments exist, no universal recipe and formula can guarantee that our language testing and assessment practices will be successful. Although this book does not provide a one-size-fits-all language testing and assessment practice, it has presented theoretical, methodological and practical concepts of language testing and assessment in context.

This final chapter concludes the book by examining the current and possible future challenges and opportunities in the field, addressing ongoing research inquiries and practical obstacles that await innovation and resolution.

Challenges

The global Covid-19 pandemic was one of the cornerstones that changed how we live today. It also sent a precautious message to us that we live in an uncertain world and should be ready to face whatever will happen next. During the pandemic, we witnessed how computer technology could provide a dynamic and adaptive capability to cope with unpredictable, devasted events that significantly impact all lives. More importantly, it has influenced how we teach, test and assess students.

Computer technology grows exponentially daily at a fast speed. How it was used yesterday can be different from today and tomorrow. Therefore, the role of computer technology in language education and, in particular, language testing and assessment needs to be constantly observed and evaluated. Similar to language tests and assessments, computer technology can be abused and used as a power to gain social control. Since computer technology and its applications will undoubtedly be a significant part of twenty-first-century language testing and assessment practices, we need to ensure its ethical use and efficacy. Computer-assisted language testing and assessment (CALTA) in the twenty-first century is a critical innovation that needs embracing and scrutinizing to ensure that it will have a sustainable and positive impact on people's learning. This chapter envisages that CALTA will be an ongoing challenge in language testing and assessment, language education and general education. We need to ensure that its practices and applications meet the quality standards in language testing and assessment. CALTA should be used meaningfully, fairly and ethically, fostering us and our future generations. CALTA will, therefore, be discussed as a major challenge in this chapter. The following sections discuss CALTA with the standards and quality criteria of language testing and assessment discussed throughout the book.

Reliability revisited

Traditionally, reliability concerns scoring consistency and accuracy. Brown (2016, p. 149) pointed out that 'reliability is desirable because it helps ensure that all examinees will have the same treatment, opportunities, and chances of success'. When evaluating the reliability of CALTA, it is helpful to ask what makes CALTA unreliable. For example, how can dishonest behaviour and test hacking be controlled and prevented in CALTA? What robust technological mechanism can deal with potential threats to CALTA reliability? Although complex encrypted scripts and password controls in a testing system may be used (Brown 2016), all software programs have some flaws and can be outdated rapidly.

In recent years, we have seen a trend to develop and use a robust multi-factor authentication method, moderation and security measures to ensure the integrity, fairness, and accuracy of language testing and assessment. Commercial testing and assessment giants such as Educational Testing Service, Pearson and Duolingo have employed technology-enhanced security measures (e.g. photographic and video records by Educational Testing Service, biometrics by Pearson and video records by Duolingo; Winke & Isbell 2017). Several educational service providers, such as universities, have used proctoring software such as ProctorU (https://www.proctoru.com/), which verifies students' or test takers' identifications, proctors, records test sessions and actively intervenes when suspicious behaviour occurs. Some people will attempt to steal an online test despite using online proctoring programs. Therefore, program developers must be vigilant to keep abreast of such attempts.

The reliability of CALTA is also associated with test and assessment data transfer. For example, electricity blackouts and unreliable internet connections can have an impact on test and assessment delivery and administration; this can be disruptive and subsequently can negatively impact students' and test takers' performance due to, for example, increased test anxiety. During online speaking tests, students' speech and responses may be recorded unintelligibly due to a slow or unreliable internet connection or a poor-quality microphone. Such issues may be addressed by regularly maintaining and upgrading IT equipment, infrastructure and software, and investing in the most reliable internet service available (Brown 2016). CALTA needs ongoing innovation and creativity to address emerging and future challenges affecting test and assessment reliability.

Validity and trustworthiness revisited

This book discusses validity in terms of test and assessment score interpretation and use for decision-making in a given situation. This criterion has been adopted mainly in standardized testing. A test and assessment that produces scores that are valid in one context does not mean it is for another. Analogous to validity, trustworthiness is a relative concept in how language testing and assessment has been purposefully and meaningfully used to improve teaching and learning. Trustworthiness in language classroom assessment goes beyond focusing on how scores are used and interpreted because scores are not the only measure used to inform decision-making. Classroom testing and assessment trustworthiness have an emotional side in that teachers have a socio-cultural connection with students. This is not the apparent case in external standardized language testing. Therefore, the validity question of CALTA in an external standardized test cannot be approached the same way as questioning the trustworthiness of classroom-based language assessment and vice versa.

Technological proficiency and strategic competence

A validity aspect of CALTA has been concerned with construct validity because computer technology affects the nature of the language constructs to be assessed. Test designers cannot assume test performance represents students' or test takers' language proficiency or learning outcomes entirely. It also reflects their technological proficiency and strategic competence. Chapelle and Douglas (2006) pointed out that when completing a computer-based test, test takers are required to have basic, relevant computer knowledge and skills to complete test tasks successfully. That is, they need to have the ability to understand how to use a computer, how to navigate the test interface, and what to do when there is a technical issue during the test. In the light of this, Chapelle and Douglas (2006) proposed that strategic competence (metacognitive strategies) should be considered part of computerized test constructs because test takers need the ability to assess and evaluate a situation unique to a computerized test environment. Strategic competence allows test takers to be adaptive and adjust to a new test environment. Chapelle and Voss (2017, p. 157) used a reading test to exemplify that strategic competence is a critical part of the construct validity of a real-life internet-based reading test.

> the construct tested would be the ability to read with strategic use of online help. The reading strategies entailed in such tasks are different from those used to read when no help is available, and therefore the definition of strategic competence becomes critical for the construct assessed. Should test takers be given access to help while reading on a reading test? One approach to the dilemma is for the test developer to decide whether or not access to help constitutes an authentic task for the reader. In other words, if examinees will be reading online with access to help, such options should also be provided in the test.

Winke and Isbell (2017, p. 9) illustrated a situation in which technological proficiency and strategic competence should be included in the construct validity of a computer-assisted writing test.

> This problem is more pronounced when the language being learned has a writing system that is very different from the students' native-language writing system. For example, Chinese character writing (by hand) is a process that is as much of a memorized motor skill as it is a complex cognitive skill. On the other hand, the process of typing Chinese on a computer involves a step that uses the Romanized alphabet system to locate and select the appropriate characters. Understanding how the cognitive construct of writing is changed when the mode of test administration is changed is an important endeavour. It is also important to ensure that the way writing is tested matches the way writing is instructed in the language classroom.

Additionally, technological proficiency and strategic competence are essential abilities that explain similar construct validity considerations that explain test performance in a smartphone platform. According to Chapelle and Voss (2017, p. 156), 'producing written language on a smartphone entails several fundamental differences from writing at a keyboard, and therefore, the device needs to be considered carefully in the design of test tasks'.

Authenticity and interactional competence

Authenticity is closely related to validity because it relates to the nature of real-life language use. Authenticity is also associated with a close alignment between CALTA and classroom teaching and learning activities in classroom-based language assessment. Although activities in CALTA can be considered authentic because people use computers for study and work, interactional competence needs to be recognized as part of the construct and content validity. Sawaki (2012, p. 434) noted that language test designers should look for a solution 'as to how to emulate real-life human communication involving reciprocal interaction with computers'. While visual information from multimedia can enhance authenticity (e.g. speaker's non-verbal expressions) in CALTA, for example, when taking a test which includes a lecture video that allows students and test takers to understand (Sawaki 2012), it can still be difficult for them to be confident in their interpretations of utterances or other non-linguistic cues in multimedia, for example, due to a small computer monitor, or unfamiliarity with the specific test situation (e.g. Chapelle & Voss 2017).

My pilot study on students' and test takers' strategic processing in an online speaking test, suggested that students and test takers reported that they aimed to appear engaging with their interviewer by looking at the webcam more constantly because their interviewer on the other side could observe this on their computer monitor. They also reported how they practised subtly glancing at the computer screen to observe their interviewer while maintaining eye contact through the webcam. Their interactional strategy seems to be a test-wiseness strategy that enhances their interactional appearance. Yet doing this might improve their CALTA performance. Accordingly, empirical research needs to address potential construct-irrelevant variance that threatens the validity of CALTA.

Students' and test takers' challenges to interact with CALTA tasks can be extended to those in non-standardized assessment contexts such as written assignments and portfolio assessments. Students and test takers may be unprepared to transition from online learning during the Covid-19 pandemic to face-to-face learning situations. They often need to navigate on their own with the complexities of new authentic language tasks they did not have during online learning. Students do not necessarily realize that effective strategies in online study do not always work to the same extent in face-to-face situations.

Scoring and face validity of automated scoring

Another validity challenge with CALTA concerns an automated scoring (AS) application that replaces human raters for judging writing and speaking. This type of validity is related to scoring validity. Winke and Isbell (2017, p. 317) pointed out that 'arguments for automated scoring that are based on convenience and cost savings may not withstand public scrutiny when the stakes are extremely high'. Although many test developers, including Educational Testing Service (ETS) and Pearson Education, have provided systematic validation evidence that their AS systems produce consistent and accurate scoring comparable with that of human raters' (e.g. Shermis 2014; Van Moere & Downey 2017), many scholars, researchers and stakeholders question the validity, suitability and usefulness of AS programs for judging students' and test takers' performance (see Ericsson & Haswell 2006; Rupp et al. 2020).

It should be noted that many positive findings about the reliability and scoring validity of automated computer programs have been published by researchers affiliated with or funded by companies that have developed AS software. While issues of AS patents, copyrights and the proprietary nature are understandable, information on exactly how automated scoring programs work is not fully available to the public, making it difficult to trust the AS scoring validity at 'face value'. Rupp et al. (2020) also caution against heavy or sole reliance on statistical analyses and evidence (e.g. correlational analyses of scores from different instruments or conditions) as empirical evidence to support an AS system. They argue that validity evidence 'may also take the form of testimonials from learners and teachers, for example, who can attest, in a more informed manner, to the fact that a particular learning environment has helped them with information-management tasks, supported effective learning and resulted in higher engagement' (pp. 483–4).

In addition, in the case of automated speaking scoring, test designers need to continue to develop AI and automated software that accurately recognizes students' and test takers' verbal and non-verbal communications, such as nodding and smiling, as part of the scoring criteria (Chapelle & Voss 2017). Rupp, Foltz and Yan (2020, p. 482) pointed out that 'it seems unrealistic to expect AS [automated scoring] systems to be able to fully replace human raters when it comes to comprehensively evaluating those qualities of performance that get to the humanistic core – creativity, subtlety, and nuance, to name but a few – or relatively complex skill applications such as those that support effective collaborative problem-solving for instance'. The social nature of writing that is part of the students' and test takers' background is insufficiently considered by AS (McNamara et al. 2015), so programmers need to incorporate this aspect into scoring to improve authenticity and fairness.

Practicality revisited

Chapter 4 discusses practicality regarding the time, cost and resources required to develop, use, take, administer and score a test. It should be noted that adopting CALTA is still not practical and feasible for many educational institutes worldwide. Disparity in computer technology infrastructure is a significant source of unfairness in CALTA. Schools, colleges and universities in underdeveloped countries do not have sufficient budgets to cover the cost of IT infrastructure, equipment and resources to realize the potential of CALTA. To consider whether CALTA is viable, it is important to consider whether or not human and technology resources are available, efficient and sufficient to make it work. It is necessary to have robust software for authoring language assessments, without which a computer-based test is not possible, as well as human and financial resources. An authoring test program is a software tool for designing and presenting a computer test and storing test data for scoring. Some basic authoring programs may be more easily learnt than others (e.g. for multiple-choice questions compared to speaking tasks). Therefore, teachers, testers and assessors involved in designing CALTA should be trained to use a given authoring program. A given institute needs time and financial and technical support because test software and technical expertise need ongoing updates (Chapelle & Voss 2017). Test tasks and questions also need to be developed and inserted into an authoring program, and new CALTA needs to be validated.

Practicality is also essential when using a proctoring application for CALTA (e.g. ProctorU), as it relates to the reliability criterion. At the beginning of the online test, each test taker must be asked to turn on their webcams to show their photo ID for verification and where they are taking the test. No one else is allowed in the room. Although there can be a proctoring program that is highly efficient, reliable and effective for online test-taking, it is essential not to forget that its use can cause stress and anxiety to test takers. For example, they have to download and activate the proctoring software and go through verification checks before taking a test. They also need to grant the proctoring program access to their webcams and computers, which can violate privacy concerns. Success in the online test can also be affected by the quality of the internet they use.

Online proctoring programs can be expensive to use. While it is possible by some international testing companies or educational institutes because they can shift the cost to test takers or students, it is not viable for most educational contexts around the world due to poverty, a lack of technology and support, the population's general literacy, other resources, and specific circumstances such as natural disasters and wars. Considering practicality in CALTA is significant as inequality and exclusivity exist across global contexts.

Ethics and fairness revisited

Ethics and fairness are essential considerations in CALTA. Ethical considerations include fairness and abuse of language tests and assessments. For example, are all students and test takers treated equally? Is CALTA used to discriminate against a particular group of people? CALTA has the potential to be unfair to people who are unfamiliar with computers or who have a low socio-economic background (Winke & Isbell 2017). A lack of familiarity with technology can result in anxiety during test-taking. For example, students or test takers can find it difficult to interpret information presented through computer technology and to manage the various types of information demands (e.g. instructions, what to do to fulfil the task requirements). For these reasons, students or test takers who do not have adequate computer skills (e.g. using keyboards for typing, using essential software such as Office and navigating test interfaces on-screen) need training and practice before participating in CALTA (Brown 2016). Familiarity training may be less demanding for new generations who grow up with computer technology (Sawaki 2012).

Another source of unfairness (also discussed in challenges in CALTA practicality above) is related to the infrastructure of computer technology, including internet speed for sufficient test completion and for transferring test data to hard drives or cloud storage and scoring (Brown 2016). Winke and Isbell (2017) urge test designers and users to examine CALTA feasibility and fairness for students and test takers who may be disadvantaged due to physical and cognitive disabilities or different first-language scripts to the target language being tested. Given that CALTA is still in its infancy, research into fairness, potential bias, and abuse of tests and assessments should ensure that all students or test takers are treated equitably. Future CALTA validation research should be more interdisciplinary when language experts, testers and assessors, educational psychologists and digital technology professionals, for example, collaborate to improve CALTA user-interface design. The questions of sufficient response times, the nature of the available help menu and whether access to online resources should be available all require careful consideration. Research investigating computational cognitive modelling during CALTA can focus on evaluating the experiences and performances of different test takers to improve CALTA operating systems.

Impact revisited

Testing and assessment impact, discussed in Chapter 4, is also relevant to CALTA. Test designers and users should investigate the immediate, short-term, mid-term and long-term effects of CALTA on students, test takers, relevant stakeholders and society. Intended and unintended consequences should be carefully considered and investigated before, during and after testing and assessment (e.g. due to CALTA formats, students' and test takers' familiarity with test formats and computer skills required to complete tasks, and the effect of automated scoring on performance). The impact of CALTA on students' or test takers' cognitive, individual and cultural characteristics that affect their test performance needs to be considered. The issues of anxiety and dishonest behaviours while participating in CALTA need to be identified and appropriately addressed.

Washback revisited

A washback impact of CALTA on teaching and learning is apparent. CALTA washback impacts include immediate feedback that prompts improvement in learning and teaching adjustment. Ensuring an alignment between teaching and learning activities and CALTA tasks remains essential. A lack of such an alignment raises the important issue of construct validity and authenticity. Finally, in classroom assessment, the extent to which both teachers and students are prepared to familiarize themselves with a given CALTA administration, test-taking strategy use, and test task completion should be understood so that time is not unduly taken from the pivotal tasks of teaching and learning the subject matter.

Further opportunities

Alongside the challenges posed by CALTA, an interconnected theme warrants further opportunities for theoretical, methodological and empirical exploration, namely the expansion of the construct definition of AL proficiency.

Language construct definition expansion

Language testing and assessment researchers and developers have faced ever-changing issues and challenges in approaching and refining a construct definition of additional language (AL) proficiency in the twenty-first century (see Chapters 1 and 2). Such challenges will continue because views of AL proficiency and performance will inevitably shift as human society evolves and faces uncertain and unknown events.

The notion of language construct definition expansion is crucial and critical in adapting testing and assessment practices to encompass the complexities of language use in diverse contexts (see also Chapters 5 and 8, which discuss the sociocognitive model of language skills). Traditional language constructs may no longer suffice to capture the multifaceted nature of language proficiency in a future globalized and technologically mediated world. There is a pressing need to broaden our understanding of language constructs to encompass a broader range of linguistic skills, including digital literacy, intercultural competence and communicative strategies in CALTA.

Purpura (2016) examines various approaches to defining the construct of AL proficiency in language testing and assessment (Chapter 2 also discusses some of these approaches). They include:

1. a trait-based perspective that views AL proficiency as an inherent and stable ability regardless of context.
2. a task-centred approach that focuses on the ability to handle real-life language tasks.
3. an interactionist perspective that acknowledges that AL proficiency may vary depending on the context.
4. a socio-interactional approach that emphasizes the collaborative construction of language performance in communicative settings.

These approaches are expected to evolve, particularly as the field explores assessment in multilingual, dynamic and AI platforms. Pivotal considerations will probably be shaped by domains related to assessing language abilities beyond English as an additional language (EAL), including multilingualism assessment and evaluating non-linear, dynamic language usage. Such developments necessitate ongoing refinements of AL construct definitions to accommodate the diverse linguistic competencies and communicative repertoires of language learners and users in contemporary multilingual and multicultural contexts.

As language testing and assessment practices evolve to reflect the complexity and diversity of language use worldwide, there is a growing recognition of the need to embrace a broader conception of AL proficiency that transcends traditional monolingual paradigms. This expanded view of language assessment encompasses the dynamic interplay between multiple languages and modalities and the ability to navigate complex socio-cultural and communicative contexts with fluency and cultural sensitivity.

Incorporating insights from multilingualism studies, sociolinguistics and dynamic systems theory (Larsen-Freeman 2012, 2017; Winke & Brunfaut 2021), researchers and practitioners can innovate new adaptive approaches to assessing AL abilities that acknowledge fluid and context-dependent language use. When a more holistic and inclusive perspective on language assessment is considered, we can better capture the richness and complexity of linguistic repertoires and promote equitable and culturally responsive assessment practices for all language learners and users.

AL constructs other than for EAL

The evolving nature of language learning and use and shifting global workforce demands will undoubtedly drive changes in the construct definition of AL proficiency over time. First, alternative perspectives on language acquisition and usage challenge traditional notions of language proficiency (Larsen-Freeman 2012, 2017), emphasizing dynamic, context-dependent language skills over static, monolingual competencies. This paradigm shift necessitates re-evaluating how AL proficiency is conceptualized and assessed to reflect multilingual individuals' diverse linguistic repertoires and communicative practices.

Second, the increasing demand for advanced-level multilinguals in diverse professional contexts has underscored the need for a more nuanced understanding of AL proficiency beyond English as an additional language. As languages such as Chinese Mandarin gain prominence in global communication, the current construct definition of EAL may not adequately capture the complexity and specificity of AL proficiency in languages other than English. Therefore, there is a growing need to develop new theoretical frameworks and assessment tools that account for the unique linguistic and cultural contexts in which alternative languages are used.

Complex, dynamic and adaptive AL proficiency

Integrating insights from second language acquisition (SLA) research, language teaching methodologies and social research have yielded invaluable contributions to language testing and assessment practices (Winke & Brunfaut 2021). One notable example is the potential to adopt the complex theory, as scholars such as Larsen-Freeman (2017) advocate. This theoretical framework posits that language learning and use are multifaceted processes shaped by linguistic, cognitive, psychological and social factors, exhibiting non-static, non-linear and non-causal dynamics. In this view, learners are viewed as active agents who interact with and adapt to their linguistic environments.

From a complex and dynamic perspective, the traditional notion that students or test takers bear sole responsibility for their test and assessment performance is called into question. Instead, the context-dependent nature of language performance suggests that many factors beyond their control influence individuals' abilities. Consequently, when defining constructs for language testing and assessment, it becomes imperative to consider the dynamic interplay between individual capacities and contextual influences.

Adopting this Complex System perspective will have far-reaching implications for test and assessment design, administration and validation. Test and assessment developers need to strive for testing and assessment that captures the dynamic nature of AL proficiency and accounts for contextual variability. Language testing and assessment research and development need to adopt methodologies that reflect the complexity of language learning or use processes, ensuring that tests and assessments accurately measure students' or test takers' evolving AL proficiency.

Concluding remarks

'Assessments can be detrimental or beneficial, but it is best they are placed on a continuum of a detrimental-to-beneficial scale, with very few being detrimental and very few being wonderfully beneficial, most being benign but not useful, or necessary but painful' (Kunnan 2018, p. 4). Language testing and assessment is not just about designing, creating, testing and assessing students and test takers for a reason. It is also about helping people transform and improve their lives and surroundings. Promoting equality, equity and social justice through language testing and assessment should be at the heart of language testing and assessment (McNamara et al. 2019). Therefore, language testers, assessors and anyone involved in language testing and assessment practices must be mindful of the socio-political and educational practices because tests and assessments give power to their users. No one test and assessment practice, even in the context of formative assessment and assessment for learning, is free from consequences – intended or not.

Discussion

1. What have you learnt about some challenges in CALTA?
2. What may be significant challenges in language testing and assessment practices in your context?
3. What opportunities exist for innovating language testing and assessment practices in your context?
4. What are your next steps in furthering your knowledge and practice in language testing and assessment?

Further reading

Fulcher, G. & Harding, L. (eds), 2022, *Routledge handbook of language testing*, 2nd edn, London and New York, Routledge.

This second edition of Fulcher and Davidson's work, initially published in 2012, features revised chapters authored by the original contributors and new contributors. It offers updated insights and perspectives on language testing and assessment.

Kunnan, A.J. (ed.), 2014, *Companion to language assessment*, John Wiley & Sons, Chichester.

This four-volume edited book comprises 140 chapters and offers an exhaustive exploration of language testing and assessment. It covers specific language skills assessment, diverse test-taker groups, various assessment methodologies, validity testing strategies, data analysis techniques and global assessment practices.

Kunnan, A.J. (ed.), 2024, *The concise companion to language assessment*, John Wiley & Sons, Oxford.

This book offers a contemporary overview of key aspects of language assessment, teaching and learning. Its coverage spans various language assessment methods, addressing multiple issues and contexts. Topics include recent advancements in language assessment technology, learning-focused assessment approaches, teacher-led assessment practices, assessment literacy for educators, plurilingual assessment frameworks and assessments for immigration processes.

Shohamy E., Or, I.G. & May, S. (eds), 2017, *Language testing and assessment*, 3rd edn, Springer, Cham.

This edited volume, comprising twenty-nine chapters, offers insights and methodologies on essential language testing and assessment topics. It covers assessing language proficiency across various domains, innovative assessment methods such as technology integration and validation techniques, and broader societal implications of language testing such as test stakes and critical perspectives.

Tsagari, D. & Banerjee J. (eds), 2017, *Handbook of second language assessment*, De Gruyter Mouton, Boston and Berlin.

This handbook provides a comprehensive overview of language assessment, covering fundamental concepts (e.g. assessment purposes, quality factors and assessing language skills). It explores assessment in various contexts, including educational and workplace settings, and addresses contemporary challenges in assessing young learners and those with disabilities.

Winke, P. & Brunfaut, T. (eds), 2021, *The Routledge handbook of second language acquisition and language testing*, Routledge, London.

This handbook includes forty-five chapters comprehensively treating language assessment methodology for second language acquisition research. It focuses on the interface between language assessment and second language acquisition research. Topics include fundamental concepts in assessment and measurement, research instruments, measuring individual differences and assessment of language development.

Appendix: Examples of Additional Language (AL) Tests and Assessments

This appendix presents and reviews some language tests and assessments. It aims to provide additional information about the designs of language assessments by various testing companies, agencies and language associations. This appendix will benefit readers by helping them to learn about multiple language tests and assessments, particularly what and how they assess. It will also help them to collect ideas for designing their tests or assessments. The following tests and assessments are presented alphabetically. Please be aware that these tests may be updated or modified by their developers, and the provided URLs may change over time.

ACTFL Oral Proficiency Interview – computer

Oral Proficiency Interview – computer (OPIc) is an internet-based, oral test for assessing foreign language proficiency levels (e.g. Arabic, Brazilian Portuguese, English, European Portuguese, French, German, Italian, Japanese, Korean, Mandarin Chinese, Pashto, Persian Farsi, Russian and Spanish, with more languages to be added). OPIc is a criterion-referenced assessment. It is owned by the American Council on the Teaching of Foreign Languages (ACTFL) and administered by Language Testing International (see https://www.actfl.org/center-assessment-research-and-development/actfl-assessments/actfl-postsecondary-assessments/oral-proficiency-interview-computer-opic; https://www.languagetesting.com/). This internet-delivered test was developed in response to the practicality limitations of its face-to-face version (e.g. location and time).

The test is based on the ACTFL Proficiency Guidelines 2012 – Speaking (see https://www.actfl.org/resources/actfl-proficiency-guidelines-2012/english/speaking), which divides functional language proficiency into Novice,

Intermediate, Advanced, Superior and Distinguished levels. OPIc, nonetheless, only utilizes the first three levels with sublevels of Low, Mid and High.

Overall, the time required to complete the test ranges from twenty to forty minutes. The test structure includes:

1 *Introduction and warm-up*: The test instructions and explanations and an illustration of a sample prompt are provided to test takers.
2 *Background survey*: Test takers answer questions about topics such as work and interests, and their responses determine the pool of prompts.
3 *Self-assessment*: Test takers are asked to self-assess their level of proficiency in a given language. This information is then used to select one of the five test forms for assessing different proficiency levels.
4 *Test tasks*: Test takers listen and respond to prompts. They can listen to the prompt a second time within five seconds of the prompt ending. The amount of time given to respond to a prompt depends on the nature of a given prompt (the time ranges from thirty seconds to two minutes).

Certified raters evaluate test performance on four criteria: function (task fulfilment), accuracy (language competence and comprehensibility), content/context (responses with content and context appropriateness), and text type (oral production and organization). See a CPIc demo test at https://opicdemo.actfltesting.org/systemcheck.

Diagnostic English Language Needs

Diagnostic English Language Needs Assessment (DELNA) is a post-entry, low-stakes assessment of enrolled tertiary students' academic language ability (see https://www.auckland.ac.nz/en/students/student-support/academic-support/delna/delna-students.html). This test was developed by the University of Auckland, New Zealand, to identify domestic and international students admitted to the university whose academic success may be affected by their language and academic literacy limitations. Hence, DELNA has a formative assessment function since it identifies strengths and weaknesses and prompts further action to support those in greatest need. There are two phases in DELNA:

1 *Phase 1 (Screening)*: Test takers complete an online test that evaluates their academic vocabulary knowledge and reading skills. The vocabulary knowledge part (approximately twenty-seven items) is based on the University Word List, whereas the reading skill part

is based on skimming and scanning. The scores range from 0 to 100. This phase is designed to identify those students who are likely to need language support and those who are not. The scores are grouped into (1) good (no support needed), (2) satisfactory (some independent study recommended), and (3) recommended for diagnosis. Test takers in Category 3 are next asked to take the diagnostic test (Phase 2).

2 *Phase 2 (Diagnostic)*: There are three sections in this test (Listening: thirty minutes, Reading: fifty minutes and Writing: thirty minutes). It does not have a Speaking component at the time of writing. Test techniques in the Listening and Reading sections include cloze, information-transfer, multiple-choice, true–false and short answers. The Writing section asks test takers to describe a diagram or graph. A six-point band is reported to test takers as assessment outcomes from 4 (lowest, suggesting the need for comprehensive language support) to 9 (highest, offering no support required). At-risk test takers (those in the low bands) are invited to make an appointment with a DELNA language adviser to discuss available language support.

Duolingo English Test

Duolingo English Test (DET) is an internet-based proficiency test for English-medium university admission (see https://englishtest.duolingo.com/). It is an adaptive test: the difficulty level of each test item depends on the test takers' performance earlier in the test. The better the performance, the more complex the following test items. Since performance can fluctuate, test item difficulty will also fluctuate. DET is scored online, ranging from 10 to 160. Test takers receive the electronic results within forty-eight hours.

The internet specifications and administration and security procedure of the test are worth noting (see LaFlair & Settles 2019 in https://s3.amazonaws.com/duolingo-papers/other/Duolingo%20English%20Test%20-%20Technical%20Manual%202019.pdf). For example, 'The browsers are locked down after onboarding, which means that any navigation away from the browser invalidates the test session. Additionally, all browser plugins must be disabled' (LaFlair & Settles 2019, p. 4). After the test has been uploaded, human proctors, with artificial intelligence assistance, are employed to check for dishonest behaviour.

The test comprises seven key sections named according to test techniques: (1) C-test (in which partial words need to be completed), (2) Yes–No Vocabulary Task (Written and Oral), (3) Elicited Imitation (Read-Aloud), (4) Extended Speaking, (5) Extended Writing, (6) Oral Interview, and (7) Writing Sample. Both (4) and (5) are not adaptive in the strictest sense because the item difficulty level is not based on performance in these sections but on performance in the previous three sections. Also, (6) and (7) are unscored, but test takers' responses are provided to the institutions receiving the test results. It is not clear why (6) and (7) are unscored and the extent of the test consequences on test takers and other stakeholders. The test items/tasks are largely restricted responses, and even in the productive sections of the writing and speaking tests, the quantity of responses is minimal (e.g. speak within thirty seconds or write fifty words). Therefore, the test design is mainly linguistic-oriented rather than communicative-oriented.

Occupational English Test

The Occupational English Test (OET) is a paper-based, specific-purpose English language test for assessing the English proficiency of healthcare professionals (e.g. doctors, nurses) who aim to register and work in an English-medium context (see https://www.occupationalenglishtest.org/test-information/). OET is an international test because it is recognized for use by various countries worldwide (see https://www.occupationalenglishtest.org/test-information/who-recognises-oet/). There are four test sections for assessing four language skills in healthcare contexts. The topics across test sections are of generic healthcare interest and accessible to candidates across all professions. Except for the Speaking Section, which is taken one-on-one in a private room, the other three sections are completed in one administration room.

1. *The Listening Section* (forty minutes) comprises three parts and has forty-two items. Test takers listen to an audio recording only once and answer the questions while listening. The main simulated situations include consultation, comprehension of short extracts of scenarios, and presentation extracts. Part 1 is based on a short-answer technique, whereas Parts 2 and 3 are based on a multiple-choice technique.
2. *The Reading Section* (sixty minutes) comprises three parts with forty-two questions. Part 1 focuses on expeditious reading (e.g. skimming and scanning) of four short passages. There are twenty questions in this section, and test techniques include short-answer, matching and sentence completion. Parts 2 and 3 measure the so-called careful reading ability and are based on a multiple-choice technique. Part 2 asks test takers to read a short text (about 100–150 words) and identify the gist, main ideas or details. Part 3 asks test takers to read two longer texts (about 800 words each).

3 *The Writing Section* (forty-five minutes) asks test takers to write a letter; the topic depends on their profession (e.g. nurse, dentist, general practitioner, pharmacist). Information relevant to the test task is provided to assist their writing.

4 *The Speaking Section* (twenty minutes) provides a task for a specific healthcare profession (e.g. nurse or doctor). It uses a role-play technique in which test takers interact with their interviewer, who plays a role as, for example, a patient or client, using provided scripts. Test takers are given cards that explain the scenario in which they are to respond. They are given three minutes to prepare for each role-play. Approximately five minutes are allocated for each of these.

Assessment criteria are used to determine test takers' proficiency levels. For example, in writing, the requirements include purpose, content, conciseness and clarity, organization and language accuracy. In contrast, the speaking criteria include intelligibility, appropriateness, fluency, accuracy and choice of language use.

TOEFL Essentials Test

The TOEFL Essentials Test is an internet-based English proficiency test recently developed by the Educational Testing Service (see https://www.ets.org/toefl/test-takers/essentials/about.html). This test can be taken at home, and security technology can monitor dishonest behaviour. The ETS website provides a discussion and assurance of test security and proctoring. Comparisons between the TOEFL Essentials and other tests can be found at https://www.ets.org/toefl/test-takers/essentials/about/compare-tests.html/. The score for each test section ranges from 1 to 12.

It is claimed that the test content is not just academic so that the test results can be used for high-stakes admissions in academic and non-academic contexts. The TOEFL Essentials Test is an adaptive test to test takers' proficiency levels, enabling it to be shorter than it would be. Test takers can complete the test in 1.5 hours. The test is based on four skills (listening, reading, writing and speaking) and fundamental language components such as grammar and vocabulary. The test is scored using both human and AI tools. Unofficial scores in reading and listening are provided at the end of the test. The test includes the following:

1 *The Listening Section* presents a range of test tasks, including (a) Listen and Reply, (2) Listen to a Conversation, (3) Academic

Listening: Announcements, and (4) Academic Listening: Talks. Test takers select answers from available options.

2 *The Reading Section* has the following test tasks: (a) Vocabulary, (b) General Reading: Daily Life, (c) Academic Reading: Tables, and (d) Academic Reading: Passages. The text lengths vary across different tasks. In (c), texts are around fifty–eighty-five words, whereas in (d), texts are about 200 words. These test tasks are mainly a selective-response or multiple-choice technique.

3 *The Writing Section* includes (a) Build a Sentence, (b) Describe a Photo, (c) Write an Email, and (d) Write for an Academic Discussion. Test takers have approximately seven minutes to complete (b) to (d) each.

4 *The Speaking Section* includes (a) Read Aloud, (b) Listen and Repeat, and (c) Virtual Interview. (a) and (b) are linguistically oriented and strictly controlled, rather than communicatively driven by the test takers, whereas (c) is somewhat communicative-oriented as test takers need to produce their answers to interview questions (within forty-five seconds, so the Speaking Section is not extended).

Additionally, test takers record their videos (two minutes each): (a) about themselves and (b) about their opinion on a topic of their choosing. This recording is, however, not scored. Further detailed information about this test can be found at https://www.ets.org/Media/Research/pdf/RM-21-03.pdf and https://www.ets.org/toefl/test-takers/essentials/content.html.

As can be seen from the selected test and assessment examples, test designers and developers have engaged in various aspects of their test specification development, including descriptions of target test takers, test purposes, test sections, time allowance, test administration, scoring and scoring reports, to name but a few. The examples presented then allow the readers to realize what to do when they plan and develop a test or assessment. Considering an example of a test can make it possible to adopt a reverse engineering activity to rationalize what the test specifications may look like.

Glossary of Language Testing and Assessment

Accuracy A broad linguistic concept that focuses on an individual's ability to control the accuracy of linguistic features, such as grammar, vocabulary and pronunciation.

Argument-based approach A validity approach which emphasizes that the test and assessment validity is not an inherent property of the test and assessment itself. Instead, it is based on the argument or evidence supporting the interpretation and use of scores for a specific purpose and situation. Validity is context-dependent and subject to ongoing evaluation and refinement.

Audience In speaking, the audience typically consists of the interlocutor (the person directly addressed) and any listeners or overhearers who may also be present. In writing, the audience refers to the readers for whom the text is intended.

Automated scoring Computerized or machine scoring for evaluating and scoring constructed-response performance of students or test takers. The scoring process employs computer algorithms based on predefined criteria and models of performance through machine training and validation.

Blueprint A document that outlines general and specific plans for developing and constructing a test and assessment. It includes how to administer and score the test and assessment. The term blueprint is often used interchangeably with test and assessment specifications.

Cognitive complexity A person's perceived or actual difficulty in using linguistic features to address a language task or activity. The person's characteristics, such as memory, metacognition, motivation and first-language background, can affect it.

Communicative competence A multi-componential proficiency to use language for successful communication. This ability comprises various competencies (e.g. language competence, strategic competence, interactional competence and sociolinguistic competence) and language modes (e.g. speaking, listening, reading and writing).

Construct An abstract concept such as communicative competence that cannot be directly observed but can be inferred through observations of behaviours or performance.

Data analysis Applying quantitative or qualitative methods to examine data (e.g. test scores, frequency counts, written reports) to understand the nature of abstract concepts or address a research issue.

Dependability The consistency of classifying test scores or performance in a criterion-referenced approach. In this method, decisions about students' performances are usually binary, such as pass/fail or mastery/non-mastery. Dependability is similar to reliability in this context.

Descriptive statistics Basic quantitative information about specific characteristics of scores or measurement scales. This includes frequency counts of score occurrences, the mean score (average), the range of scores, and measures of score variation such as variance and standard deviation.

Direct assessment A method that involves asking students or test takers to demonstrate the language skills being evaluated directly. For instance, students are asked to write an essay because the test aims to measure their writing ability.

Edumetric An approach to testing and assessment to enhance teaching and learning within an educational setting. It involves using assessments to support and monitor students' learning progress. Common edumetric assessments include formative and summative assessments in the language classroom.

Error of measurement Interferences, nuances or mistakes that impact observed test scores can potentially limit the ability to draw accurate inferences about language abilities or skills based solely on these scores.

Ethics The principles guiding the appropriate design and use of tests and assessments for a given purpose. It encompasses considerations of fairness and the potential impact of tests. An ethical language test is fair and lacks unintended consequences or hidden intentions. Additionally, ethical considerations extend to addressing misconduct or misuse of language tests and assessments.

Fairness Ensuring equal opportunities for all students or test takers to participate in and complete a test or assessment. This includes equal treatment during test administration, marking and scoring. The test can be deemed unfair if test takers do not receive equal treatment throughout the testing and assessment process.

Feedback Information regarding the quality of students' or test takers' performance or processes. It informs them about their current language proficiency, learning status and areas for improvement. It emphasizes their strengths and weaknesses, empowering them to enhance their skills.

Fluency Smooth, eloquent and effortless language use. The speed of language processing is natural. For example, speakers are fluent when they produce speech at a natural pace without obvious hesitations or long pauses.

Illocutionary acts Using speech utterances to express or impose a specific function (e.g. please open the door).

Impact The consequences or effects of tests or assessments on students, test takers or society. It encompasses both intended and unintended outcomes for individuals and society.

Implicature Implied meanings beyond literal utterances (e.g. 'I have an appointment with the dentist on Saturday' by a wife to mean 'You have to drive me there' for the husband who knows that his wife does not drive). It is related to Grice's (1975) cooperative principle of maxims.

Indirect testing and assessment Methods where students or test takers are asked to perform a test or assessment that does not directly measure a specific language skill of interest (e.g. using grammar or vocabulary tests to assess students' ability to read or write).

Inductive reasoning A logical process where specific observations, examples or evidence are used to form general principles or conclusions. It involves moving from particular instances to broader generalizations.

Inferencing A form of inductive reasoning that interprets a given test score or performance to understand an underlying construct.

Inferential statistics Statistical methods based on probability testing about a relationship or differences between variables of interest.

Interlocutor Another person or speaker with whom students or test takers exchange information. In a speaking test, an interlocutor may be the interviewer.

Interactional competence The ability to interact with other interlocutors or audiences during communication, usually in face-to-face or technology-mediated communication.

Inter-rater reliability The level of agreement or correlation between scores of two or more raters who rate the same piece of performance, such as writing or speaking.

Intercultural competence The ability to use language appropriate for and sensitive to one's audience, such as interlocutors, groups of speakers, and readers whose cultures, values, beliefs and cultural identities differ from those of the person.

Intra-rater reliability The extent of scoring consistency and accuracy of a given rater in evaluating students' or test takers' performance.

Item writers Language experts who can create test tasks, items, and questions for testing and assessing a particular skill or construct according to the test and assessment specifications provided.

Item writing Crafting and creating test and assessment items, tasks or questions based on the test and assessment specifications provided.

Language assessment literacy (LAL) Knowledge about the purposes and functions of different tests and assessments within educational and social settings. For instance, educators with language assessment literacy can analyse the rationale behind testing and assessment practices, design assessment tasks to evaluate specific skills or learning objectives, and apply assessment quality criteria or standards to evaluate tests and assessments.

Linguistic complexity The level of a person's linguistic system (e.g. declarative and procedural knowledge of, for example, lexico-grammatical, phonological and morphological principles) that influences the size, choice, richness, variability and choices of their language production.

Listening comprehension The ability to construct, understand and interpret meanings and discourses from spoken texts.

Listening models Conceptual illustration of the abstract concepts and their internal processes involved in listening. Models provide a structured way to understand how individuals perceive, process and comprehend spoken language.

Listening purposes The reasons individuals attend to spoken texts. Listening purposes include obtaining new or updated information, learning and integrating information.

Locutionary acts Speech utterances for literal expressions of intended meaning (e.g. 'Can you open the door, please?').

Mixed methods research Combining, sequencing or integrating quantitative and qualitative research designs within a single study. This approach allows researchers to gain a more comprehensive understanding of a research topic or problem.

Model A graphical representation of key theoretical aspects illustrating the direction or flow of specified components. Models provide a visual framework for understanding complex phenomena.

Monolingualism Being proficient in only one language, typically one's native or first language.

Multilingualism Being able to speak, understand or use more than one language. Being multilingual does not imply that one must be highly proficient in these languages.

Perlocutionary acts Speech utterances for presenting an agenda (e.g. persuading, scaring) to the interlocutor or listener (e.g. 'I warn you'). It is typically more forceful than illocutionary acts.

Politeness Using socially agreeable utterances or expressions that do not cause communication breakdowns.

Practicality Feasibility of a test or assessment in terms of time and cost for developing, administering and scoring.

Productive language skills Language skills that involve speaking, writing and interacting with other people.

Psychometric A measurement approach that aims to develop tests or assessments to measure an abstract construct of interest based on predetermined standards (e.g. reliability and validity).

Qualitative analysis Analysis methods for understanding data such as interviews, observations, images or textual data.

Qualitative research A naturalistic and humanistic approach that focuses on understanding processes and issues from students', teachers' and stakeholders' perspectives. Data can be from interviews and verbal reports.

Quantitative analysis Data analysis that involves analysing numerical data such as test scores, questionnaire responses and frequency counts. It aims to infer statistical results about a relationship between variables.

Quantitative research A statistical approach that involves collecting and analysing numerical data, such as test scores and frequencies. It aims to understand linear and causal relationships between variables of interest.

Receptive language skills Involve reading and listening, and they enable individuals to comprehend information and understand the world.

Reliability The consistency and accuracy of test scores or scoring procedures. Test scores may fluctuate due to factors such as target language constructs, test administration and raters.

Research A systematic inquiry into a particular topic area of interest. It requires planning, data collection and data analysis.

Scoring methods The procedures used to evaluate test performance. Objective scoring applies to test tasks with unequivocal answers, while subjective scoring involves scorers making subjective judgements about test takers' performances, such as in essay or speaking tasks.

Scoring rubric The assessment matrix for evaluating performance, particularly in written and spoken responses. They consist of descriptors for different performance levels. Each level is assigned a number (i.e. score) to represent the quality of a given performance or response.

Social dimension of language assessment A perspective that emphasizes the influence of social factors on language learning and use. Social factors such as interlocutors' support and the choice of assessment tasks can impact students' or test takers' language performance.

Speech acts Using speech to convey direct (explicit) or indirect (implicit) actions to the listener or interlocutor.

Standardization A systematic procedure and administration of language tests and assessments to ensure that a test is administered, scored or interpreted similarly for all students and test takers.

Task complexity The extent to which a language task structure constrains a person's ability to be attentive in retrieving and memorizing information during their language use. In language assessment, task complexity is related to a given test condition, such as access to resources, planning time and time allowance, as well as the level of stakes of the task (e.g. low, medium or high).

Test administration The procedures for administering the test or assessment to students or test takers.

Test and assessment specifications The blueprint for creating and developing a test or assessment. They include purposes, constructs, students or test takers, the number of sections, administration, and scoring procedures.

Test and assessment techniques Specific methods used to engage students' or test takers' responses or reactions to questions or tasks. They range from restricted- to constructed-response techniques.

Test coordinator A person responsible for overseeing test and assessment activities, including working with item writers, test validators, programmers, editors, test administrators and raters.

Test format The structure in which test tasks and sections are arranged to create a test or assessment. It encompasses the sequence of test instructions and sections as designed. Test and assessment formats are also linked to the mode of test delivery, such as paper-based, computer-based, or portfolio assessment.

Test task Questions or prompts for students or test takers to respond to or answer. These tasks assess their knowledge or skills and evaluate their language accuracy, fluency and competence levels.

Validation The process of ensuring a test and assessment has achieved desirable qualities and intended outcomes. It may involve piloting test questions or tasks and providing rater training.

Validity The extent to which inferences and decisions based on a test score are meaningful and appropriate in a given context. Validity is not inherent to a test or assessment itself. It concerns test interpretation and use in decision-making.

Variables Aspects that can vary in values or degrees (e.g. language knowledge, motivation and anxiety).

Washback The impact of test and assessment use on language teaching and learning. Introducing a test can change teachers' and students' behaviours, thoughts or attitudes towards language learning.

References

Abedi, J., 2014, 'Accommodations in the assessment of English language learners' in *Companion to language assessment*, ed. A.J. Kunnan, John Wiley & Sons, Oxford, pp. 1–15.

Abedi, J., Zhang, Y., Rowe, S.E. & Lee, H., 2020, 'Examining effectiveness and validity of accommodations for English language learners in mathematics: An evidence-based computer accommodation decision system', *Educational Measurement: Issues and Practice*, vol. 39, no. 4, pp. 41–52.

Afflerbach, P. (ed.), 2016, *Handbook of individual differences in reading: Reader, text, and context*, Routledge, New York and London.

Alderson, J.C., 2000, *Assessing reading*, Cambridge University Press, Cambridge.

Alderson, J.C. & Banerjee, J., 2001, 'Language testing and assessment (Part I)', *Language Teaching*, vol. 34, no. 4, pp. 213–36.

Alderson, J.C. & Banerjee, J., 2002, 'Language testing and assessment (Part 2)', *Language Teaching*, vol. 35, no. 1, pp. 79–113.

Alderson, J.C., Haapakangas, E., Huhta, A., Nieminen, L. & Ullakonoja, R., 2015, *The diagnosis of reading in a second or foreign language*, Routledge, New York and London.

Al-Mahrooqi, R. & Denman, C., 2018, 'Alternative assessment' in *The TESOL encyclopedia of English language teaching*, eds J.I. Liontas & C. Coombe, John Wiley & Sons, Hoboken, pp. 1–7.

American Educational Research Association (AERA), American Psychological Association (APA) & National Council on Measurement in Education (NCME), 1999, *Standards for educational and psychological testing*, American Educational Research Association, Washington.

American Educational Research Association (AERA), American Psychological Association (APA) & National Council on Measurement in Education (APA), 2014, *Standards for educational and psychological testing*, American Educational Research Association, Washington.

Anderson, J.R., 2000, *Learning and memory: An integrated approach*, 2nd edn, John Wiley and Sons, New York.

Anderson, L.W. & Krathwohl, D.R. (eds), 2001, *A taxonomy for learning, teaching, and assessing: A revision of Bloom's taxonomy of educational objectives*, Longman, New York.

Ariza, E.N.W. & Morehouse, J.L., 2018, 'Non-traditional assessment' in *The TESOL encyclopedia of English language teaching*, eds J.I. Liontas & C. Coombe, John Wiley & Sons, Hoboken, pp. 1–7.

Aryadoust, V., Ng, L.Y. & Sayama, H., 2021, 'A comprehensive review of Rasch measurement in language assessment: Recommendations and guidelines for research', *Language Testing*, vol. 38, no. 1, pp. 6–40.
Bachman, L.F., 1990, *Fundamental considerations in language testing*, Oxford University Press, Oxford.
Bachman, L.F., 2000, 'Modern language testing at the turn of the century: Assuring that what we count counts', *Language Testing*, vol. 17, no. 1, pp. 1–42.
Bachman, L.F., 2010, 'Second language assessment' in *International encyclopedia of education* (vol. 4), eds P. Peterson, E. Baker & B. McGaw, Elsevier, Oxford, pp. 140–7.
Bachman, L.F., 2014, 'Ongoing challenges in language assessment' in *Companion to language assessment*, ed. A.J. Kunnan, John Wiley & Sons, Oxford, pp. 1–18.
Bachman, L.F. & Damböck, B., 2017, *Language assessment for classroom teachers*, Oxford University Press, Oxford.
Bachman, L. & Palmer, A., 1996, *Language testing in practice: Developing language assessments and justifying their use in the real world*, Oxford University Press, Oxford.
Bachman, L. & Palmer, A., 2010, *Language assessment in practice*, Oxford University Press, Oxford.
Bailey, K.M., 1996, 'Working for washback: A review of the washback concept in language testing', *Language Testing*, vol. 13, no. 3, pp. 257–79.
Bandura, A. & National Institute of Mental Health, 1986, *Social foundations of thought and action: A social cognitive theory*, Prentice Hall, Maidenhead.
Biggs, J.B. & Tang, C., 2011, Teaching for quality learning at university, 4th edn, McGraw Hill Education & Open University Press, Maidenhead.
Black, P. & Wiliam, D., 1998, 'Assessment and classroom learning', *Assessment in Education*, vol. 5, no. 1, pp. 7–74.
Black, P. & Wiliam, D., 2009, 'Developing the theory of formative assessment', *Educational Assessment, Evaluation and Accountability*, vol. 21, no. 1, pp. 5–31.
Black, P. & Wiliam, D., 2018, 'Classroom assessment and pedagogy', *Assessment in Education: Principles, Policy & Practice*, vol. 25, no. 6, pp. 551–75.
Bloom, B.S., Engelhart, M.D., Furst, E.J., Hill, W.H. & Krathwohl, D.R., 1956, *Taxonomy of educational objectives: The classification of educational goals. Handbook I: Cognitive domain*, David McKay Company, New York.
Bonner, S.M., 2013, 'Validity in classroom assessment: Purposes, properties, and principles' in *SAGE handbook of research on classroom assessment*, ed. J.H. McMillan, SAGE, Thousand Oaks, pp. 87–106.
Braun, V. & Clarke, V., 2006, 'Using thematic analysis in psychology', *Qualitative Research in Psychology*, vol. 3, no. 2, pp. 77–101.
Braun, V. & Clarke, V., 2019, 'Reflecting on reflexive thematic analysis', *Qualitative Research in Sport, Exercise and Health*, vol. 11, no. 4, pp. 589–97.
Brown, A., 2012, 'Interlocutor and rater training' in *Routledge handbook of language testing*, eds G. Fulcher & F. Davidson, Routledge, London and New York, pp. 413–25.
Brown, H.D. & Abeywickrama, P., 2019, *Language assessment: Principles and classroom practice*, 3rd edn, Pearson Longman, White Plains.

Brown, J.D., 2005, *Testing in language programs: A comprehensive guide to English language assessment*, McGraw Hill, New York.
Brown, J.D. (ed.), 2012, *Developing, using, and analyzing rubrics in language assessment with case studies in Asian and Pacific languages*, National Foreign Language Resource Center, Hawaii.
Brown, J.D., 2016, 'Language testing and technology' in *Routledge handbook of language learning and technology*, eds F. Farr & L. Murray, Routledge, New York and London, pp. 141–59.
Brown, J.D., 2022, 'Classical test theory' in *Routledge handbook of language testing*, eds G. Fulcher & L. Harding, Routledge, London, pp. 447–61.
Buck, G., 2001, *Assessing listening*, Cambridge University Press, Cambridge.
Burkett, T., 2018, 'Norm-referenced testing and criterion-referenced testing' in *The TESOL encyclopedia of English language teaching*, eds J.I. Liontas & C. Coombe, John Wiley & Sons, Hoboken, pp. 1–5.
Canale, M., 1983, 'On some dimensions of language proficiency' in *Issues in language testing research*, ed. J. Oller, Newbury House, Cambridge, pp. 333–42.
Canale, M. & Swain, M., 1980, 'Theoretical bases of communicative approaches to second language teaching and testing', *Applied Linguistics*, vol. 1, no. 1, pp. 1–47.
Carr, N., 2011, *Designing and analysing language tests*, Oxford University Press, Oxford.
Celce-Murcia, M., 2007, 'Rethinking the role of communicative competence in language teaching' in *Intercultural language use and language learning*, eds E.A. Soler & M.P. Safont Jordà, Springer, Dordrecht, pp. 41–57.
Chalhoub-Deville, M.B., 2019, 'Multilingual testing constructs: Theoretical foundations', *Language Assessment Quarterly*, vol. 16, no. 4–5, pp. 472–80.
Chapelle, C.A., 2021, *Argument-based validation in testing and assessment*, SAGE, London.
Chapelle, C.A. & Douglas, D., 2006, *Assessing language through computer technology*, Cambridge University Press, Cambridge.
Chapelle, C.A. & Lee, H., 2022, 'Conceptions of validity' in *Routledge handbook of language testing*, 2nd edn, eds G. Fulcher & L. Harding, Routledge, London, pp. 17–31.
Chapelle, C.A. & Voss, E., 2017, 'Using technology in language assessment' in *Language testing and assessment*, 3rd edn, eds E. Shohamy, I.G. Or & S. May, Springer, Cham, pp. 149–61.
Cheng, L. & Curtis, A., 2012, 'Test impact and washback: Implications for teaching and learning' in *Cambridge guide to second language assessment*, eds C. Coombe, P. Davidson, B. O'Sullivan & S. Stoynoff, Cambridge University Press, Cambridge, pp. 89–95.
Chong, S.W. & Reinders, H. (eds), 2023, *Innovation in learning-oriented language assessment*, Palgrave Macmillan, Cham.
Clapham, C., 1996, *The development of IELTS: A study of the effects of background knowledge on reading comprehension*, Cambridge University Press, Cambridge.
Council of Europe, 2020, *Common European framework of reference for languages: Learning teaching, assessment – companion volume*, Council of Europe, Strasbourg.

Cronbach, L.J., 1971, 'Test validation' in *Educational measurement*, 2nd edn, ed. R.L. Thorndike, American Council on Education, Washington DC, pp. 443–507.

Cronbach, L.J. & Meehl, P.E., 1955, 'Construct validity in psychological tests', *Psychological Bulletin*, vol. 52, no. 4, pp. 281–302.

Curtis, A., 2018, 'Portfolio' in *The TESOL encyclopedia of English language teaching*, eds J.I. Liontas & C. Coombe, John Wiley & Sons, Hoboken, pp. 1–7.

Davidson, F., 2012, 'Test specifications and criterion-referenced assessment' in *Routledge handbook of language testing*, eds G. Fulcher & F. Davidson, Routledge, London and New York, pp. 197–207.

Davidson, F. & Lynch, B.K., 2002, *Testcraft: A teacher's guide to writing and using language test specifications*, Yale University Press, New Haven.

Davies, A., 1982, 'Language testing parts 1 and 2' in *Cambridge surveys 1*, ed. V. Kinsella, Cambridge University Press, Cambridge, pp. 127–59.

Davies, A., 2012, 'Ethical codes and unexpected consequences' in *Routledge handbook of language testing*, eds G. Fulcher & F. Davidson, Routledge, London and New York, pp. 455–68.

Davies, A., 2014, 'Fifty years of language assessment' in *Companion to language assessment*, ed. A.J. Kunnan, John Wiley & Sons, Oxford, pp. 1–19.

Davies, A., 2017, 'Ethics, professionalism, rights, and codes' in *Language testing and assessment*, 3rd edn, eds E. Shohamy, I.G. Or & S. May, Springer, Cham, pp. 397–415.

Dörnyei, Z. & Ryan, S., 2015, *The psychology of the language learner revisited*, Routledge, New York and London.

Doughty, C.J., 2018, 'Cognitive language aptitude', *Language Learning*, vol. 69, no. S1, pp. 101–26.

Douglas, D., 2000, *Assessing languages for specific purposes*, Cambridge University Press, Cambridge.

Douglas, D., 2010, *Understanding language testing*, Hodder Education, London.

Duckor, B. & Holmberg, C.L., 2023, *Feedback for continuous improvement in the classroom: New perspectives, practices, and possibilities*, Corwin Press, Thousand Oaks.

Eckes, T. & Grotjahn, R., 2006, 'A closer look at the construct validity of C-tests', *Language Testing*, vol. 23, no. 3, pp. 290–325.

Elliott, M., 2013, 'Test taker characteristics' in *Examining listening*, eds A. Geranpayeh & L. Taylor, Cambridge University Press, Cambridge, pp. 36–76.

Ellis, R., 2015, *Understanding second language acquisition*, Oxford University Press, Oxford.

Ellis, R. & Shintani, N., 2014, *Exploring language pedagogy through second language acquisition research*, Routledge, London and New York.

Ericsson, P.F. & Haswell, R. (eds), 2006, *Machine scoring of student essays: Truth and consequences*, Utah State University Press, Logan.

Fantini, D.K., 2009, 'Implementing intercultural competence assessment: Issues and tools' in *SAGE handbook of intercultural competence*, ed. D.K. Deardorf, SAGE, Thousand Oaks, pp. 477–91.

Ferri, G. & Magne, V., 2021, 'Exploring the language ideology of nativeness in narrative accounts of English second language users in Montreal', *Critical Inquiry in Language Studies*, vol. 18, no. 3, pp. 229–46.

Field, J., 2008, *Listening in the language classroom*, Cambridge University Press, Cambridge.
Field, J., 2011, 'Cognitive validity' in *Examining speaking*, ed. L. Taylor, Cambridge University Press, Cambridge, pp. 65–111.
Field, J., 2013, 'Cognitive validity' in *Examining listening*, eds A. Geranpayeh & L. Taylor, Cambridge University Press, Cambridge, pp. 77–151.
Flowerdew, J. & Miller, L., 2005, *Second language listening: Theory to practice*, Cambridge University Press, Cambridge.
Fox, J., 2017, 'Using portfolios for assessment/alternative assessment' in *Language testing and assessment*, 3rd edn, eds E. Shohamy, I.G. Or & S. May, Springer, Cham, pp. 135–47.
Fulcher, G., 2003/2014, *Testing second language speaking*, London and New York, Routledge.
Fulcher, G., 2010, *Practical language testing*, Hodder Education, London.
Fulcher, G., 2012a, 'Assessment literacy for the language classroom', *Language Assessment Quarterly*, vol. 9, no. 2, pp. 113–32.
Fulcher, G., 2012b, 'Scoring performance tests' in *Routledge handbook of language testing*, eds G. Fulcher & F. Davidson, Routledge, New York and London, pp. 378–92.
Fulcher, G., 2017, 'Standards and frameworks' in *Handbook of second language assessment*, eds D. Tsagari & J. Banerjee, De Gruyter Mouton, Boston and Berlin, pp. 29–44.
Fulcher, G. & Harding, L. (eds), 2022, *Routledge handbook of language testing*, 2nd edn, Routledge, London and New York.
Gass, S. & Mackey, A., 2006, 'Input, interaction and output: An overview', *AILA Review*, vol. 19, pp. 3–17.
Geranpayeh, A., 2013, Scoring validity, in *Examining listening*, eds A. Geranpayeh & L. Taylor, Cambridge University Press, Cambridge, pp. 242–72.
Goodman, K., 1967, 'Reading: A psychological guessing game', *Journal of the Reading Specialist*, vol. 6, no. 4, pp. 126–35.
Grabe, W., 2009, *Reading in a second language: Moving from theory to practice*, Cambridge University Press, Cambridge.
Grabe, W. & Kaplan, R.B., 1996/2014, *Theory and practice of writing: An applied linguistic perspective*, Routledge, London and New York.
Grabe, W. & Stoller, F.L., 2020, *Teaching and researching reading*, 3rd edn, Routledge, New York and London.
Gray, W.S., 1960, 'The major aspects of reading' in *Psychology of reading: Foundations of instruction*, eds M.C. Robeck & J.A.R. Wilson, John Wiley & Sons, New York.
Green, A., 2014, *Exploring language assessment and testing: Language in action*, Routledge, Abingdon.
Green, A., 2020, *Exploring language assessment and testing: Language in action*, 2nd edn, Routledge, Abingdon.
Green, R., 2013, *Statistical analyses for language testers*, Palgrave Macmillan, Basingstoke.
Green, R., 2017, *Designing listening tests: A practical approach*, Palgrave Macmillan, London.
Grice, H.P., 1975, 'Logic and conversation' in *Syntax and semantics*, eds P. Cole & J. Morgan, Academic Press, New York, pp. 113–27.

Griffiths, C., 2012, 'Learning styles: Traversing the quagmire' in *Psychology for language learning: Insights from research, theory and practice*, eds S. Mercer, S. Ryan & M. Williams, Palgrave Macmillan, Basingstoke, pp. 151–68.
Grosjean, F., 1989, 'Neurolinguists, beware! The bilingual is not two monolinguals in one person', *Brain and Language*, vol. 36, no. 1, pp. 3–15.
Guba, E.G., 1981, 'Criteria for assessing the trustworthiness of naturalistic inquiries', *Educational Communication and Technology Journal*, vol. 29, no. 2, pp. 75–91.
Guba, E.G. & Lincoln, Y.S., 1989, *Fourth generation evaluation*, SAGE, Thousand Oaks.
Hambleton, R. & Rodgers, J., 1995, 'Item bias review', *Practical Assessment, Research, and Evaluation*, vol. 4, no. 1, pp. 1–3.
Harding, L. & Kremmel, B., 2017, 'Teacher assessment literacy and professional development' in *Handbook of second language assessment*, eds D. Tsagari & J. Banerjee, De Gruyter Mouton, Boston and Berlin, pp. 413–27.
Hasrol, S.B., Zakaria, A. & Aryadoust, V., 2022, 'A systematic review of authenticity in second language assessment', *Research Methods in Applied Linguistics*, vol. 1, no. 3, Article 100023.
Hayes, J.R., 1996, 'A new framework for understanding cognition and affect in writing' in *The science of writing: Theories, methods, individual differences and applications*, eds C.M. Levy & S. Ransdell, Lawrence Erlbaum Associates, Mahwah, pp. 1–27.
He, L. & Jiang, Z., 2020, 'Assessing second language listening over the past twenty years: A review within the socio-cognitive framework', *Frontiers in Psychology*, vol. 11, pp. 1–15.
Hinkel, E., 2002, *Second language writer's text: Linguistic and rhetorical features*, Routledge, London and New York.
Hudson, T., 2007, *Teaching second language reading*, Oxford University Press, Oxford.
Hughes, A., 2003, *Testing for language teachers*, 2nd edn, Cambridge University Press, Cambridge.
Hughes, A. & Hughes, J., 2020, *Testing for language teachers*, 3rd edn, Cambridge University Press, Cambridge.
Hughes, R. & Reed, B.S., 2017, *Teaching and researching speaking*, 3rd edn, Routledge, New York.
Hyland, K., 2016, *Teaching and researching writing*, 3rd edn, Routledge, London.
Hymes, D., 1972, 'On communicative competence' in *Sociolinguistics: Selected readings*, eds J.B. Pride & J. Holmes, Penguin, Harmondsworth, pp. 269–93.
Inbar-Lourie, O., 2017, 'Language assessment literacy' in *Language testing and assessment*, 3rd edn, eds E. Shohamy, I.G. Or & S. May, Springer, Cham, pp. 257–70.
Jiao, H. & Chen, Y.-H., 2014, 'Differential item and testlet functioning analysis' in *Companion to language assessment*, ed. A.J. Kunnan, John Wiley & Sons, Oxford, pp. 1–19.
Jin, Y., 2018, 'Practicality' in *The TESOL encyclopedia of English language teaching*, eds J.I. Liontas & C. Coombe, John Wiley & Sons, Hoboken, pp. 1–6.
Kane, M.T., 2016, 'Validity as the evaluation of the claims based on test scores', *Assessment in Education: Principles, Policy & Practice*, vol. 23, no. 2, pp. 309–11.

Kane, M.T., 2022, 'Articulating a validity argument' in *Routledge handbook of language testing*, eds G. Fulcher & L. Harding, Routledge, London and New York, pp. 32–47.
Kang, O. & Ginther, A., 2018, *Assessment in second language pronunciation*, Routledge, London and New York.
Kang, O. & Moran, M., 2018, 'Different varieties of world Englishes: Perceptual judgments and speech characteristics' in *Assessment of L2 listening: Moving towards authenticity*, eds G. Ockey & E. Wagner, John Benjamins, Amsterdam and Philadelphia, pp. 113–26.
Kenyon, D. & MacGregor, D., 2012, 'Pre-operational testing' in *Routledge handbook of language testing*, eds G. Fulcher & F. Davidson, Routledge, London and New York, pp. 295–306.
Kessler, M., Solheim, I. & Zhao, M., 2021, 'Can task-based language teaching be "authentic" in foreign language contexts? Exploring the case of China', *TESOL Journal*, vol. 12, no. 1, pp. 1–16.
Koda, K., 2005, *Insights into second language reading: A cross-linguistic approach*, Cambridge University Press, Cambridge.
Kramsch, C., 1986, 'From language proficiency to interactional competence', *Modern Language Journal*, vol. 70, no. 4, pp. 366–72.
Kunnan, A.J., 1999, 'Recent developments in language testing', *Annual Review of Applied Linguistics*, vol. 19, pp. 235–53.
Kunnan, A.J., 2012, 'Language assessment for immigration and citizenship' in *Routledge handbook of language testing*, eds G. Fulcher & F. Davidson, Routledge, London and New York, pp. 162–77.
Kunnan, A., 2018, *Evaluating language assessments*, Routledge, New York.
Kunnan, A.J., 2022, 'Revisiting language assessment for immigration and citizenship: The case of US citizenship and the Naturalization Test 96', in *Routledge handbook of language testing*, eds G. Fulcher & L. Harding, 2nd edn, Routledge, London and New York, pp. 96–116.
Lado, R., 1961, *Language testing: The construction and use of foreign language tests*, Longman, London.
LaFlair, G. & Settles, B., 2019, *Duolingo English test: Technical manual.* Retrieved 28 January 2025, from https://s3.amazonaws.com/duolingo-papers/other/Duolingo%20English%20Test%20-%20Technical%20Manual%202019.pdf
Lanteigne, B., 2018, 'Assessment development process' in *The TESOL encyclopedia of English language teaching*, eds J.I. Liontas & C. Coombe, John Wiley & Sons, Hoboken, pp. 1–8.
Lam, R., 2023, 'E-Portfolios: What we know, what we don't, and what we need to know', *RELC Journal*, vol. 54, no. 1, pp. 208–15.
Larsen-Freeman, D., 2012, 'A complexity theory approach to second language development/acquisition' in *Alternative approaches to second language acquisition*, ed. D. Atkinson, Routledge, London and New York, pp. 48–72.
Larsen-Freeman, D., 2017, 'Complexity: The lessons continue' in *Complexity and language development: In celebration of Diane Larsen-Freeman*, eds L. Ortega & Z. Han, John Benjamins, Amsterdam and Philadelphia, pp. 11–50.
Leung, C., 2022, 'Action-oriented plurilingual mediation: A search for fluid foundation' in *Reflecting on the Common European Framework of Reference*

for Languages and its companion volume, eds D. Little & N. Figueras, Multilingual Matters, Bristol, pp. 78–94.

Levelt, W.J.M., 1989, *Speaking: From intention to articulation*, MIT Press, Cambridge, MA.

Lewkowicz, J. & Leung, C., 2021, 'Research timeline: Classroom-based assessment', *Language Teaching*, vol. 54, no. 1, pp. 47–57.

Lincoln, Y.S. & Guba, E.G., 1985, *Naturalistic inquiry*, SAGE, Newbury Park.

Lissitz, R.W. (ed.), 2009, *The concept of validity: Revisions, new directions, and applications*, Information Age Publishing, Charlotte.

Loewen, S., 2020, *Introduction to instructed second language acquisition*, 2nd edn, Routledge, New York and London.

Lopez, A.A., Turkan, S. & Guzman-Orth, D., 2017, 'Assessing multilingual competence' in *Language testing and assessment*, 3rd edn, eds E. Shohamy, I.G. Or & S. May, Springer, Cham, pp. 91–102.

Luoma, S., 2004, *Assessing speaking*, Cambridge University Press, Cambridge.

Lynch, B.K., 2002, *Language assessment and program evaluation*, Edinburgh University Press, Edinburgh.

MacMillan, F.M., 2017, 'Assessing reading' in *Handbook of second language assessment*, eds D. Tsagari & J. Banerjee, De Gruyter Mouton, Boston and Berlin, pp. 113–29.

McKinley, J. & Rose, H. (eds), 2017, *Doing research in applied linguistics: Realities, dilemmas, and solutions*, Routledge, Abingdon.

McNamara, D.S., Crossley, S.A., Roscoe, R.D., Allen, L.K. & Dai, J., 2015, 'A hierarchical classification approach to automated essay scoring', *Assessing Writing*, vol. 23, no. 1, pp. 35–59.

McNamara, T., 1996, *Measuring second language performance*, Longman, London and New York.

McNamara, T. & Roever, C., 2006, *Language testing: The social dimension*, Blackwell, Oxford.

McNamara, T., Knoch, U. & Fan, J., 2019, *Fairness, justice, and language assessment*, Oxford University Press, Oxford.

McNeish, D., 2018, 'Thanks coefficients alpha: We'll take it from here', *Psychological Methods*, vol. 23, no. 3, pp. 412–33.

Mercer, S., 2012, 'Self-concept: Situating the self' in *Psychology for language learning: Insights from research, theory and practice*, eds S. Mercer, S. Ryan & M. Williams, Palgrave Macmillan, Basingstoke, pp. 10–25.

Mercer, S., Ryan, S. & Williams, M. (eds), 2012, *Psychology for language learning: Insights from research, theory and practice*, Palgrave Macmillan, Basingstoke.

Messick, S., 1989, 'Validity' in *Educational measurement*, ed. R.L. Linn, Macmillan, New York, pp. 13–103.

Messick, S., 1995, 'Validity of psychological assessment: Validation of inferences from persons' responses and performances as scientific inquiry into score meaning', *American Psychologist*, vol. 50, no. 9, pp. 741–9.

Midraj, J. 2018, 'Self-assessment' in *The TESOL encyclopedia of English language teaching*, eds J.I. Liontas & C. Coombe, John Wiley & Sons, New York.

Miles, M.B., Huberman, A.M., & Saldaña, J., 2014, *Qualitative data analysis: An expanded sourcebook*, 2nd edn, SAGE, Los Angeles.

Newton, P.E., 2012, 'Clarifying the consensus definition of validity', *Measurement: Interdisciplinary Research & Perspective*, vol. 10, nos 1–2, pp. 1–29.

Norman, D.A., 2004, *Emotional design: Why we love (or hate) everyday things*, Basic Civitas Books, New York.
O'Sullivan, B., 2012a, 'A brief history of language testing' in *Cambridge guide to second language assessment*, eds C. Coombe, P. Davidson, B. O'sullivan & S. Stoynoff, Cambridge University Press, Cambridge, pp. 9–19.
O'Sullivan, B., 2012b, 'The assessment development process' in *Cambridge guide to second language assessment*, eds C. Coombe, P. Davidson, B. O'Sullivan & S. Stoynoff, Cambridge University Press, Cambridge, pp. 47–58.
Ockey, G. & Wagner, E., 2018, *Assessing L2 listening: Moving towards authenticity*, John Benjamins, Amsterdam and Philadelphia.
Ortiz, S.O. & Cehelyk, S.K., 2024, 'The bilingual is not two monolinguals of same age: Normative testing implications for multilinguals', *Journal of Intelligence*, vol. 12, no. 3, pp. 1–25.
Oxford, R.L., 2017, *Teaching and researching language learning strategies: Self-regulation in context*, 2nd edn, Routledge, New York and London.
Paltridge, B. & Phakiti, A. (eds), 2015, *Research methods in applied linguistics: A practical resource*, Bloomsbury, London.
Paltridge, B., Harbon, L., Hirsh, D., Shen, H., Stevenson, M., Phakiti, A. & Woodrow, L., 2009, *Teaching academic writing: An introduction for teachers of second language writers*, University of Michigan Press, Ann Arbor.
Phakiti, A., 2003, *An empirical investigation into the relationships of state-trait strategy use to EFL reading comprehension test performance: A structural equation modeling approach*, PhD thesis, University of Melbourne.
Phakiti, A., 2007, *Strategic competence and EFL reading test performance*, Peter Lang, Frankfurt am Main.
Phakiti, A., 2018, 'Assessing higher-order thinking skills', in *The TESOL encyclopedia of English language teaching*, eds J.I., Liontas & C. Coombe, John Wiley & Sons, Hoboken.
Phakiti, A., 2023, 'How to run statistics' in *Current approaches in second language acquisition research*, eds S. Gass & A. Mackey, Wiley-Blackwell, Hoboken, pp. 276–303.
Phakiti, A., 2024, *Independent versus integrated writing tasks for IELTS writing: A mixed methods study*, British Council, Cambridge Assessment English and IDP: IELTS Australia.
Phakiti, A. & Leung, C., 2024, *Assessment for language teaching*, Cambridge University Press, Cambridge.
Phakiti, A. & Isaacs, T., 2021, 'Classroom assessment and validity: Psychometric and edumetric approaches', *The European Journal of Applied Linguistics and TEFL*, vol. 10, no. 1, pp. 3–24.
Phakiti, A. & Steinhoff, A., 2023, 'Five golden rules for successful classroom assessment based on what we have learnt from JD Brown', *Language Teaching Research Quarterly*, vol. 37, pp. 76–90.
Phakiti, A., De Costa, P., Plonsky, L. & Starfield, S. (eds), 2018, *The Palgrave handbook of applied linguistics research methodology*, Palgrave, London.
Pill, J. & Smart, C., 2021, 'Raters: Behavior and training' in *Routledge handbook of second language acquisition and language testing*, eds P. Winker & T. Brunfaut, Routledge, New York and London, pp. 135–44.
Plakans, L., 2022, 'Writing integrated tasks' in *Routledge handbook of language testing*, 2nd edn, eds G. Fulcher & L. Harding, Routledge, New York and London, pp. 357–71.

Poehner, M.E. & Infante, P., 2017, 'Dynamic assessment in the language classroom' in *Handbook of second language assessment*, eds D. Tsagari & J. Banerjee, De Gruyter Mouton, Boston and Berlin, pp. 275–90.

Popham, W.J., 1978, *Criterion-referenced measurement*, Prentice Hall, Englewood Cliffs.

Popham, W.J., 1981, *Modern educational measurement*, Prentice Hall, Englewood Cliffs.

Popham, W.J., 2017, *Classroom assessment: What teachers need to know*, 8th edn, Pearson, London.

Purpura, J.E., 2008, 'Assessing communicative language ability: Models and their components' in *Language testing and assessment*, 2nd edn, eds E. Shohamy & N.H. Hornberger, Springer Science + Business Media LLC, New York, pp. 53–68.

Purpura, J.E., 2016, 'Second and foreign language assessment', *Modern Language Journal*, vol. 100, no. S1, pp. 190–208.

Purpura, J.E., 2024, 'Learning-oriented language assessment' in *The concise companion to language assessment*, ed. A.J. Kunnan, Wiley, Oxford.

Rea-Dickins, P. & Scott, C., 2007, 'Washback from language tests on teaching, learning and policy: Evidence from diverse settings', *Assessment in Education: Principles, Policy & Practice*, vol. 14, no. 1, pp. 1–7.

Read, J., 2015, 'Researching language testing and assessment' in *Research methods in applied linguistics: A practical resource*, eds B. Paltridge & A. Phakiti, Bloomsbury, London, pp. 471–86.

Roever, C. & Phakiti, A., 2018, *Quantitative methods for second language research: A problem solving approach*, Routledge, New York and London.

Rossi, O. & Brunfaut, T., 2021, 'Text authenticity in listening assessment: Can item writers be trained to produce authentic-sounding texts?', *Language Assessment Quarterly*, vol. 18, no. 4, pp. 398–418.

Rost, M., 2024, *Teaching and researching listening*, 4th edn, Routledge, New York and London.

Rupp, A.A., Foltz, P.W. & Yan, D., 2020, 'Theory into practice: Reflection on the handbook' in *Handbook of automated scoring: Theory into practice*, eds D. Yan, A.A. Rupp & P.W. Foltz, CRC Press, Boca Raton, New York and London, pp. 475–87.

Salaberry, M.R. & Kunitz, S. (eds), 2019, *Teaching and testing L2 interactional competence: Bridging theory and practice*, Routledge, New York and London.

Saville, N. & Khalifa, H., 2017, 'The impact of language assessment' in *Handbook of second language assessment*, eds D. Tsagari & J. Banerjee, De Gruyter Mouton, Boston and Berlin, pp. 77–94.

Sawaki, Y., 2012, 'Technology in language testing' in *Routledge handbook of language testing*, eds G. Fulcher & F. Davidson, Routledge, London and New York, pp. 426–37.

Sawaki, Y., 2017, 'Norm-referenced vs criterion-referenced approach to assessment' in *Handbook of second language assessment*, eds D. Tsagari & J. Banerjee, De Gruyter Mouton, Boston and Berlin, pp. 45–60.

Schissel, J.L., 2018, 'Test impact and washback' in *The TESOL encyclopedia of English language teaching*, eds J.I. Liontas & C. Coombe, John Wiley & Sons, Hoboken, pp. 1–6.

Schreier, M., 2014, 'Qualitative content analysis' in *SAGE handbook of qualitative data analysis*, ed. U. Flick, SAGE, London, pp. 170–83.
Shaw, D. & Weir, C. (eds), 2007, *Examining writing*, Cambridge University Press, Cambridge.
Shermis, M.D., 2014, 'State-of-the-art automated essay scoring: Competition, results, and future directions from a United States demonstration', *Assessing Writing*, vol. 20, no. 1, pp. 53–76.
Shin, D., 2012a, 'Item writing and writers' in *Routledge handbook of language testing*, eds G. Fulcher & F. Davidson, Routledge, London and New York, pp. 237–48.
Shin, S.-Y., 2012b, 'Web-based language testing' in *Cambridge guide to second language assessment*, eds C. Coombe, P. Davidson, B. O'Sullivan & S. Stoynoff, Cambridge University Press, Cambridge, pp. 274–79.
Shohamy, E., 1988, 'A proposed framework for testing the oral language of second/foreign language learners', *Studies in Second Language Acquisition*, vol. 10, no. 2, pp. 165–79.
Shohamy, E., 2013, 'Expanding the construct of language testing with regards to language varieties and multilingualism' in *International experience in language testing and assessment: Selected papers in memory of Pavlos Palou*, eds D. Tsagari, S. Papadima-Sophocleous & S. Ioannou-Georgiou, Peter Lang, Frankfurt am Main, pp. 17–32.
Shohamy, E., 2017, 'Critical language testing' in *Language testing and assessment*, 3rd edn, eds E. Shohamy, I.G. Or & S. May, Springer, Cham, pp. 441–54.
Skehan, P., 1988, 'State of the art article: Language testing part 1', *Language Teaching*, vol. 21, no. 4, pp. 211–21.
Skehan, P., 1989, 'State of the art article: Language testing part 2', *Language Teaching*, vol. 22, no. 1, pp. 1–13.
Smith, M. & Stanfield, C.W., 2017, 'Testing aptitude for second language learner' in *Language testing and assessment*, 3rd edn, eds E. Shohamy, I.G. Or & S. May, Springer, Cham, pp. 77–90.
Spolsky, B., 1977, 'Language testing: Art or science?' in *Proceedings of the fourth International Congress of Applied Linguistics* (vol. 3), ed. G. Nickel, Hochschuverlag, Stuttgart, pp. 7–28.
Spolsky, B., 1995, *Measured words*, Oxford University Press, Oxford.
Spolsky, B., 2017, 'History of language testing' in *Language testing and assessment*, 3rd edn, eds E. Shohamy, I.G. Or & S. May, Springer, Cham, pp. 375–84.
Stanley, K., 2017, *Validating psychological constructs, historical, philosophical, and practical dimensions*, Palgrave Macmillan, London.
Stevenson, M. & Phakiti, A., 2014, The effects of computer-generated feedback on the quality of writing, *Assessing Writing*, vol. 19, no. 1, pp. 51–65.
Stevenson, M. & Phakiti, A., 2019, 'Automated feedback and second language writing' in *Feedback in second language writing: Contexts and issues*, Cambridge, Cambridge University Press, pp. 125–42.
Sun, Y. & Doman, E., 2018, 'Peer assessment' in *The TESOL encyclopedia of English language teaching*, eds J.I. Liontas & C. Coombe, John Wiley & Sons, Hoboken, pp. 1–7.

Taylor, L., 2009, 'Developing assessment literacy', *Annual Review of Applied Linguistics*, vol. 29, pp. 21–36.

Taylor, L., 2012, 'Accommodation in language testing' in *Cambridge guide to second language assessment*, eds C. Coombe, P. Davidson, B. O'Sullivan & S. Stoynoff, Cambridge University Press, Cambridge, pp. 307–15.

Tsagari, D. & Cheng, L., 2017, 'Washback, impact, and consequences revisited' in *Language testing and assessment*, 3rd edn, eds E. Shohamy, I.G. Or & S. May, Springer, Cham, pp. 359–72.

Turner, C.E. & Purpura, J.E., 2017, 'Learning-oriented assessment in second and foreign language classrooms' in *Handbook of second language assessment*, eds D. Tsagari & J. Banerjee, De Gruyter Mouton, Boston and Berlin, pp. 255–73.

Urquhart, S. & Weir, C., 1998, *Reading in a second language: Process, product and practice*, Longman, New York.

Van Moere, A. & Downey, R., 2017, 'Technology and artificial intelligence in language assessment' in *Handbook of second language assessment*, eds D. Tsagari & J. Banerjee, De Gruyter Mouton, Boston and Berlin, pp. 341–57.

Vandergrift, L. & Goh, C., 2012, *Teaching and learning second language listening: metacognition in action*, Routledge, New York.

Wall, D., 2012, 'Washback' in *Routledge handbook of language testing*, eds G. Fulcher & F. Davidson, Routledge, London and New York, pp. 79–92.

Weigle, S., 2002, *Assessing writing*, Cambridge University Press, Cambridge.

Weir, C.J., 1990, *Communicative language testing*, Prentice Hall, New York.

Weir, C.J., 2005, *Language testing and validation: An evidence-based approach*, Palgrave Macmillan, London.

Winke, P.M., 2018, 'Aptitude testing' in *The TESOL encyclopedia of English language teaching*, eds J.I. Liontas & C. Coombs, John Wiley & Sons, Hoboken.

Winke, P. & Brunfaut, T. (eds), 2021, *Routledge handbook of second language acquisition and language testing*, Routledge, New York and London.

Winke, P.M. & Isbell, D.R., 2017, 'Computer-assisted language assessment' in *Language, education and technology*, 3rd edn, eds S.L. Thorne & S. May, Springer, Cham, pp. 313–25.

Xi, X., 2010, 'How do we go about investigating test fairness?', *Language Testing*, vol. 27, no. 2, pp. 147–70.

Yan, D., Rupp, A.A. & Foltz, P.W. (eds), 2020, *Handbook of automated scoring: Theory into practice*, CRC Press, Boca Ratan, London and New York.

Young, R.F., 2022, 'Social dimensions of language testing' in *Routledge handbook of language testing*, 2nd edn, eds G. Fulcher & L. Harding, Routledge, London and New York, pp. 63–80.

Zechner, K. & Evanini, K. (eds), 2020, *Automated speaking assessment: Using language technologies to score spontaneous speech*, Routledge, New York and London.

Zhang, M., Bridgeman, B. & Davis, L., 2020, 'Validity considerations for using automated scoring in speaking assessment' in *Automated speaking assessment: Using language technologies to score spontaneous speech*, eds K. Zechner & K. Evanini, Routledge, New York and London, pp. 21–31.

Zheng, Y. & Cheng, L., 2018, 'How does anxiety influence language performance? From the perspectives of foreign language classroom anxiety and cognitive test anxiety', *Language Testing in Asia*, vol. 8, no. 13, pp. 1–19.

Index

Page numbers relating to Figures are in **bold**, whereas numbers relating to Tables will be in *italics*.